⟋ **W9-DEE-176**

T·H·I·R·D E·D·I·T·I·O·N

ADVERTISING MEDIA SOURCEBOOK

ARNOLD M. BARBAN
University of Alabama

DONALD W. JUGENHEIMER
Fairleigh Dickinson University

PETER B. TURK
University of Akron

NTC Business Books
a division of *NTC Publishing Group* • Lincolnwood, Illinois USA

1992 Printing

Published by NTC Business Books, a division of NTC Publishing Group.
© 1989 by NTC Publishing Group, 4255 West Touhy Avenue,
Lincolnwood (Chicago), Illinois 60646-1975 U.S.A.
Manufactured in the United States of America.
Library of Congress Catalog Card Number: 88-62120

1 2 3 4 5 6 7 8 9 VP 9 8 7 6 5 4 3 2

Contents

Acknowledgments

The source examples are reproduced through the courtesy of the following firms and organizations:

Arbitron Ratings Company
Birch Radio, Inc.
Buyer's Guide to Outdoor Advertising
Editor & Publisher Market Guide
Leading National Advertisers, Inc.
Media Records, Inc.
Mendelsohn Media Research, Inc.
Nielsen Media Research Company
Radio Advertising Bureau
Sales & Marketing Management
SAMI/Burke, Inc.
Scarborough's Newspaper Ratings Company, Ltd.
Simmons Market Research Bureau: *1987 Study of Media and Markets*
Standard Rate and Data Service
Statistical Research, Inc.

The authors express their appreciation to Professor Lee F. Young of the University of Kansas, who contributed significantly as a coauthor of the first two editions of this book.

Foreword

Whether you are a student just beginning to learn about media or an advertising professional who lives, sleeps, and breathes the subject every day of the year, *Advertising Media Sourcebook* is a must buy.

But be careful. Under no circumstances is it to be stacked neatly on the shelf with all those other "to be read" books. *Advertising Media Sourcebook* must be well used and it must become well worn. If it is, the price you paid for it will come back to you with rich dividends.

Putting together a supermarket (actually a hypermarket) of media tools, techniques, and terminology was no easy task. But with dozens of years experience teaching media, Arnold, Don, and Peter have earned an A+ for a job more than well done.

During my thirty years at Leo Burnett, CBS, and JWT, I was constantly amazed at how people who, unfortunately, felt they knew everything there was to know about media also, unfortunately, believed everyone else was equally astute.

That just isn't the way it is!

The media world changes so rapidly that even the most knowledgeable media pro has difficulty remembering where to go when to get what. And for the media novice, simply getting started often leads to frustration.

With *Advertising Media Sourcebook* some of that frustration will rapidly disappear. Of course, everyone will have his or her own system for using this fine book. I have my own very special "5 Step Recipe."

1. Every day for thirty-five days, review one of the "Media/Marketing Sources" in Section One. In a little over a month, I guarantee you will know more about where to go for what than 90 percent of everyone in the media business.
2. Do the same with the eight concepts in the "Media Calculation Guide." That will take another week.
3. Never be afraid to ask for help. That's what the "Advertising Media Source Contacts" listing is for. Call these companies. They have answers to more questions than there are questions!
4. Remember all those times a new media buzzword was tossed around and you were too embarrassed to ask what it meant. That's what the "Glossary of Advertising Media Terms" is for. If you don't know what it means, *l-o-o-k i-t u-p!*
5. And finally, don't neglect the wonderful series of exercises. You learn by doing. As a matter of fact, take the *Advertising Media Sourcebook* along when you travel. It is amazing how quickly it will help pass the time on those long delayed flights or when you're in your hotel room and don't want to watch "The Tonight Show" or read *What's New in Cedar Rapids!*

Congratulations Arnold, Don, and Peter. *Advertising Media Sourcebook* is a job very well done!

Ron Kaatz, Associate Professor
Medill School of Journalism
Northwestern University

Introduction

Basic Media Considerations

Buying advertising time or space in broadcast or print media is only the final step in the advertising media selection process. Actually, a series of decisions is involved in determining how a product or service will be communicated to the buying public.

Media buying is the tactical implementation of an advertising strategy. It is based on marketing factors, such as a knowledge of the product and its positioning with respect to competition and distribution. It should include an analysis of the potential buyer, both in demographic and psychographic terms. Media selection is also based on pure quantitative considerations, such as audience size and prices.

Before sophisticated advertisers or their advertising agencies commit advertising budgets to actual expenditures, a thorough study of marketing factors that affect the salability and the promotability of products and services is necessary. Thus, the advertising decision-maker must employ not only resources that provide information for the actual purchase of media time and space, but also those resources that help determine the most effective and efficient way to use the funds available.

This activity leads in turn to a study of markets—of populations, their buying capabilities and inclinations, their collective and individual behaviors; and of competitors, their sales success and their advertising activity. Eventually, the media units are studied, along with audience sizes and characteristics. The best way to learn these processes is through exposure to actual conditions and resources and through practice in utilizing them.

This third edition of *Advertising Media Sourcebook* provides actual examples of some of the many media resources that exist in the U.S. advertising industry, along with thorough descriptions and explanations of those resources. It then provides practice assignments that demonstrate some of the applications of these sources.

Not all the available sources can be shown, of course, but a sampling for most media and for the most common situations are included. Rapid developments in marketing practice may alter some of the actual formats of these resources, nonetheless, the decision processes and outcomes will remain much the same. These examples and exercises are intended to provide a basis for making realistic media selection decisions, fitting these decisions into a professional educational process that will continue to be useful in a variety of career situations.

The Advertising Media Process

What follows is a description of the advertising media decision-making process as diagrammed in Figure 1. Use of that diagram will aid comprehension of the dynamic nature of the advertising media process.

The first stage of the process involves searching for background information about consumers of the product or service to be promoted, as well as information about the product or service itself and about the optimal market areas for the promotional effort. In addition, information about the marketing and advertising and the media policies and practices of the primary competitors can be gathered at this stage.

At this point, the media evaluation, selection, and buying process can be divided into three distinct stages: objectives, strategies, and tactics. In the objectives stage, "goals" are set: first come the overall marketing objectives; then the advertising objectives, which are based on and correspond with the marketing objectives; finally, the media objectives, which are based on and correspond with both the marketing and the advertising objectives.

Only after the objectives are considered and firmly established can the strategic or planning stage begin. The target markets and the target groups are established, and the general kinds of media to be used and their relative importance are then outlined. Other audience and media considerations must be taken into account, along with the need for continuity within the media plan and between the media plan and the remainder of the marketing and advertising plans.

Tactical implementation involves the choice of the specific advertising vehicles and units to be used. Estimates and actual costs are determined; then the actual ordering and scheduling of media time and space begin. It is important that this actual buying phase follows the establishment of objectives and strategies.

The process is not yet complete, however. A number of logistical support functions are needed. Certain outside factors, such as changes by the competition, new regulations, raw materials shortages, and the like, can influence any media plan. Eventually, the advertisements will appear in the media, and there will be some degree of impact on the audience and in the marketplace. The record of this media contribution to the effectiveness of the overall advertising program is difficult to measure, but it must be done. It, in turn, becomes an input to the next campaign's media process.

FIGURE 1.
OVERVIEW OF THE DECISION-MAKING PROCESS

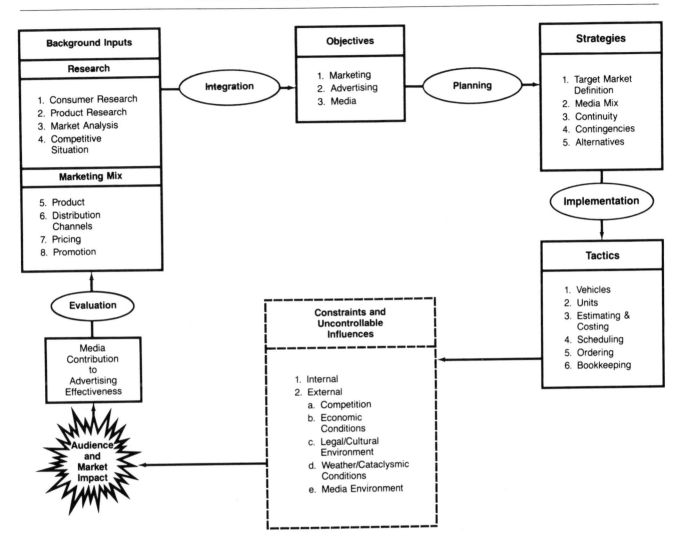

Steps in the Process of Evaluating, Selecting, and Buying Advertising Media

This outline presents the basic steps in the advertising media process. The order in which these items are considered may need to be altered to meet specific situations and problems.

Research Inputs

- ☐ Analyze the product or service to be advertised.
- ☐ Perform consumer research.
- ☐ Analyze the market.
    - ☐ Determine market potential.
- ☐ Gather background information on the activities of the competition.

Goals

- ☐ Establish the marketing objectives.
    - ☐ Determine plans for product development.
        - ☐ Utilize the marketing concept.
    - ☐ Outline introduction patterns (for new or altered products).
    - ☐ Establish pricing policy.
    - ☐ Develop general patterns of timing (by year, season, month, week, and/or day of week).
    - ☐ Determine distribution availabilities and geographic patterns.
    - ☐ Initiate plans for dealing with competition.
    - ☐ Examine need for service operations.
    - ☐ Plan promotional support.
    - ☐ Outline goals of promotional activities.
    - ☐ Establish specific level of accomplishment that is desired against which eventual success is measured.
- ☐ Establish the advertising objectives.
    - ☐ Support marketing objectives.
    - ☐ Consider other promotional efforts that will support advertising.
    - ☐ Outline basic creative considerations.
    - ☐ Determine budget levels.
        - ☐ Allocate budget to various functions, goals, products, and so forth.
    - ☐ Specify timing patterns of advertising.
    - ☐ Establish levels to achieve in awareness, knowledge, desire for product and sales.
    - ☐ Introduce general media characteristics that are to be considered.
- ☐ Establish the media objectives.
    - ☐ Support marketing and advertising objectives.
    - ☐ Outline basic audience characteristics to be considered.
    - ☐ Establish need for reach, frequency, continuity, and impact.
        - ☐ Determine the relative importance of reach, frequency, continuity, and impact.
        - ☐ Attempt to establish specific levels of reach, frequency, continuity, and impact that are to be achieved.
        - ☐ Consider media "wave" patterns.
    - ☐ Establish cost efficiency goals and criteria for advertising media to be selected.
    - ☐ Examine need for flexibility in advertising media.

Strategies

☐ Evaluate proposed advertising budget.
  ☐ Relate budget investment to sales expectations.
  ☐ Justify budgetary changes and trends.
☐ Determine the target group.
  ☐ Outline specific demographic and/or psychographic characteristics of the target group.
  ☐ Establish the numerical size of the target group.
☐ Determine the target market.
  ☐ Outline specific characteristics of the target market.
  ☐ Establish geographic and numerical size of the target market.
☐ Attempt to determine the types of media to be used in the campaign.
  ☐ Rank the media in terms of their order of importance.
    ☐ Relate the rankings to the desired media, group, and market characteristics.
  ☐ Rate the relative importance of the various media considerations.
  ☐ Begin to eliminate some media that do not meet criteria.
  ☐ Rate the media in terms of their contributions to the marketing, advertising, and media objectives.
  ☐ Establish primary and secondary rankings for the media to be used.
  ☐ Provide specific reasons for using each medium.
☐ List the media that are not to be used.
  ☐ Provide specific reasons for not using each medium.
☐ Determine the specific abilities of each medium.
  ☐ For each medium, analyze the ability to reach the target group.
  ☐ For each medium, analyze the ability to teach the target market.
  ☐ For each medium, estimate the size of audience.
  ☐ For each medium, estimate the effective reach to prospects.
  ☐ For each medium, estimate the quality of audience.
  ☐ For each medium, estimate the cost efficiencies.
☐ Ascertain that all media objectives (as well as marketing and advertising objectives) can be met with the media that have been selected.
☐ Evaluate the environment of the media.
☐ Consider merchandising and other promotional support that will be required.
☐ Outline needs for continuity.
  ☐ Relate continuity to timing of the advertising effort.
    ☐ Establish periods of introductory and sustaining phases.
    ☐ Examine needs and uses of flight and hiatus periods.
☐ Develop contingency plans to meet unexpected occurrences.
  ☐ Develop specific action to be taken if sales expectations are not being met.
  ☐ Develop specific action to be taken if sales expectations are being exceeded.
  ☐ Develop specific action to be taken if a competitor takes some unexpected action.
☐ Check back to marketing, advertising, and media objectives to be certain that all objectives can be met with these plans.
☐ Write an executive summary or overview that will go at the beginning of the media plan.

Tactics

☐ Outline specific goals and uses for each medium to be used.
☐ Consider cost efficiencies of each medium.

☐ Select specific media vehicles.
   ☐ Rank the vehicles in terms of their order of importance and applicability.
      ☐ Relate the rankings to the desired media, group, and market characteristics.
   ☐ Consider cost efficiencies of each vehicle.
      ☐ Relate vehicle audiences to anticipated sales levels.
   ☐ Begin to eliminate some vehicles that do not fit the desired pattern.
   ☐ Relate the remaining vehicles to goals, applicability, media environment, targets, and the like.
   ☐ Review competitive considerations.
   ☐ Provide specific reasons for using each vehicle.
   ☐ Establish rankings of the vehicles in their order of use.
☐ Select the units of advertising to be used.
   ☐ Relate the units to the creative considerations.
   ☐ Relate the units to the budgetary considerations.
   ☐ Relate the units to availability of desired units and vehicles and media.
   ☐ Relate the units to cost efficiencies.
☐ Estimate the costs of vehicles and units to be used.
   ☐ Work out various possible arrangements of vehicles and units.
   ☐ Utilize process of elimination until most satisfactory pattern is decided upon.
☐ Check on actual costs of vehicles and units.
   ☐ Compare actual costs to estimates.
   ☐ Make adjustments as necessary.
☐ Check on availability of units and vehicles.
☐ Relate availability to units selected and estimates.
☐ Reserve desired media time and/or space.
☐ Order appropriate time and/or space.
☐ Schedule units of advertising on specific advertising vehicles.
☐ Report plans to client, traffic department, creative department, account management, media representatives, and so on, as appropriate.
   ☐ Report coordination requirements to appropriate departments and personnel.

FIGURE 2.
ESTIMATES OF EXPENDITURES IN U.S. ADVERTISING MEDIA

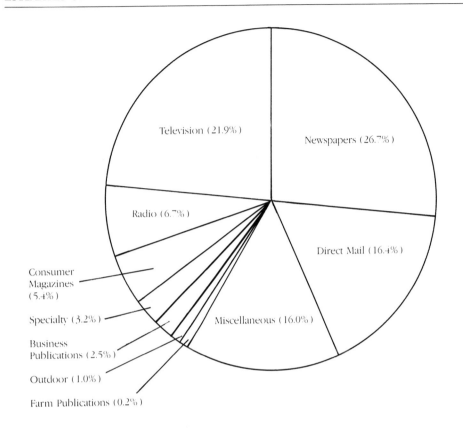

Projections are based on figures from the Newspaper Advertising Bureau, Inc.

Guide to Advertising Media Sources

Principle Sources of Advertising Media Information

1. *Advertising Age*
2. Advertising agency media estimating guides
3. American Business Press, Inc. (ABP)
4. Arbitron Ratings Company
5. Audit Bureau of Circulations (ABC)
6. Birch Radio, Inc.
7. Business/Professional Advertising Association (B/PAA) Media Data
8. Broadcast Advertisers Reports (BAR)
9. Business Publications Audit of Circulation (BPA)
10. *Buyer's Guide to Outdoor Advertising*
11. *State and Metropolitan Area Data Book*
12. *Editor & Publisher Market Guide*
13. C. E. Hooper, Inc., "Hooperatings"
14. Interactive Market Systems (IMS)
15. Leading National Advertisers (LNA), Inc.
16. Magazine Publishers Association, Inc. (MPA)
17. Media Records, Inc.
18. Mediamark Research, Inc. (MRI)
19. Mendelsohn Media Research, Inc. (MMR)
20. Nielsen Media Research Company
21. PRIZM
22. Radio Expenditure Reports
23. SAMI/Burke, Inc.
24. *Sales and Marketing Management Survey of Buying Power*
25. Scarborough's Newspaper Ratings Company, Ltd.
26. Simmons Market Research Bureau: *Study of Media and Markets*
27. Sindlinger Report
28. *Standard Directory of Advertisers*
29. *Standard Directory of Advertising Agencies*
30. Standard Rate and Data Service
31. Telmar
32. Verified Audit Circulation Corporation (VAC)

Cross-Reference Guide to Advertising Media Sources

	General Information	Competitive Activities	Market Information (geographic)	Audience Information (target groups)	Advertising Rates
Nonmedia Information (general marketing)	1,* 11, 18, 19, 26, 28, 29	1, 23	11, 12, 18, 19, 21, 24, 26, 30	18, 19, 26	
Multimedia or Intermedia	1, 18, 19, 26	1, 15	21	2, 14, 31	2
Daily Newspapers		17		5, 18, 19, 25, 26	2, 30
Weekly Newspapers					30
Consumer Magazines	16	15		18, 19, 26	2, 30
Farm Publications				5, 32	2, 30
Business Publications			7, 9	7, 32	2, 30
Network Television		8, 15		4, 18, 19, 20, 26	2
Spot Television		8, 15		4, 18, 19, 20, 26	2, 30
Network Radio		8, 22		13, 18, 19, 20 26, 27	2
Spot Radio		22		4, 6, 13, 20, 26	2, 30
Direct Mail					2, 30
Outdoor		15			2, 10
Transit					2

*Item numbers correspond to the list of *Principle Sources of Advertising Media Information.*

S·E·C·T·I·O·N O·N·E

Reference Sources

In this section, a number of representative sources are included to provide a feel for the spectrum of data references. Not every source can be included in any guide, but a broad range covering most types of data and kinds of media is provided as examples.

With each source example, there is an explanation of the purpose of the source, a description of how to read and understand the data, and practical application of the source to a realistic advertising media situation.

MEDIA/MARKETING SOURCES

SAMI® Market Resume

Sales and Marketing Management Survey of Buying Power

Editor & Publisher Market Guide

Leading National Advertisers (LNA) Multi-Media Report Service

Media Records ("Newspaper Ad Activity"/"Brand Data Activities")

MEDIA AUDIENCE MEASUREMENT SOURCES

Nielsen Television Index (NTI) Pocketpiece

Arbitron Ratings/Television ("Daypart Summary")

Arbitron Ratings/Television ("Weekly Program Estimates")

Arbitron Ratings/Radio

Birch Radio Qualitative Report

Mendelsohn Media Research Survey of Adults and Markets of Affluence (SAMA)

Simmons Market Research Bureau Publications: Total Audiences ("Demographic Status")

Simmons Market Research Bureau Multi-Media Audiences: Adults "Buying Styles"

Scarborough's Newspaper Audience Ratings Study

Standard Rate and Data Service Newspaper Circulation Analysis ("Section II—ADI Market Areas")

MEDIA COST SOURCES AND ESTIMATORS

Network Television Cost Estimator

Cable Television Network/"Superstation" Cost Estimator

Spot Television Cost Estimator

Network Radio Cost Estimator

Spot Market Radio Cost Estimator

Daily Newspaper Cost/Coverage Estimator

Standard Rate and Data Service Newspaper Rates and Data

Standard Rate and Data Service Consumer Magazine and Agri-Media Rates and Data

Standard Rate and Data Service Spot Television Rates and Data

Outdoor Billboard (Thirty-Sheet) Cost Estimator

Buyer's Guide to Outdoor Advertising

MEDIA AUDIENCE REACH ESTIMATORS

Nielsen Television Index (NTI) Brand Cumulative Audience Report

Spot Market Television Reach Table

Network Radio Reach and Frequency Table

Spot Market Radio Reach Table

Daily Newspaper Reach Table

Simmons Market Research Bureau Publications: Twelve-Issue Reach and Frequency

Simmons Market Research Bureau Publications: Duplication of Audiences

Hofmans's Model for Estimating the Reach of Three or More Publications (Single Insertion)

Outdoor Reach and Frequency Table

Source 1

SAMI® Market Resume ("Ready-to-Eat-Cereals")

Research Firm

SAMI/Burke, Inc.

Frequency

Sales audits and projections are taken monthly and can be reported that often. Trends are more likely to be valued for established brands and, therefore, quarterly (twelve-week) and past year (fifty-two-week) levels are always used. These sales data are available on contract only and can be customized for client needs. This is proprietary information and the results are strictly confidential.

Data Collection

Data are collected from sales movement in the retail process (cereals from food store operations). Sales movement is based on shipments from store warehouses to the outlet shelves. Movement is measured in cases (or pounds for some categories) and in dollar volume based on retail price. Because sales reflect warehouse and not cashier lines, trends are very important.

Function/Purpose

The primary function of this data is to supply sales and marketing staffs field information on consumer response. Some aspects, however, are important to media planners when the advertiser uses market-by-market advertising plans. Market sales vitality and market potential have significant effect on advertising allocations (ad dollars per market). These data are incorporated into media spending allocation programs used by many companies.

Format Explanations

Working with these data takes some effort and patience. Here are some guidelines to assist you:

1. Base Measurements. Dollar volume is found by cases shipped multiplied by the manufacturer's retail price per package or case. SAMI/Burke will break out dollars by package size if desired.
2. Time Frame. Five periods are reported: current (past) four weeks; current (past) twelve weeks; current (past) fifty-two weeks; history, twelve weeks from a year ago; and history, fifty-two weeks from a year ago.
3. Category or Brand. Category is the sum of all brands competing. These figures tell how good general demand is in the market. Brand figures refer to each of the manufacturer's products. Brand data is almost always compared with category data.
4. Share of Category. This is the percentage of all dollar volume credited to one brand. You can also learn the market's share of national sales. It is not shown on the summary but is easily calculated. Divide total U.S. dollar volume into market's dollar volume. For example (from excerpt shown): Current four weeks for Syracuse (last market heading) is $3,500,000. Divide this figure by the projected national volume ($405,000,000) and multiply answer by 100 (for accurate decimal location). Syracuse share of national dollar volume is 0.86 percent.
5. Special Reading Note: The top five rows (bold face print) are data in dollars, the remaining rows (light face print) are in share percentages.

Illustration

Media planning uses these data in allocation formulas too detailed for this space. (See Single-Source Exercise 1, p. 84 for detailed discussion.) The purpose of the allocation formula is to spread advertising dollars between markets according to market size in relation to market sales. These are fairly objective and uniform methods to decide how much advertising investment each market is entitled to.

SAMI MARKET RESUME

MANUFACTURER · CONTRACT NO.
ISSUES COVERED 252 – 277
PERIOD COVERED 12/07/85 – 12/04/87

CATEGORY **READY-TO-EAT CEREAL**
UNITS **DOLLAR VOLUME**
PAGE **0501-001A**

DESCRIPTION DETAIL
A-CURRENT 4 WEEK SHARE OF CATEGORY
B-CURRENT 12 WEEK SHARE OF CATEGORY
C-YEAR AGO 12 WEEK SHARE OF CATEGORY
D-CURRENT 52 WEEK SHARE OF CATEGORY
E-YEAR AGO 52 WEEK SHARE OF CATEGORY

EASTERN MARKETS

DESCRIPTION		TOTAL U.S.	ALBNY/SCNTDY	BALT/WASH	BOSTN/PROV	BUFF/RCHSTR	HRTFRD NW HVN	NEW YORK	PHILA	PRTLND CONCRD	SCRNTN WLK-BR	SYRA-CUSE
READY-TO-EAT CEREAL	A	405W	2,346M	6,768M	10292M	4,558M	3,811M	23431M	11888M	2,534M	1,576M	3,500M
	B	1,237W	7,330M	20287M	32274M	14229M	11875M	73112M	36473M	7,658M	4,885M	10788M
	C	1,146W	8,827M	18449M	28290M	13423M	10675M	64981M	32194M	6,803M	4,605M	10075M
	D	5,384W	32883M	87613M	124W	63147M	51852M	316W	156W	33376M	21515M	48108M
	E	4,949W	31750M	84190M	124M	56163M	47097M	286W	140W	28915M	20421M	42578M
KELLOGG SUGAR FRST FLK	A	4.91	3.80	6.05	4.18	3.98	4.27	5.74	4.89	3.11	3.34	3.16
	B	5.40	4.07	6.34	4.47	4.27	4.64	6.05	5.24	3.41	3.43	3.65
	C	5.50	3.86	6.53	4.48	4.55	4.73	6.03	5.17	3.09	3.64	3.70
	D	5.47	3.90	6.41	4.48	4.38	4.64	6.01	5.24	3.20	3.42	3.61
	E	5.64	4.04	6.76	4.60	4.62	4.67	6.06	5.30	3.29	3.71	3.75
KELLOGG RICE KRISP	A	4.79	4.41	4.16	4.58	4.58	4.74	4.41	4.32	3.98	4.53	4.52
	B	3.99	3.65	3.83	4.00	4.55	3.97	3.92	3.82	3.92	4.07	3.60
	C	3.62	3.50	3.58	3.74	3.38	3.81	3.80	3.62	3.64	3.71	3.44
	D	3.72	3.62	3.64	3.83	3.71	3.95	3.94	3.84	3.62	3.89	3.51
	E	3.89	3.86	3.88	4.07	3.93	4.13	4.14	4.04	3.85	4.10	3.75
G MILLS CHEERIOS	A	4.06	4.38	4.51	5.35	4.74	4.88	4.49	4.33	6.04	4.00	4.34
	B	4.41	5.28	4.81	5.44	5.13	5.05	4.63	4.71	6.12	4.87	4.99
	C	4.76	5.54	5.24	5.57	5.50	5.61	4.68	4.69	6.54	4.75	5.22
	D	4.54	5.41	5.09	5.46	5.15	5.20	4.56	4.56	6.26	4.85	5.01
	E	4.80	5.49	5.28	5.43	5.31	5.42	4.90	4.78	6.39	4.76	5.39
KELLOGG CORN FLAKES	A	3.98	3.40	4.38	3.41	3.60	3.53	5.73	3.53	2.94	3.70	3.02
	B	4.03	3.46	4.31	3.74	3.49	3.70	5.84	3.43	2.86	3.59	3.24
	C	4.11	3.33	4.50	3.55	3.70	3.67	5.78	3.50	3.08	3.67	3.35
	D	4.14	3.51	4.33	3.72	3.61	3.79	5.82	3.47	3.00	3.62	3.33
	E	4.33	3.64	4.57	3.70	3.96	3.82	5.87	3.77	3.18	3.82	3.58
KELLOGG RAISIN BRAN	A	3.35	3.12	3.12	3.81	3.47	3.67	3.85	3.80	3.20	2.94	2.92
	B	3.67	3.72	3.28	4.50	3.32	4.06	3.92	3.77	3.57	2.86	3.34
	C	3.91	4.20	3.71	4.62	3.59	4.27	4.11	3.84	3.95	2.92	3.61
	D	3.74	3.92	3.43	4.44	3.31	3.95	3.95	3.78	3.73	2.93	3.47
	E	4.00	4.41	3.76	4.81	3.67	4.55	4.16	3.94	3.94	3.08	3.74
G MILLS CHEERIOS HNY/NT	A	2.87	3.16	2.76	3.34	2.86	3.63	2.79	3.25	3.31	2.51	2.54
	B	2.94	3.33	3.04	3.28	3.08	3.41	2.93	3.46	3.43	3.00	2.63
	C	2.97	3.60	3.07	3.47	3.69	3.66	3.06	3.74	3.73	3.16	3.07
	D	2.99	3.43	3.19	3.23	3.36	3.48	2.88	3.41	3.40	2.99	2.74
	E	3.02	3.42	3.08	3.31	3.58	3.57	2.99	3.59	3.62	3.09	2.94
KELLOGG FROOT LOOP	A	2.78	2.62	2.97	2.36	2.36	2.32	2.43	2.16	2.54	2.09	2.37
	B	2.65	2.31	2.79	2.22	2.32	2.25	2.28	2.02	2.37	1.91	2.26
	C	2.73	2.49	2.96	2.56	2.41	2.55	2.58	2.23	2.46	1.99	2.53
	D	2.84	2.53	2.96	2.37	2.43	2.44	2.52	2.21	2.45	1.96	2.47
	E	3.16	2.84	3.26	2.80	2.85	2.67	2.80	2.51	2.72	2.22	2.88

M = 000   W = 000,000
*** = VOLUME % CHANGE-GREATER THAN 999.9%
THE TOTAL U.S. COLUMN REPRESENTS PROJECTED DATA.
THE INDIVIDUAL MARKET COLUMNS REPRESENT ACTUAL DATA.

Source 2

Sales and Marketing Management Survey of Buying Power

Research Firm

Published by *Sales and Marketing Management* magazine with data bases provided by Market Statistics.

Frequency

This is an annual publication available in the third calendar quarter.

Data Collection

Market Statistics is a private survey company that uses governmental (Census) data as a foundation for each analysis. The techniques of analysis and projection are not discussed. This is, however, the oldest private survey firm and is a supplier of data to our largest media research firms.

Function/Purpose

This data base is used for geographic evaluations. It provides comparative data on region, state, and metropolitan markets, as well as countries and cities. Data cover demographics, economics, and distribution (sales) for each area segment.

Though it has many applications, most advertisers use the *Survey* for selection of test markets and/or for advertising investment decisions (which market will receive more ad dollars).

Format Explanations

Each volume (there are four) explains the meaning of each category term. There are too many to list here, but two unique terms deserve explanation.

> Effective Buying Income per Household. Includes all sources of household income *less* (minus) personal taxes on income and contributions to Social Security.

> Buying Power Index. This weighted, comparative index is a special feature of all SBP reports. It is widely used to estimate a market's potential for popularly priced consumer products. A complete description of how it is developed follows.

Illustration

Although advertisers can use any of the individual tabulations, most will combine factors through the buying power index (BPI). This index gives marketers a sensitive but convenient way to compare areas.

There is a standard format for BPI; however, many advertisers will customize the index to their special needs. To demonstrate: Assume a marketer of middle-priced contemporary furniture is choosing outlet markets in West Virginia (the excerpt shown). The company has chosen young adults (25–34 yrs.) as the demographic; EBI household income of $20,000–34,999 as the economic factor; and furniture sales. Using the Charleston metro area as the example, here are the steps in preparing the Charleston BPI:

1. All categories must be converted to whole numbers. Note that age and EBI are now in percentages. To convert just multiply the segment percentage by the total for the market.

Age 25–34

$$269.6 \text{ (Tot. Pop.)} \times .178 \text{ (\% } 25\text{–}34) = 47,989$$

EBI Income HH

$$106,000 \text{ (Tot. HH)} \times .296 \text{ (\% } \$20\text{–}34.99K \text{ HH)} = 31,376$$

Furniture Sales is already expressed in whole numbers: $62,623,000.

2. Find the percentage of the United States for each category. The U.S. totals are listed elsewhere in each SBP report. In this case, it means dividing the Charleston figure by the U.S. figure and multiplying by 100.

Age

$$\frac{47,989(\text{Chas.})}{42,690,100(\text{U.S.})} \times 100 = 0.1124\% \text{ of U.S.\%}$$

EBI HH

$$\frac{31,376(\text{Chas.})}{23,919,400(\text{U.S.})} \times 100 = 0.1312\% \text{ of U.S.\%}$$

Furniture Sales

$$\frac{\$62,623(\text{Chas.})}{\$77,157,654(\text{U.S.})} \times 100 = 0.0812\% \text{ of U.S.\%*}$$

*000s are dropped from sales to ease calculation.

3. Apply recommended weights to each of the three percentages from Step two. SBP does not believe each factor is of equal value to the index. It recommends these weights (but marketers can create their own): Age = .5; Income = .3; Sales = .2.

The BPI calculation is then

$$(\text{US \% of age})(.5) + (\text{US \% of HHs income})(.3) + (\text{U.S. \% of sales})(.2) = \text{BPI}.$$

The Charleston calculation, for ages 25–34 earning \$20,000–\$34,999 who purchase furniture, would then be

$$\text{Charleston BPI} = .0562 + .0394 + .0162 = .1118$$

The Charleston BPI would then be compared with others to determine priority. The higher the BPI, the stronger the market.

WEST VIRGINIA

W.VA. S&MM ESTIMATES	POPULATION—12/31/86								RETAIL SALES BY STORE GROUP 1986						
METRO AREA County City	Total Population (Thousands)	% Of U.S.	Median Age of Pop.	18–24 Years	25–34 Years	35–49 Years	50 & Over	House-holds (Thousands)	Total Retail Sales ($000)	Food ($000)	Eating & Drinking Places ($000)	General Mdse. ($000)	Furniture/ Furnish./ Appliance ($000)	Auto-motive ($000)	Drug ($000)
				% of Population by Age Group											
CHARLESTON	269.6	.1109	33.5	10.1	17.8	19.6	27.8	106.0	1,699,144	350,106	121,331	196,010	62,623	497,995	61,814
Kanawha	225.7	.0928	33.9	10.3	17.7	19.1	28.9	90.2	1,532,684	315,615	110,562	188,830	59,986	438,774	58,141
• Charleston	58.7	.0241	37.2	9.8	17.0	17.4	35.3	26.0	794,321	120,006	66,743	140,481	26,918	224,911	24,054
Putnam	43.9	.0181	31.9	9.2	18.9	21.9	22.2	15.8	166,460	34,491	10,769	7,180	2,637	59,221	3,673
SUBURBAN TOTAL	210.9	.0868	32.7	10.1	18.1	20.1	25.8	80.0	904,823	230,100	54,588	55,529	35,705	273,084	37,760

W.VA. S&MM ESTIMATES	EFFECTIVE BUYING INCOME 1986							W.VA. S&MM ESTIMATES	EFFECTIVE BUYING INCOME 1986						
METRO AREA County City	Total EBI ($000)	Median Hsld. EBI	A	B	C	D	Buying Power Index	**METRO AREA** County City	Total EBI ($000)	Median Hsld. EBI	A	B	C	D	Buying Power Index
			% of Hslds. by EBI Group: (A) $10,000–$19,999 (B) $20,000–$34,999 (C) $35,000–$49,999 (D) $50,000 & Over								% of Hslds. by EBI Group: (A) $10,000–$19,999 (B) $20,000–$34,999 (C) $35,000–$49,999 (D) $50,000 & Over				
CHARLESTON	3,062,052	22,821	23.2	29.6	16.1	10.4	.1081	Fayette	445,669	15,450	31.8	25.1	9.5	3.5	.0173
Kanawha	2,627,323	22,676	23.4	29.0	15.8	10.9	.0937	Gilmer	57,961	13,366	31.1	23.8	4.1	3.4	.0021
• Charleston	790,062	20,535	24.0	23.7	13.2	14.1	.0342	Grant	82,295	17,029	29.5	25.2	11.0	5.5	.0028
Putnam	434,729	23,549	22.0	33.3	17.5	7.4	.0144	Greenbrier	318,850	16,098	30.6	26.1	8.7	5.2	.0130
SUBURBAN TOTAL	2,271,990	23,457	23.0	31.5	17.0	9.2	.0739	Hampshire	121,926	15,600	32.1	24.9	8.6	4.2	.0045

Source 3

Editor & Publisher Market Guide

Research Firm

Editor & Publisher magazine

Frequency

This compilation of information on towns and cities is published annually.

Data Collection

As the primary trade magazine for the newspaper industry, *Editor & Publisher* has a natural access to local market information. Newspapers are asked to assist with gathering municipal, utility, banking, and retail information for a standardized profile of each market.

Function/Purpose

This is a relatively unique source of market information. When used in conjunction with data bases such as *Survey of Buying Power* (see page 14), this adds valuable descriptive detail on each area. For smaller towns, this is nearly an exclusive source.

Because of its encyclopedic nature, *Market Guide* can fulfill diverse needs: tracking retail distribution, identifying geographic locations from highway and rail access, and most importantly, providing needed data on prospective field or test market locations.

Format Explanations

States and cities are arranged in alphabetical order. Each listing covers thirteen standardized elements (or fourteen if you count the newspaper listing). The order of items is consistent throughout to expedite reference. All information headings are self-explanatory. Note that "Population" and "Household" sizes are updated each year from the last U.S. Census.

Illustration

As a descriptive reference, use is fully dependent on the needs of the client. For example, some years back, a national firm that specializes in laundry and bath products was selecting markets for a field test. A major consideration in selection was water condition because laundry products' performance is affected by water hardness. Along with the other standard demographic and isolation measures, *Market Guide* "tap water" listings were included so that a balance of hard and soft water areas was used for the test.

insecticide distributing center. Distribution Headquarters (14 Counties) State Hwy. Department. Central SE part of state, 44 mi. from Montgomery.

2 - TRANSPORTATION: Railroads-Seaboard-Coastline; Southern.
Motor Freight Carriers-4.
Intercity Bus Lines-Greyhound; Trailways.

3 - POPULATION:
Corp. City 80 Cen. 12,587; E&P 87 Est. 13,489
County 80 Cen. 28,050; E&P 87 Est. 29,248

4 - HOUSEHOLDS:
City 80 Cen. 4,160; E&P 87 Est. 4,646
County 80 Cen. 9,525; E&P 87 Est. 10,285

5 - BANKS	**NUMBER**	**EST. DEP.**
Commercial	3	$56,395,000

6 - PASSENGER AUTOS: County 18,814

7 - ELECTRIC METERS: Residence 3,963

8 - GAS METERS: Residence 2,080

9 - PRINCIPAL INDUSTRIES: Industry, No. of Wage Earners-Woodworking 497; Textiles 511; Fertilizer-Insecticides 116; College 615; Truck Body 115; College/State University (5,732 students, 180 faculty).
Principal Pay Day-Fri.

10 - CLIMATE: Min. & Max. Temp.-Spring 56-81; Summer 69-91; Fall 56-76; Winter 38-58.

11 - TAP WATER: Alkaline, slightly hard; fluoridated

12 - RETAILING: Principal Shopping Center-10 blocks on 4 sts., Troy Plz.; Park Lane.

Nearby Shopping Centers

Name (No. of stores)	**Miles from Downtown**	**Principal Stores**
Parklane(6)	NA	Piggly Wiggly, Sears, Fred's Dollar Store
Troy Plz.(8)	NA	Winn-Dixie
Southland Village	NA	Piggly Wiggly, TG&Y

Principal Shopping Days-Mon. through Sat., 1 pm Sun.

13 - RETAIL OUTLETS: Department Stores-Rosenberg's; Leon's; Stanton's; Wal-Mart; Town Sq.
Variety Stores-Fred's.
Discount Stores-Bargaintown USA; Top Dollar.
Chain Drug Stores-SupeRx; Harco.
Chain Supermarkets-Piggly Wiggly; IGA; Winn-Dixie; Junior Foods; Food World.
Other Chain Stores-Diana Shops; Goodyear; Sears; Kenwin; Eleanor Shops; Baxter Shoes; Firestone; Kitchen Withit Shoes.

14 - NEWSPAPERS: MESSENGER (m-tues to fri; S) 2,896; sworn Oct. 1, 1986.
Local Contact for Advertising and Merchandising Data: Deedie Domizio, Adv. Mgr., MESSENGER, 113 N. Market St.; PO Box 727, Troy, AL 36081; Tel. (205) 566-4270.
National Representative: General Advertising Service.

TUSCALOOSA

1 - LOCATION: Tuscaloosa County (MSA). E&P Map B-3, County Seat. 50 mi. SW of Birmingham; largest city between Birmingham & Mobile; U.S. Hwy. 82, 11, 43, I-20, I-59. Industrial, lumber, agricultural cattle raising, university and institutional town.

2 - TRANSPORTATION: Railroads-Amtrak (passenger); Norfolk-Southern (freight); L&N; Mississippi; Southern.
Barge Lines-To Port of Mobile, New Orleans, Chicago, Houston & points on Tennessee, Tombigbee, Mississippi & Ohio Rivers.
Motor Freight Carriers-14.
Intercity Bus Lines-Greyhound; Trailways; ATS Trans. Service.
Airlines-Atlantic Southeastern; American Eagle; Delta.

3 - POPULATION:
Corp. City 80 Cen. 75,143; E&P 87 Est. 74,857
NDM-ABC: (80) 137,541
County/MSA 80 Cen. 137,473; E&P 87 Est. 143,151

4 - HOUSEHOLDS:
City 80 Cen. 26,147; E&P 87 Est. 27,456
NDM-ABC: (80) 46,820
County/MSA 80 Cen. 46,800; E&P 87 Est. 51,177

5 - BANKS	**NUMBER**	**EST. DEP.**
Savings & Loan	3	$325,000,000
Commercial	6	$685,000,000

6 - PASSENGER AUTOS: County 94,606

7 - ELECTRIC METERS: Residence 56,671

8 - GAS METERS: Residence 29,626

9 - PRINCIPAL INDUSTRIES: Industry, No. of Wage Earners (Av. Wkly. Wage)-Tire Plant 2,080 ($510); Lumber 1,800 ($325); Chem. 157 ($475); Coal 2,000 ($580).
Principal Industrial Pay Days-Tues., Fri., 1st & 15th.

10 - CLIMATE: Min. & Max. Temp.-Spring 59-83; Summer 70-92; Fall 51-76; Winter 34-56. Rainfall 54 in.; Growing Season 232 days.

11 - TAP WATER: Alkaline, very soft; fluoridated.

12 - RETAILING: Principal Shopping Centers-4 blocks on University Blvd.; 4 on Greensboro Ave.; 3 on 6th St.
Neighborhood Shopping Centers-15th St. & 5th Ave.; 12th to 14th Aves. on 5th St.; 18th to 22nd Sts. on G'boro Ave.; Alberta City; 10th Ave. & 15th St.; West Park; 82 Bypass; Also 6 blocks in Northport; McFarland at 15th St.; McFarland at Skyland.

Nearby Shopping Centers

Name (No. of stores)	**Miles from Downtown**	**Principal Stores**
Parkview(29)	2	A&P
City Center	2	City Furn.
Westgate	3	Winn-Dixie, Harco
Leland(13)	4	Winn-Dixie (Kwik-Chek), Harco
Northgate	2	Food Center
McFarland Mall(51)	6	Gayfer's, Zayre, Winn-Dixie
Woodsquare	2	
K mart	5	K mart
Bama(13)	3	Kroger, Wal-Mart
University Mall(95)	5	Sears, Pizitz, JCPenney, Parisians, Bruno
Northwood	4	Kroger, McCrory's Piggly Wiggly

Principal Shopping Days-Dept. Stores-Mon., Thur., Fri. Food: Thur., Fri., Sat., Mon.
Stores Open Evenings-Food-Fri. (some 6 nights, 8 open 24 hours).
Shopping Centers-6 nights until 9.

13 - RETAIL OUTLETS: Department Stores-Adrians; JCPenney; Pizitz; Sears; Raymon's; Gayfer's; Parisians.
Variety Stores-Woolworth; McCrory's.
Discount Stores-Top Dollar; K mart; Fred's; Wal-Mart; Family Dollar; Zayre; Dollar General.
Chain Supermarkets-A&P; Piggly Wiggly 4; Winn-Dixie 3; Food World 2; Kroger 2; Consumer Warehouse 2; Bruno's.
Other Chain Stores-Women's Apparel: Eleanor Shop, Smart & Thrifty; Shoes: Butler's; Paint: Glidden, Sherwin-Williams; Hdwe.: Westcash, Lowe's, Homecrafters; Jewelry: Lorch's, Busch's; Auto Parts: Bumper to Bumper, Carport, Sellers Auto; General: Radio Shack, Baskin-Robbins, Singer, Hancock Fabric, Otasco.

14 - NEWSPAPERS: NEWS (e) 34,556; (S) 38,953; Mar. 31, 1987 ABC.
Local Contact for Advertising and Merchandising Data: Joe H. Junkin, Ret. Adv. Mgr., NEWS, 2001 6th St.; PO Drawer 1, Tuscaloosa, AL 35402; Tel. (205) 345-0505.
National Representative: Branham/Newspaper Sales.

TUSCUMBIA
See FLORENCE

ALASKA SURVEYS

METROPOLITAN STATISTICAL AREAS

Anchorage-Anchorage Borough.

POPULATION ESTIMATES
(Thousands)

Age Group	**1970**	**1980**	**1988**
Under 5 Years	32	38	47
5-14 Years	71	70	87
15-24 Years	64	82	102
25-44 Years	88	146	182
45-64 Years	41	55	69
65 and Over	7	12	15
TOTAL	303	403	502

Based on U.S. Census

Alaska II-7

RETAIL SALES ESTIMATES
(Millions)

Kind of Business	**1977 Census**	**1982 Census**	**1988 Est.**
Bldg. Mat./Hdwr	150	340	638
General Mdse	227	334	501
Food	427	692	918
Automobiles	241	410	791
Gasoline Stations	103	206	204
Apparel	69	127	184
Furniture	59	128	234
Eat-Drink Places	254	405	599
Drugs	80	136	201
TOTAL SALES	1,831	3,227	4,776

ANCHORAGE

1 - LOCATION: Anchorage County. E&P Map B-3 (MSA). Largest city in Alaska. Wholesale and retail distribution center for area extending 800 mi. W. Headquarters for Alaska's corporations, banks, communications, health facilities, petroleum industry, military establishment. Hub of rail, air and highway transportation. On main highway connecting W Alaska and U.S. via Canada; 550 mi. W of Juneau; 350 mi. S of Fairbanks; 1,450 mi. NW of Seattle.

2 - TRANSPORTATION: Railroads-Alaska.
Motor Freight Carriers-23.
Freight Steamship Lines-6.
Intercity Bus Lines-Alaska-Yukon Motorcoaches; Kenai Peninsula Bus Lines; Anchorage Transit (People Mover); Mat-Valley Commuter; Greyline.
Airlines-20. Intermediate stop of international flights: China Air; Flying Tigers; Air France; British Airways; Japan Airlines; KLM; Korean; Lufthansa; Sabena; Scandinavian Airways. Interior: Delta; Alaska; Northwest; Reeve Aleutian; Air Cal; TWA; Mark Air; United; Southcentral; Eastern; Hawaiian; Air Pac; ERA; Swiss Air. Air Taxi 60; Helicopters 14.

3 - POPULATION:
Corp. City 80 Cen. 173,017; E&P 87 Est. 249,375
MSA/County 80 Cen. 173,017; E&P 87 Est. 249,375
NDM-ABC: (80) 225,877

4 - HOUSEHOLDS:
City 80 Cen. 60,042; E&P 87 Est. 89,974
MSA/County 80 Cen. 60,042; E&P 87 Est. 89,974
NDM-ABC: (80) 77,404

5 - BANKS	**NUMBER**	**DEPOSITS**
Savings & Loan	1	$40,839,000
Commercial	15	$3,977,227,000

6 - PASSENGER AUTOS: County 135,573

7 - ELECTRIC METERS: Residence 85,558

8 - GAS METERS: Residence 58,645

9 - PRINCIPAL INDUSTRIES: Industry, No. of Wage Earners (Av. Wkly. Wage N.A.)-Gov't 26,600; Whol. & Ret. Trade 29,000; Irons 4,250; Constr. 8,500; Mfg. 2900; Petroleum; Servs. 27,200; Trans., Commun., Util. 9,700; Insurance, R.E., Finance 9,350; Mining 4,400.

10 - CLIMATE: Av. Temp. Jan. 13 degrees; July 57 degrees. An. rainfall 9 in.; av. an. snowfall 70 in.

11 - TAP WATER: Neutral, hard; fluoridated.

12 - RETAILING: Principal Shopping Centers-33 blocks on 4th, 5th and 6th Aves.; 20 blocks on Northern Lights Blvd.; 20 blocks on Dimond Blvd.; 10 blocks Northway Drive.

Nearby Shopping Centers

Name (No. of stores)	**Miles from Downtown**	**Principal Stores**
Aurora Vlg.(12)	3	Carr's, Payless, Pay 'N Pak
Boniface	6	Pay'N Save, Safeway
Country Village	4	Discount Fabrics
Dimond(160)	6	Safeway, Pay'N Save, Lamont's
Carr's Dimond	6	Carr's, Payless
Eastgate(11)	4	Carr's, Payless
Mountain View	2	Market Basket
Northern Lts.(15)	2	Safeway, Pay'N Save
Northway Mall(73)	NA	Safeway, Pay'N Save, Lamont's
Post Office Mall		Book Cache
Southcenter	5	
Spenard University	4	Lamont's, Pay'N Save
Univ. Ctr.(34)	NA	Safeway, Book Cache
Sears Mall(30)	3	Sears, Carr's, Payless
West Side City	8	
Eagle River(6)	15	Carr's, Payless

Principal Shopping Days-Thur., Fri., Sat., Sun.
Stores Open Evenings-Mon. through Fri.

13 - RETAIL OUTLETS: Department Stores-Nordstrom; JC Penney; Sears; Lamont's 3; Sportswest 2.
Discount Stores-Fred Myer 2; Price Savers; Cosco.
Variety Stores-Woolworth; B&J.
Chain Drug Stores-Pay'N Save 6; Payless 9; Rexall; Long's 2.
Chain Supermarkets-Carr's 9; Safeway 6; Proctor's; Prairie Mkt. 2; Foodland 3.
Other Chain Stores-Klopfensteins (men's); Zale's 3; Kinney Shoes 3; Pay 'N Pak; Jay Jacobs 2; McMahan's Furn.; Pacific Fabrics; Singer 2; Discount Fabrics; Leed's Shoes 2; Singer; Baskin-Robbins 4; Book Cache 13; Waldenbooks; Dalton Books; The Office Place; Computerland; Qwik Stop 28; 7-Eleven 7.

14 - NEWSPAPERS: DAILY NEWS (m) 54,712; (S) 67,971; Mar. 31, 1987 ABC.
Local Contact for Advertising & Merchandising Data: Marge Campbell, Dir. of Mktg. & Research, DAILY NEWS, 1001 Northway Dr.; PO Box 14-9001, Anchorage, AK 99514-9001; Tel. (907) 257-4200.
National Representative: Cresmer, Woodward, O'Mara & Ormsbee.
TIMES (e) 35,696; (S) 47,135; Mar. 31, 1987 ABC.
Local Contact for Advertising and Merchandising Data: Arlene Sayers, Adv. Dir., TIMES, 820 Fourth Ave., Anchorage, AK 99501; Tel. (907) 263-9000.
National Representative: Branham/Newspaper Sales.

FAIRBANKS

1 - LOCATION: Fairbanks North Star County, E&P Map B-2, Judicial Seat. Only city and main business center for 227,000 sq. mi. of interior. In heart of Tanana Valley. 470 mi. by rail from coastal town of Seward; Northern terminus Alaska Hwy. from the states through Canada; northern terminus of Richardson Hwy.; 365 mi. from Valdez; connected with Anchorage and Seward by Richardson, Glennallen, Seward, Hart and Parks Hwys. International and two other airports; airline distribution and supply center for interior and N Alaska, including $1.5 billion national defense installations employing 21,400 military and civilian personnel. University of Alaska campus adjoins city; 4,761 on-campus students. University's research facilities include 1,400 to 1,500 technical and scientific personnel.

2 - TRANSPORTATION: Railroads-Northern terminus Alaska Railroad.
Motor Freight Carriers-20.
Bus Lines-Alaskan Coachways & Alaskan-Yukon Motorcoaches, connecting with Canadian lines to U.S. on Alaska Highway. Alaska Overland serves Fairbanks area and Clear (70 mi. SW).
Barge & River Lines-1.
Airlines-Alaska; Markair; Alaska Central Air; Friendship Air; Delta; Polar; Aurora Air Service; Charter 20; Charter Helicopter service 4.

3 - POPULATION:
Corp. City 80 Cen. 22,645; E&P 87 Est. 30,726
CZ-ABC: (80) 27,561
RTZ-ABC: (80) 55,538
City & RTZ-ABC: (80) 83,099
County 80 Cen. 53,983; E&P 87 Est. 70,855

4 - HOUSEHOLDS:
City 80 Cen. 8,145; E&P 87 Est. 10,937
County 80 Cen. 18,224; E&P 87 Est. 24,743
CZ-ABC: (80) 9,621
RTZ-ABC: (80) 16,410
City & RTZ-ABC: (80) 26,031

5 - BANKS	**NUMBER**	**DEPOSITS**
Savings & Loan	2	$508,100,000
Commercial	8	(incl. above)
Credit Unions	6	(incl. above)

6 - PASSENGER AUTOS: 42,914

7 - ELECTRIC METERS: Residence 27,057

8 - GAS METERS: Bus. & Residence N.A.

9 - PRINCIPAL INDUSTRIES: Industry, No. of Wage Earners (Av. Wkly. Wage)-Constr. 1,603 ($3,120); Gov't excluding military 9,489 ($2,955); Servs. 5,758 ($1,730); Ret. & Whol. 6,110 ($1,815); Trans., Commun., Util. 2,712 ($3,431); Fin., Ins., R.E. 1,108 ($2,143); Other Mfg. 589 ($2,441).
Principal Pay Days-1st & 15th.

10 - CLIMATE: Min. & Max. Temp.-Spring 19-40; Summer 48-80; Fall 20-32; Winter -17-3. First killing frost, Sept. 2; last killing frost, May 21.

11 - TAP WATER: City system, after treatment 120 ppm hardness; 8.6 alkaline. Outside city 150 to 400 ppm hardness in wells from 30 to 400 feet.

Source 4

Leading National Advertisers (LNA) Multi-Media Report Service ("Class/Brand YTD $")

Research Firm

Leading National Advertisers, Inc.

Frequency

This summary of brand media expenditures is published each year at three-month intervals ("YTD" = Year to Date) for six national media.

Data Collection

These reports are a cooperative effort among several monitoring services. Consumer magazine and newspaper supplement activity are provided by the Publishers Information Bureau (PIB). Spot and cable television and network radio and television activity are reported by Broadcast Advertisers Reports, Inc. (BAR). Outdoor activity is measured by LNA.

Reporting is a two-stage process. First, monitoring for the medium is done through various means. For example, BAR tracks network television through a continuous audio tape record of each of the wired networks. Once every message unit is catalogued, industry sources provide estimated costs. Because the actual prices paid are often secret, LNA uses only standard rates that reflect no special discounting.

Function/Purpose

Tracking the level and direction of product advertising of competing brands is a major component of marketing strategy.

Few brands in active consumer segments are willing to ignore what their competitors are doing in advertising. To do so would be dangerous because the pattern and extent of advertising has some direct relationships to sales.

Competitive spending patterns are also valuable in media planning. Numerous studies of competitive situations have proved that the brand's comparative proportion of message units among competitors ("share of voice") in a particular medium can have significant influence on consumer awareness, comprehension, attitude, and sales.

Format Explanations

The LNA format is very straightforward and easy to read. The column "Class" refers to LNA definitions of the product/service category. The remaining columns are self-explanatory.

Illustration

The excerpt page is from the nine-month summary (January–September). Figures reflect the cumulative expenditures up to that point. This listing covers nearly all "cold,—cough-&-sinus remedies." Assume a planner was checking the network television share of voice for *nighttime liquid cold medicines for adults*. Once the competitors were identified, the data could be arranged as follows:

Brand	Nine-Month Net TV Expenditures	Net TV Share of Voice %
Comtrex	$2,019,300	22.3%
Cotylenol	4,476,700	49.4
Nyquil	2,568,600	28.3
	$9,064,600	100.0%

L͞N͞A CLASS/BRAND YTD $ (000)

BRANDS BY CLASSIFICATION	CLASS	6-MEDIA TOTAL	MAGAZINES	NEWSPAPER SUPPLEMENTS	NETWORK TELEVISION	SPOT TELEVISION	NETWORK RADIO	OUTDOOR
D212 COLD,-COUGH-&-SINUS-REMEDIES------------								
AMERICAN HOME PRODUCTS CORP								
BRONITIN FOR ASTHMA	D212-0	119.1	- -	- -	- -	119.1	- -	- -
DRISTAN AF ASPIRIN FREE TABLETS	D212-0	613.0	- -	- -	395.1	217.9	- -	- -
DRISTAN CAPSULES	D212-0	1,236.3	- -	- -	652.4	583.9	- -	- -
DRISTAN LONG LASTING NASAL MIST	D212-0	2,532.4	97.7	- -	2,042.8	391.9	- -	- -
DRISTAN LONG LASTING VAPORMIST	D212-0	4.4	- -	- -	- -	4.4	- -	- -
DRISTAN MULTI-PRODUCT ADVERTISING	D212-0	.1	- -	- -	- -	.1	- -	- -
DRISTAN NASAL MIST	D212-0	305.0	- -	- -	246.6	58.4	- -	- -
DRISTAN TABLETS	D212-0	938.4	- -	- -	793.2	145.2	- -	- -
DRISTAN TABLETS & CAPSULES	D212-0	7,824.6	407.4	- -	6,876.3	540.9	- -	- -
PRIMATENE MIST	D212-0	92.8	40.7	- -	- -	52.1	- -	- -
PRIMATENE MIST & TABLETS	D212-0	6,148.2	445.4	- -	5,246.2	456.6	- -	- -
VIRO-MED LIQUID & TABLETS	D212-0	.2	- -	- -	- -	.2	- -	- -
VIRO-MED TABLETS	D212-0	456.9	- -	- -	414.7	42.2	- -	- -
BAYER A G								
ALKA-SELTZER PLUS COLD TABLETS	D212-0	3,385.6	- -	- -	3,057.8	327.8	- -	- -
BEECHAM GROUP P L C								
NICE SUGARLESS COUGH LOZENGES	D212-0	139.2	- -	- -	- -	139.2	- -	- -
SOMINEX BED TIME COLD MEDICINE	D212-0	2.0	- -	- -	- -	2.0	- -	- -
SUCRETS CHILDRENS LOZENGES	D212-4	5.3	- -	- -	5.3	- -	- -	- -
SUCRETS LOZENGES	D212-0	42.7	- -	- -	42.7	- -	- -	- -
BRISTOL-MYERS CO								
BUFFERIN COLD TABLETS	D212-0	8.5	- -	- -	- -	8.5	- -	- -
COMTREX NIGHTIME COLD MEDICINE LIQUID	D212-0	2,187.2	97.9	- -	2,019.3	70.0	- -	60.0
COMTREX COLD MEDICINE LIQUID & TABLETS	D212-0	95.7	- -	- -	- -	35.7	- -	- -
COMTREX COLD TABLETS & CAPSULES	D212-0	1.5	- -	- -	- -	1.5	- -	- -
COMTREX MULTI-PRODUCT ADVERTISING	D212-0	7,581.1	693.3	- -	6,463.5	424.3	- -	- -
CONGESPIRIN CHILDRENS COLD LIQUID & TABLETS	D212-4	964.3	172.5	- -	791.8	- -	- -	- -
4-WAY LONG ACTING NASAL SPRAY	D212-0	25.0	- -	- -	8.2	16.8	- -	- -
4-WAY NASAL SPRAY	D212-0	1,308.6	- -	- -	1,292.0	16.6	- -	- -
QUADRIN COUGH SYRUP	D212-0	15.6	- -	- -	- -	15.6	- -	- -
CREOMULSION CO								
CREOMULSION REGULAR/CHILDRENS COUGH SYRUP	D212-0	279.9	- -	- -	- -	279.9	- -	- -
DOW CHEMICAL CO								
CEPASTAT LOZENGES	D212-0	262.2	- -	- -	- -	- -	262.2	- -
NOVAHISTINE ELIXIR	D212-0	2,210.5	- -	- -	1,919.4	291.1	- -	- -
JOHNSON & JOHNSON								
COLDMAX COLD PRODUCTS	D212-0	29.5	- -	- -	- -	29.5	- -	- -
COLDMAX COLD TABLETS	D212-0	73.1	- -	- -	- -	73.1	- -	- -
COTYLENOL COLD MEDICINE ADULT & CHILDREN	D212-0	1.0	- -	- -	- -	1.0	- -	- -
COTYLENOL COLD MEDICINE ADULT STRENGTH	D212-0	4,645.7	- -	- -	4,476.7	169.0	- -	- -
COTYLENOL COLD FORMULA MULTI-PRODUCT ADVERTISING	D212-0	2.1	2.1	- -	- -	- -	- -	- -
SINE-AID SINUS TABLETS	D212-0	2,290.8	- -	- -	2,022.4	268.4	- -	- -
TYLENOL SINUS CAPSULES	D212-0	200.4	- -	- -	186.2	14.2	- -	- -
TYLENOL SINUS TABLETS & CAPSULES	D212-0	35.7	- -	- -	- -	35.7	- -	- -
LUDENS INC								
LUDENS COUGH DROPS	D212-0	36.2	- -	- -	- -	36.2	- -	- -
MORTON THIOKOL INC								
HEAD & CHEST COLD MEDICINE MULTI-PRODUCT ADVERTISING	D212-0	1,776.7	- -	- -	1,731.6	45.1	- -	- -
PROCTER & GAMBLE CO								
CHLORASEPTIC LOZENGES	D212-0	.7	- -	- -	- -	.7	- -	- -
CHLORASEPTIC LOZENGES & SPRAY	D212-0	3.5	- -	- -	- -	3.5	- -	- -
CHLORASEPTIC MULTI-PRODUCT ADVERTISING	D212-0	1,385.4	- -	- -	1,219.2	- -	166.2	- -
RICHARDSON-VICKS INC								
CREMACOAT COUGH MEDICINE	D212-0	69.1	23.6	- -	- -	45.5	- -	- -
SURROUND COUGH SYRUP	D212-0	33.1	- -	- -	- -	33.1	- -	- -
VICKS BLUE COUGH DROPS	D212-0	10.4	- -	- -	- -	10.4	- -	- -
VICKS COUGH DROPS	D212-0	501.1	- -	- -	- -	501.1	- -	- -
VICKS DAYCARE COLD CAPSULES	D212-0	476.5	- -	- -	- -	476.5	- -	- -
VICKS DAYCARE COLD REMEDY	D212-0	14.3	- -	- -	- -	14.3	- -	- -
VICKS FORMULA 44 COUGH SYRUP	D212-0	1.3	- -	- -	- -	1.3	- -	- -
VICKS FORMULA 44-D COUGH SYRUP	D212-0	2,153.9	- -	- -	2,063.3	90.6	- -	- -
VICKS HEADWAY COLD TABLETS & CAPSULES	D212-0	1,137.1	- -	- -	1,042.9	94.2	- -	- -
VICKS NYQUIL NIGHTTIME COLDS MEDICINE	D212-0	3,218.5	- -	- -	2,568.6	649.9	- -	- -
VICKS SINEX LONG ACTING NASAL SPRAY	D212-0	1,905.1	- -	- -	1,722.0	183.1	- -	- -
VICKS SINEX NASAL SPRAY	D212-0	12.1	- -	- -	- -	12.1	- -	- -
VICKS VAPORUB	D212-0	236.9	- -	- -	- -	236.9	- -	- -
VICTORS COUGH DROPS	D212-0	29.0	- -	- -	- -	29.0	- -	- -
ROBINS A H CO INC								
DIMETANE ALLERGY & DECONGESTANT TABLETS	D212-0	567.1	567.1	- -	- -	- -	- -	- -
ROBITUSSIN COUGH MEDICINES	D212-0	3,700.4	74.4	- -	375.1	3,250.9	- -	- -
SANDOZ LTD								
ACTREV COLD TABLETS & LIQUID	D212-0	30.6	- -	- -	- -	30.6	- -	- -
TRIAMINIC COLD TABLETS	D212-0	1,325.5	- -	- -	1,284.4	41.1	- -	- -
TRIAMINIC SYRUP	D212-0	3,016.2	- -	- -	2,978.8	37.4	- -	- -
TRIAMINICIN COLD TABLETS	D212-0	326.6	- -	- -	- -	326.6	- -	- -
SCHERING-PLOUGH CORP								
AFRIN NASAL SPRAY	D212-0	10.1	10.1	- -	- -	- -	- -	- -
CORICIDIN D DECONGESTANT TABLETS	D212-0	10.1	10.1	- -	- -	- -	- -	- -
DURATION NASAL SPRAY	D212-0	1,805.3	24.8	- -	1,660.1	120.4	- -	- -
ST JOSEPH CHILDRENS PRODUCTS	D212-4	770.0	93.8	- -	653.2	23.0	- -	- -
SCOT-TUSSIN PHARMACAL CO INC								
SCOT-TUSSIN COUGH MEDICINE	D212-0	.6	- -	- -	- -	.6	- -	- -
SMITHKLINE BECKMAN CORP								
CONTAC COLD CAPSULES	D212-0	4,337.5	- -	- -	4,159.5	178.0	- -	- -
CONTAC MULTI-PRODUCT ADVERTISING	D212-0	15.2	- -	- -	- -	15.2	- -	- -
CONTAC SEVERE COLD FORMULA	D212-0	3,468.8	- -	- -	3,213.7	255.1	- -	- -

---CONTINUED---

Source 5

Media Records ("Newspaper Ad Activity"/"Brand Data Activities")

Research Firm

Media Records, Inc.

Frequency

This summary of brand newspaper expenditures is published each calendar quarter. Each successive quarter also includes the "year-to-date" summaries.

Data Collection

Media Records gathers competitive activity space reports from publishers of daily newspapers and national Sunday supplements. Publishers report the contracted number of column inches run for each company and brand. These data are organized by brand within specifiied product/service categories. The cost of the space is calculated by multiplying the inches used by the publication's open (no discount) rate. Charges for color, preprints, and other production charges are included when appropriate.

Function/Purpose

Media Records gives advertisers current surveillance of competitor's newspaper campaigns. Source users can learn how much competitors are investing, market by market and by newspaper. Indications of display space and insert activity are also noted. Because the cost data do not reflect discounts, expenditures are treated as comparatives and not as absolute expenditures.

Format Explanations

Page space limitations require Media Records to use a series of abbreviations to fit the desired format. The following explanations will assist interpretation.

The second column after the market designation indicates the initial of the newspaper. Should the analyst be unsure of the reference, the name can be verified through other sources.

The third column from the left indicates the publication status. Here are the possible options:

     M = Morning newspaper, weekdays M–F

     E = Evening newspaper, weekdays M–F

     SA = Saturday newspaper

     S = Sunday newspaper

     AD = Preprinted advertising insert

The remainder of the columns concerns estimated dollars (from the left): per month, per quarter, and for the year to date. Summaries at the bottom of each company or brand are broken out with and without supplements.

Illustration

The excerpt page is from the third quarter and nine-month summary (January–September). Assume a planner was interested in the expenditures for beer in July for the San Antonio market. Based on the excerpt here is that summary:

Brand	July Expenditures
Budweiser	$2,837* ($1,923 + $914)
Bud and Bud Light	8,580 ($4,500 + $4,080)
Busch and Natural Light	6,505* ($4,434 + $2,071)

*Figure shown is the total for both newspapers.

*** BEERS***

BUDWEISER (CONTINUED)

CITY	NEWS PAPER		JUL.	AUG.	SEP.	QTR.	TOTAL
NEW YORK	N	S	11229			11229	38472
NEW YORK	P	AD	5621			5621	16353
NEW YORK	T	S					2489
NEWARK	SL	M	16049		16049	32098	49354
NEWARK	SL	S		2351	19945	22296	22296
OAKLAND	T	S		312	312	624	14522
ORANGE CTY	R	S	3223	161		3384	15552
ORANGE CTY	R	AD	4921	16048		20969	45496
PASADENA	SN	M	293			293	293
PHILA	I	M	20496	14218	9048	43762	92879
PHILA	I	S			4734	4734	16944
PHILA	N	E		1662	1292	2954	5724
PHOENIX	AR	M					1807
PHOENIX	AR	S					2131
PHOENIX	G	E					1859
PITTSBURGH	P	E					1502
PITTSBURGH	P	S					5595
PITTSBURGH	PG	M					1570
PROVIDENCE	J	M					5504
PROVIDENCE	J	S					7337
SAN ANT	EN	S		2400		2400	7672
SAN ANT	EN	AD	1923	1992	1992	5907	17752
SAN ANT	EN	SA					1763
SAN ANT	L	S		409		409	2331
SAN ANT	L	AD	914			914	6760
SAN ANT	L	SA			2144	2144	2631
SAN DIEGO	T	E	411			411	7279
SAN DIEGO	U	M	411	10116		10527	11722
SAN DIEGO	U	S		1960	1738	3698	26556
SAN FRAN	C	M					3397
SAN FRAN	E&C	S	68969	57333	23060	149362	319354
SAN JOSE	MN	S					4268
SAN JOSE	MN	AD	201	9759		9960	21310
ST LOUIS	PD	M		1910	1203	3113	10141
ST LOUIS	PD	S	5224	6824	1231	13279	71258
ST PAUL	PPD	S		3783		3783	3783
ST PAUL	PPD	AD		3109		3109	3109
STATE COLL	CT	E			159	159	159
TALLAHASEE	D	M	332			332	332
TOLEDO	B	E	1557	926	1221	3704	12080
TOLEDO	B	S		545	545	1090	2874
WASHINGTON	P	M					18670
WASHINGTON	P	S					28933
WSTCH RCKL	RD	E					3514
WSTCH RCKL	RD	S					518

TOTAL ACCOUNT EXPENDITURES -   QTR $1411002   YTD $3840513
TOTAL EXPENDITURE EXCL. SUPPLEMENTS $1391420 $3805816
PROJECTED 125 MARKETS EXCL. SUPPLS. $1730175 $4713463

BUDWEISER & BUDWEISER LIGHT

CITY	NEWS PAPER		JUL.	AUG.	SEP.	QTR.	TOTAL
ASBURY PK	P	E		566		566	566
BERGEN CTY	R	E					556
CAMDEN	CP	E			1359	1359	1359
CLEVELAND	PD	M	11573			11573	11573
DALLAS	N	M	6541		13596	20137	39370
DALLAS	TH	AD	5978		12402	18380	36224
HOUSTON	C	AD	6543		13086	19629	38969
HOUSTON	P	M	6441		12690	19131	38071
LA/TORR	B	E					2970
LA/TORR	B	S					8911
LA/TORR	NP	E					2970
LOS ANGELS	T	M					37370
SAN ANT	EN	S					1262
SAN ANT	EN	AD	4500		9000	13500	25593
SAN ANT	L	AD	4080		11323	15403	27766
SAN DIEGO	T	E		5077		5077	5077
SAN DIEGO	U	M					5077

TOTAL ACCOUNT EXPENDITURES -   QTR $124755   YTD $283684
TOTAL EXPENDITURE EXCL. SUPPLEMENTS $124755 $283684
PROJECTED 125 MARKETS EXCL. SUPPLS. $206310 $444179

BUDWEISER LIGHT

CITY	NEWS PAPER		JUL.	AUG.	SEP.	QTR.	TOTAL
ALLENTOWN	C	M	793			793	793
BOCA RATON	N	M	371			371	371
BOSTON	G	M	18056	16586	5689	40331	76600
BOSTON	G	S	2475			2475	2475
BOSTON	H	M	3192		13023	16215	39198
BOSTON	H	S	1788			1788	8386
CHARLOTTE	O	M					1215
CHICAGO	T	M					91
CLEVELAND	PD	M		9169		9169	9169
DENVER	P	S					5947
HOUSTON	P	S					6435
INDPLS	S	S					2415

BUDWEISER LIGHT (CONTINUED)

CITY	NEWS PAPER		JUL.	AUG.	SEP.	QTR.	TOTAL
LA/TORR	B	E	3228	1407		4635	4635
LA/TORR	NP	E	1626			1626	1626
LEXINGTON	HL	M					346
MACON	T&N	M					169
MACON	T&N	S					188
NEWARK	SL	M	3620	6878		10498	18342
NEWARK	SL	S		6112		6112	6112
PHOENIX	AR	M					103
PHOENIX	G	E					155
SAN ANT	L	AD					1340
SAN FRAN	E&C	S					6636
TOLEDO	B	E		1684		1684	1684
WASH SBRN	MJ	M		390		390	390
WSTCH RCKL	RD	E	699			699	699

TOTAL ACCOUNT EXPENDITURES -   QTR $96786   YTD $195520
TOTAL EXPENDITURE EXCL. SUPPLEMENTS $96786 $195520
PROJECTED 125 MARKETS EXCL. SUPPLS. $115820 $245723

BUSCH

CITY	NEWS PAPER		JUL.	AUG.	SEP.	QTR.	TOTAL
DALLAS	N	M					3319
NASHVILLE	B	E					1005
NASHVILLE	T	M					1005
NASHVILLE	T	S					3711
SAN FRAN	E&C	S					10936
ST LOUIS	PD	S		15140	24983	40123	63686

TOTAL ACCOUNT EXPENDITURES -   QTR $40123   YTD $83662
TOTAL EXPENDITURE EXCL. SUPPLEMENTS $40123 $83662
PROJECTED 125 MARKETS EXCL. SUPPLS. $54166 $121346

BUSCH & NATURAL LIGHT

CITY	NEWS PAPER		JUL.	AUG.	SEP.	QTR.	TOTAL
DALLAS	N	M	6541		6901	13442	26427
DALLAS	TH	M	6067		6434	12501	24367
HOUSTON	C	AD	9622		6447	16069	32330
HOUSTON	P	M	9614		6441	16055	32015
SAN ANT	EN	AD	4434		4434	8868	18915
SAN ANT	L	AD	2071		2278	4349	14702

TOTAL ACCOUNT EXPENDITURES -   QTR $71284   YTD $148756
TOTAL EXPENDITURE EXCL. SUPPLEMENTS $71284 $148756
PROJECTED 125 MARKETS EXCL. SUPPLS. $121896 $254373

CARLSBERG

CITY	NEWS PAPER		JUL.	AUG.	SEP.	QTR.	TOTAL
BOSTON	G	M					34879
BOSTON	G	S					22429
BOSTON	H	M					5186
ST LOUIS	PD	M		3896		3896	3896

TOTAL ACCOUNT EXPENDITURES -   QTR $3896   YTD $66390
TOTAL EXPENDITURE EXCL. SUPPLEMENTS $3896 $66390
PROJECTED 125 MARKETS EXCL. SUPPLS. $5260 $83378

CARLSBERG LIGHT

CITY	NEWS PAPER		JUL.	AUG.	SEP.	QTR.	TOTAL
LOS ANGELS	T	M	9343	9343		18686	18686

TOTAL ACCOUNT EXPENDITURES -   QTR $18686   YTD $18686
TOTAL EXPENDITURE EXCL. SUPPLEMENTS $18686 $18686
PROJECTED 125 MARKETS EXCL. SUPPLS. $19993 $19993

CERVECERIA CUAUTHEMOC BEERS

CITY	NEWS PAPER		JUL.	AUG.	SEP.	QTR.	TOTAL
LOS ANGELS	T	M			45806	45806	45806

TOTAL ACCOUNT EXPENDITURES -   QTR $45806   YTD $45806
TOTAL EXPENDITURE EXCL. SUPPLEMENTS $45806 $45806
PROJECTED 125 MARKETS EXCL. SUPPLS. $49012 $49012

CHIHUAHUA & TECATE

CITY	NEWS PAPER		JUL.	AUG.	SEP.	QTR.	TOTAL
LOS ANGELS	T	M					14014
SAN DIEGO	T	E					1195
SAN DIEGO	U	M					1195
SAN FRAN	C	M					4812
SAN FRAN	E	E					4812

TOTAL ACCOUNT EXPENDITURES -   QTR   YTD $26028
TOTAL EXPENDITURE EXCL. SUPPLEMENTS $26028
PROJECTED 125 MARKETS EXCL. SUPPLS. $35299

CLASSIC

CITY	NEWS PAPER		JUL.	AUG.	SEP.	QTR.	TOTAL
LONG ISL	N	E					36695

TOTAL ACCOUNT EXPENDITURES -   QTR   YTD $36695
TOTAL EXPENDITURE EXCL. SUPPLEMENTS $36695
PROJECTED 125 MARKETS EXCL. SUPPLS. $38163

COORS

CITY	NEWS PAPER		JUL.	AUG.	SEP.	QTR.	TOTAL
AKRON	BJ	M		1113		1113	1113
ATLANTA	J	E					619

Media Audience Measurement Sources

Source 6

Nielsen Television Index (NTI) Pocketpiece

Research Firm

Nielsen Media Research Company

Frequency

Published twice monthly, this report covers forty-eight weeks of each year.

Data Collection

This source employs the "people meter" technology. It is an electronic metering device installed with each set in the selected household. Each member of the Nielsen household panel uses this personalized meter which operates in the same way that remote control does with a television set. The people meter operation began in 1987 with an expected final sample size of 4,000 households. The audit created by this demographic measurement is called the *national audience composition* (NAC).

Function/Purpose

Reporting of program audiences is the primary function of this report. Program-by-program audience data are presently limited to the so-called wired networks—ABC, CBS, and NBC—although cable network and national satellite station estimates are shown as categories of audience interest. Program audiences for cable and "superstations" are available in special reports.

The frequency of the report and its rapid delivery schedule (twelve days following the survey period) make it a valuable trend or tracking survey for major advertisers and network executives.

Format Explanations

The revised version of the Pocketpiece still features the traditional networks on the top half of each day or night section. The change in format now reports all other viewing activity in the bottom portion. Although some of the viewing options ("Pay Services"—HBO, etc.—and "PBS") are noncommercial, there is still interest in the impact such sources have on commercial television alternatives.

Household Estimates. Three types of data are used in this portion: ratings, share of audience in percentages, and numerical projections of households. Each program is segmented into fifteen-minute blocks for reporting with the exceptions shown with the asterisk (*). These are thirty-minute averages involving the current and preceding quarter hours.

Average Audience Ratings. This figure reports the percentage of U.S. television households viewing the program during an *average minute* for each segment (either a quarter or half hour). The average audience rating shown immediately above the dark horizontal line is for that quarter-hour segment. The "average" means Nielsen computes a mean of the fifteen continuous estimates.

If the analyst wishes only a summary for the program, the first percentage shown for each program (e.g., "Dynasty," 15.2) is the average of all quarter hours for that program.

Share of Audience. This is a percentage based on all U.S. television household viewing at the time. It is a relative measure of popularity.

Illustration

An agency client has purchased a participation that ran in the 10:30 P.M.–10:45 P.M. segment of "Dynasty." Here are the likely summary figures drawn for the analysis:

Average Household Rating (program)	15.2
Average Household Rating (10:30 P.M.–10:45 P.M.)	15.2
Share of Audience	26

A-6 *Nielsen* NATIONAL TV AUDIENCE ESTIMATES — EVE.WED. SEP.30, 1987

TIME	7:00	7:15	7:30	7:45	8:00	8:15	8:30	8:45	9:00	9:15	9:30	9:45	10:00	10:15	10:30	10:45		
HUT	52.9	54.2	55.5	57.7	57.3	58.9	60.5	62.2	62.7	63.1	63.4	62.5	60.6	59.4	58.4	55.6		

ABC TV

PERFECT STRANGERS | HEAD OF THE CLASS | HOOPERMAN | SLAP MAXWELL (PAE) | ←————DYNASTY———→ (PAE)

AVERAGE AUDIENCE (Hhlds (000) & %)
SHARE AUDIENCE %
AVG. AUD. BY 1/4 HR %

14,440		15,150		15,420		13,110		13,470			
16.3		17.1		17.4		14.8		15.2	15.5 *		14.9 *
28		28		28		24		26	26 *		26 *
15.8	16.8	16.6	17.7	17.3	17.5	15.1	14.5	15.5	15.5	15.2	14.7

CBS TV

←————OLDEST ROOKIE————→ | ←———MAGNUM, P.I.———→ (R)(PAE) | ←———EQUALIZER———→

9,570			13,200			12,400			
10.8	10.4 *	11.2 *	14.9 *	14.1 *	15.7 *	14.0	14.2 *		13.9 *
18	18 *	18 *	24	22 *	25 *	24	24 *		24 *
10.2	10.5	11.0	11.4	13.8	14.4	15.5	16.0	14.2	14.1	14.1	13.6

NBC TV

←———HIGHWAY TO HEAVEN———→ | ←———A YEAR IN THE LIFE———→ | ←———ST. ELSEWHERE———→

11,960			10,720			12,490			
13.5	12.9 *	14.0 *	12.1 *	11.7 *	12.5 *	14.1	13.8 *		14.3 *
23	22 *	23 *	19	19 *	20 *	24	23 *		25 *
12.7	13.1	14.0	14.0	11.6	11.9	12.5	12.5	13.5	14.1	14.6	14.1

INDEPENDENTS

| AVERAGE AUDIENCE | 13.7 | 13.0 | 13.1 | 14.2 | 13.6 | 13.4 | 11.0 | 9.2 |
| SHARE AUDIENCE % | 26 | 23 | 23 | 23 | 22 | 21 | 18 | 16 |

SUPERSTATIONS

| AVERAGE AUDIENCE | 3.2 | 2.6 | 2.6 | 3.1 | 2.9 | 2.8 | 2.6 | 2.3 |
| SHARE AUDIENCE % | 6 | 5 | 4 | 5 | 5 | 4 | 4 | 4 |

PBS

| AVERAGE AUDIENCE | 1.8 | 2.2 | 2.8 | 3.5 | 3.1 | 2.9 | 2.2 | 1.7 |
| SHARE AUDIENCE % | 3 | 4 | 5 | 6 | 5 | 5 | 4 | 3 |

CABLE ORIG.

| AVERAGE AUDIENCE | 4.1 | 5.1 | 4.8 | 4.6 | 5.5 | 6.0 | 5.7 | 5.0 |
| SHARE AUDIENCE % | 8 | 9 | 8 | 7 | 9 | 10 | 10 | 9 |

PAY SERVICES

| AVERAGE AUDIENCE | 1.7 | 2.3 | 2.6 | 3.0 | 3.7 | 4.0 | 3.9 | 3.3 |
| SHARE AUDIENCE % | 3 | 4 | 4 | 5 | 6 | 6 | 7 | 6 |

U.S. TV HOUSEHOLDS: 88,600,000

For explanation of symbols, See page B.

A-7

Source 7

Arbitron Ratings/Television ("Daypart Summary")

Research Firm

Arbitron Ratings Company

Frequency

This report covers 210 markets with a variable frequency of from four to seven reports per year depending on market size. Each season of the year is represented.

Data Collection

Arbitron uses personal diaries placed by random telephone contact for nearly all scheduled markets. Sample sizes vary (200 to 2,000). In eleven of the largest markets, a sample of electronic meter households is used to supplement the diaries. The sample size of the electronic sample varies from between 300 to 500 per market.

Function/Purpose

These reports are generally designed to assist buyers and sellers of spot television time in estimating the size and composition of television audiences.

The "Daypart Summary" gives researchers a fast recap on hourly blocks of the broadcast day on a station-by-station basis. Because broad time-blocks are used, program titles are excluded. This summary is an expedient source for verifying station history in a daypart.

Format Explanations

This summary reports data in raw (headcount) and percentage form (ratings). The figures are based on the average of each fifteen-minute segment within the block. See page 26 for a full discussion of the "HUT/Total" recaps.

Two geographic areas are reported on—total survey area or TSA and area of dominant influence or ADI. The TSA is the larger of the two incorporating the ADI counties and other counties that meet minimum reporting standards set by Arbitron. The ADI area is also a predetermined list of counties that have been assigned to a home market. Each area consists of all counties in which the home-market commercial stations and satellite stations reported in combination received a preponderance of the counties' total viewing hours. These assignments are reviewed annually.

Audience descriptions follow standard breaks according to age and gender. A variety of age breaks are reported in anticipation of a variety of age profiles desired by different advertisers.

Illustrations

Assume that a buyer is considering a purchase in the late news period in this market. For the sake of illustration, the target audience is women 18–49 years. Because this is a market in the eastern time zone, the late news will run from 11:00 P.M.–11:30 P.M. This report shows a very dominant position for WKTV. Its ADI rating for household is 14.0 and that is 3.5 times greater than the next closest competitor. In target viewers under the TSA area, WKTV is still dominant with an average of 5,000. Remember, this is a seven-day average. Individual shows may be higher or lower. Under the ADI ratings, WKTV has a 7.0 rating for women 18–49; that rating is 3.5 times greater than the closest competitor's.

Subsequent steps of analysis would incorporate these data with cost information to calculate cost per rating point (CPRP) or cost per thousand impressions (CPM).

Daypart Audience Estimates Summary

TOTAL SURVEY AREA, IN THOUSANDS (000's)

Source 8

Arbitron Ratings/Television ("Weekly Program Estimates")

Research Firm

Arbitron Ratings Company

Frequency

Individual market reports are made throughout the year, with the largest markets reported as many as seven times and smaller markets receiving no fewer than four reports. Arbitron reports on 210 individual markets each year.

Data Collection

This report is compiled from two survey methods. The vast majority of markets are measured by individual diaries placed by telephone. The diary sample size varies from 200 to 2,000 per market. The largest television markets are measured by a sample of electronic meters. Currently, the sample sizes for metered markets ranges from 300 to 500.

Function/Purpose

The general purpose of these reports is to evaluate the audience size and composition of program segments and other commercial positions. The role for the "Weekly Program Estimates" section is to allow evaluation of program segments on a day-to-day basis. The evaluation may be in consideration of a purchase of time or it may be for postcampaign monitoring.

Estimates are provided for each half-hour segment ("within program audiences") and for commercial positions between programs ("station break averages"). The latter are produced by averaging the audience totals for the fifteen minutes preceding the fifteen minutes following the break position.

Format Explanations

The formats for each section of the television ratings report by Arbitron are very similar. Data are organized around two geographic areas, TSA and ADI, with each offering a special area perspective. Advertisers with products or services in wide distribution would be more interested in the total survey area of each market because the likelihood of wasted coverage is remote. Firms with tighter distribution patterns might be more interested in the ADI figures.

The data are reported in raw projections (headcount) and in percentages (ratings and shares); it is segmented according to standard divisions of age and gender.

At the bottom of each period section is a summary line identified as "HUT/Total." This deserves some explanation. HUT stands for homes using television, which is a summary rating for that time segment. All viewing is reported regardless of the location of the station or the origination of the programming. In most reports, the sum of the ratings for the listed stations will *not* match the HUT figure. The advent of public broadcasting and multitiered cable systems means that part of the rating sample will have as many as twenty different channels to choose from. Noting every possible channel would make these reports very long and much more difficult to use. The compromise is to show the nonhome station activity in the summary line only. The "total" aspect reflects the same situation in headcount or viewers.

Illustration

Much of this format has already been described elsewhere (see page 24, and above). Still some attention should be given to the "Station Break Average Estimates" section because of its unique reporting situation.

Assume the buyer has been offered a thirty-second position preceding the popular "Bill Cosby Show." What audience value should be assigned to this position? The weekly program estimate for 8:00 P.M.–8:30 P.M. includes viewing up to thirty minutes following the break position. Logic suggests that thirty minutes away from the break is too long for accuracy. The same would be true for the show preceding "Cosby." The report system does not reflect any estimates for less than fifteen minutes, and diaries do not ask if people viewed between programs. The compromise position is for the report to average the values of the two flanking fifteen-minute segments and report the break as an average. In our example, the household "compromise figure" is 36, or 36,000 homes for the 8:00 P.M. break. Obviously, any such "estimate" is truly that and must be used with caution (i.e., susceptible to substantial error).

Weekly Program Estimates

Time Period Average Estimates

DAY AND TIME / STATION / PROGRAM	WK1 4/30	WK2 5/7	WK3 5/14	WK4 5/21	RTG R	SHR S	FEB 86	NOV 85	JUL 85	MAY 85	TV HH	PERSONS 18+	12-24	12-34	WOMEN TOT 18+	18-49	12-24	18-34	25-49	25-54	WKG WMN 18+	MEN TOT 18+	18-49	18-34	25-49	25-54
	1	2	3	4	5	6	58	59	60	61	11	13	15	16	18	19	20	21	22	23	24	25	26	27	28	29
RELATIVE STD-ERR 25% THRESHOLDS (1 σ) 50%					5 1						10 2	16 4	20 5	18 4	13 3	12 3	18 4	15 3	11 2	11 2	12 3	12 3	12 3	16 4	11 2	11 2
6:30P- 7:00P																										
WKTV NBC NGHT NWS	*	*	*	*	23	42	40	45	46	46	26	44	2	9	24	7	2	5	6	7	3	20	9	3	9	11
WUTR ABC WRLD NWS	*	*	*	*	8	14	16	18	22	23	10	15	2	3	8	4	1	2	3	4	3	7	3	1	2	2
WTVH CBS EVE NEWS	*	*	*	*	4	7	5	4	3	3																
HUT/TOTAL	*	*	*	*	54		66	59	48	55	36	59	4	12	32	11	3	7	9	11	6	27	12	4	11	13
7:00P- 7:30P																										
WKTV NW NWLYWD GM	*	*	*	*	12	22	24	26	14	20	17	29	9	11	17	7	5	3	5	6	3	12	6	3	5	5
WUTR WHEEL OF FOR	*	*	*	*	16	30	27	23	31	33	21	40	4	8	23	9	3	4	6	8	5	17	6	2	6	7
WTVH ENTRTNMT TON	*				5	8																				
SS ARRV POM		*																								
--4 WK AVG--					4	7	9	13	16	10																
HUT/TOTAL	*	*	*	*	53		67	65	43	58	38	69	13	19	40	16	8	7	11	14	8	29	12	5	11	12
7:30P- 8:00P																										
WKTV NW PRCE RGHT	*	*	*	*	14	25	23	23	20	20	23	42	10	16	25	9	6	5	7	10	4	18	8	5	5	6
WUTR JEOPARDY-S	*	*	*	*	11	21	28	21	25	32	17	27	3	7	17	7	1	3	6	8	5	11	5	1	4	4
WTVH MASH-S	*	*	*	*	6	10	9	12	14	12																
HUT/TOTAL	*	*	*	*	54		66	65	42	57	40	69	13	23	42	16	7	8	13	18	9	29	13	6	9	10
8:00P- 8:30P																										
WKTV BILL COSBY	*	*	*	*	37	54	54	58	47	51	51	83	29	50	51	35	19	24	25	27	11	32	21	13	16	18
WUTR BELVE IT NOT	*	*			2	3					3	3			1					1	1	2	1	1	1	1
20/20 SP		*																								
--4 WK AVG--					3	5	8	4	3	9	4	5		1	2				1	1	1	2	1		1	1
WTVH SIMON-SIMON	*	*	*	*	8	11	13	9	18	14																
HUT/TOTAL	*	*	*	*	67		74	74	58	64	55	88	29	51	53	35	19	24	25	28	12	34	22	13	17	19
8:30P- 9:00P																										
WKTV FAMILY TIES	*	*	*	*	30	46	50	56	41	43	44	70	29	49	44	33	20	22	23	25	12	26	20	13	16	17
WUTR BELVE IT NOT	*	*			3	4					3	3			1	1		1	1	1		2	1	1	1	1
20/20 SP		*																								
--4 WK AVG--					4	5	7	5	3	10	4	5		1	3	1			1	1		2	1		1	1
WTVH SIMON-SIMON	*	*	*	*	7	11	14	10	19	15																
HUT/TOTAL	*	*	*	*	64		73	70	55	63	48	75	29	50	47	34	20	22	24	26	12	28	21	13	17	18

Time Period Average Estimates

Station Break Average Estimates

DAY, TIME AND STATION	TEENS TOTAL 12-17	CHILDREN 2-11	6-11	PERSONS 18-49	12-24	12-34	WOMEN TOT 18+	18-49	12-24	18-34	25-49	25-54	WKG WMN 18+	MEN TOT 18+	18-49	18-34	25-49	25-54	TNS TOT 12-17	CHD TOT 2-11
	30	31	32	37	38	39	41	42	43	44	45	46	47	48	49	50	51	52	53	54
THRES 25% HOLDS 50%	17 4	24 6	19 5	6 1	19 5	10 2	6 1	10 2	31 10	21 6	11 3	10 2	19 5	7 1	11 2	20 5	12 3	11 3	34 11	31 10
6:30P																				
WKTV	2	1	1	11	4	8	19	10	6	10	12	13	12	17	12	7	17	18	6	3
WUTR				5	3	6	6	3	4	6	6	9	6	4	3	3	3			
WTVH				2	1	3	2		1	2	3	1	5	2	2	2	4			
H/P/T	2	1	1	28	18	21	42	26	16	21	31	32	37	43	29	22	31	34	18	29
7:00P																				
WKTV	6	4	4	7	11	8	10	8	11	6	7	6	9	8	7	6	6	7	14	7
WUTR	1	7	4	7	3	4	14	7	4	5	9	11	10	13	7	3	9	10	5	16
WTVH				1			2	1			1	1		3	1		1	3		
4 WK				1			2	1			1	1	1	3	1		2	3		
H/P/T	7	11	8	31	29	27	45	33	30	30	35	35	40	43	30	24	29	31	27	35
7:30P																				
WKTV	5	12	8	11	13	12	12	11	7	12	11	10	12	10	10	13	8	9	11	27
WUTR	2	3	1	6	5	5	9	5	1	4	7	7	6	8	6	3	7	6	9	7
WTVH				4	4	4	3	3	5	4	2	3	4	5	4	4	5	2	5	5
H/P/T	7	15	9	34	35	30	45	33	33	29	35	35	41	44	35	28	32	33	35	50
8:00P																				
WKTV	13	25	16	35	39	38	36	42	50	52	35	34	27	27	28	29	27	27	31	43
WUTR		1					1				1	1	2	2	1		1	1		
4 WK		1					2				1	1	2	2	1		1	1		
WTVH				2	1	2	5	2	2	2	2	1	4	3	2	4	3	2	
H/P/T	13	26	16	50	51	48	59	56	64	60	53	54	48	50	45	36	45	46	49	51
8:30P																				
WKTV	14	17	9	31	35	35	29	38	48	46	32	30	29	20	25	28	25	24	30	31
WUTR		1		1			1	1		2	1	1		2	1		1	1		
4 WK		1		1			2	1		1	1	1		2	1		1	1		1
WTVH				2	1	2	5	2	2	2	2	1	4	3	2	4	3	2	1	
H/P/T	14	18	9	50	48	48	56	56	60	60	55	54	53	47	44	39	44	46	44	39
9:00P																				
WKTV	5	7	4	30	25	29	25	30	24	35	28	26	27	24	30	34	27	26	13	11
WUTR	2	1	1	8	2	6	9	11	4	11	12	11	9	5	6	6	8	7		3
4 WK	2	1	1	7	2	5	10	10	3	8	12	11	7	6	5	4	7	6		2
WTVH				4	4	4	4	8	5	5	3	2	4	4	3	5	5	3	1	
H/P/T	7	8	5	53	44	50	57	56	48	59	58	57	57	52	51	51	51	53	34	14
9:30P																				
WKTV	3	5	2	26	21	25	23	26	19	30	25	23	27	22	27	31	23	23	8	3
WUTR	2	1	1	9	2	6	9	11	4	11	12	11	9	6	6	6	9	8		
4 WK	2	1	1	7	1	5	10	10	4	8	12	11	7	6	5	4	6	6		2
WTVH				4	4	4	3	5	8	5	3	2	4	4	3	5	5	3	1	
H/P/T	5	6	3	50	35	42	53	50	33	52	52	51	51	50	49	50	51	19	7	

TIME ADI TV HH RTG	TV HH	WOMEN TOT 18+	18-49	18-34	25-49	MEN TOT 18+	18-49	18-34	25-49	CHD TOT 2-11
5	11	18	19	21	22	25	26	27	28	31
5 1	.10 2	13 3	12 3	15 3	11 2	12 3	12 3	16 4	11 2	24 6
6:30P										
24	27	24	7	4	6	20	9	4	8	1
10	12	10	4	2	4	9	4	2	3	
3										
57	39	34	11	6	10	29	12	5	11	1
7:00P										
17	22	20	7	4	6	16	7	3	7	3
12	15	16	7	3	5	12	5	2	4	4
4 53	37	36	14	7	11	28	12	5	11	7
7:30P										
13	20	21	8	4	6	15	7	4	5	8
14	19	20	8	4	6	14	6	2	5	5
5 54	39	41	16	8	12	29	13	6	10	13
8:00P										
25	36	38	22	15	16	25	15	9	10	19
7 7	11	10	4	1	3	7	3	1	2	2
60	47	48	26	16	19	32	18	10	12	21
8:30P										
33	48	48	34	23	24	29	21	13	16	21
3 7	4	2	1		1	2	1		1	1
60	52	50	35	23	25	31	22	13	17	22
9:00P										
28	41	40	29	19	20	28	22	14	16	11
7 7	10	9	5	2	4	5	3	1	3	1
66	51	49	34	21	24	33	25	15	19	12
9:30P										
27	38	35	23	16	17	29	22	14	15	6
11 6	16	17	9	4	8	8	4	2	4	1
66	54	52	32	20	25	37	26	16	19	7

Source 9

Arbitron Ratings/Radio

Research Firm

Arbitron Ratings Company

Frequency

Over 250 markets are surveyed at least once per year. The largest 10 percent of these are surveyed from three to four times per year.

Data Collection

The radio data are collected from personal diaries placed with each member of the household (12+ years of age). Market sample populations are generated from telephone listings. Sample sizes are statistically derived and vary widely (250 to 13,000 households) depending on the market.

Function/Purpose

The focus in radio audience measurement is upon station listeners rather than to a program title as found in television. Measurement is segmented into basic age and gender groups. Audiences are reported in two ways: as an average audience (per quarter hour) within a portion of the day, and as the cumulative or different people listening to at least one quarter-hour segment within the day portion (daypart).

The *average audience* tells planners how many people listen at a given time. This "static" measure estimates the number of people that will have an opportunity to be exposed to the message in any particular time segment.

The *cumulative audience* tells the planner how many different people will hear at least some of the station's programming. *Cume* is less of a measure of station loyalty than it is a measure of the station's ability to attract a more diverse audience (different listeners over multiple time periods).

Format Explanations

This source provides three data expressions—an estimated number of listeners (headcounts), a percentage of total market audience segment (ratings), and a percentage of all those listening at a given time (share).

Radio Ratings reports audiences by basic age and gender groups. As the example illustrates, a number of adult age configurations are shown. In addition, adult males, adult female, and teen segments are reported separately.

The geographic dimensions are called "Total Area" and "Metro Survey Area." The total area includes the metropolitan counties and other counties that satisfy minimum reporting standards for the home market. This total area is, in part, dependent upon the home stations' signal strengths and their audience popularity. The metropolitan survey area corresponds to the government's Office of Management and Budget definitions.

Illustration

The excerpt shown here is an Iowa–Illinois border area called the Quad Cities. The daypart excerpt is from Monday through Friday, 6:00 A.M.–10:00 A.M. (known as morning drive time).

Assume that the buyer has a target audience of adults 25–49 years old located within the metro survey area. The request is to recommend the top three stations. The only section heading needed is "Adults 25–49." Selecting which stations to recommend is more complicated. Station KIIK is the first choice regardless of the data category used. The same is true for WLLR in the second position. Third place is in dispute because KRVR (1.7), WHBF-FM (1.6), WMRZ (1.5), and WOC (1.5) are virtually tied, based on average ratings per quarter hour.

With this situation, the buyer is likely to shift analysis to the cumulative estimates to break the deadlock. Based on Monday through Friday, WHBF-FM becomes a clearer choice with 18,100 listeners over the five-day period. Although on any individual quarter-hour basis WHBF-FM has a modest 2,200 listeners, the station's audience turnover in a five-day period is a powerful 8 to 1 (18,100/2,200). This would give the station a hold on the third position.

||| Adults |||

Average Quarter-Hour and Cume Listening Estimates

QUAD CITIES (DAVNPRT-RI-MOLINE)
SPRING 1985

MONDAY-FRIDAY 6.00AM-10.00AM

Adults 18+ / Adults 18-34 / Adults 18-49

STATION CALL LETTERS	18+ TA AVG (00)	18+ TA CUME (00)	18+ MSA AVG (00)	18+ MSA CUME (00)	18+ MSA RTG	18+ MSA SHR	18-34 TA AVG	18-34 TA CUME	18-34 MSA AVG	18-34 MSA CUME	18-34 RTG	18-34 SHR	18-49 TA AVG	18-49 TA CUME	18-49 MSA AVG	18-49 MSA CUME	18-49 RTG	18-49 SHR
KBQC	8	72	8	72	.3	1.0	5	50	5	50	.4	1.8	8	72	8	72	.4	1.7
KFMH	15	86	13	69	.5	1.7	15	86	13	69	1.1	4.7	15	86	13	69	.7	2.7
KIIK	276	1097	159	651	5.6	20.4	177	713	91	407	7.9	32.9	263	1049	148	614	8.0	31.1
KKZX	7	107	7	107	.2	.9	5	74	5	74	.4	1.8	7	89	7	89	.4	1.5
KRVR	81	359	72	262	2.6	9.2	19	66	16	38	1.4	5.8	40	153	35	104	1.9	7.4
WHBF	95	454	87	387	3.1	11.2	10	49	6	35	.5	2.2	26	165	21	126	1.1	4.4
WHBF FM	47	397	35	283	1.2	4.5	27	223	20	169	1.7	7.2	35	310	25	227	1.3	5.3
WJRE	10	61	9	42	.3	1.2	3	36	3	17	.2	.7	4	38	3	19	.1	.6
WKEI	33	106	28	89	1.0	3.6	5	5	1	5	.1	.4	10	30	8	21	.4	1.7
WLLR	146	671	87	428	3.1	11.2	51	242	30	155	2.6	10.8	111	499	66	312	3.6	13.9
WMRZ	27	172	27	163	1.0	3.5	12	76	12	76	1.0	4.3	23	154	23	145	1.2	4.8
WOC	108	470	96	393	3.4	12.3	7	48	3	29	.3	1.1	26	154	21	128	1.1	4.4
WXLP	81	462	40	251	1.4	5.1	75	431	38	224	3.3	13.7	77	458	40	251	2.2	8.4
KKRQ	11	41					11	41					11	41				
WGN	46	215	12	55	.4	1.5	7	28	3		.3	1.1	22	104	7	38	.4	1.5
WLS	26	235	6	74	.2	.8	15	186	4		.3	1.4	26	227	6	66	.3	1.3
WMT	66	241	6	31	.2	.8	9	68	2		.2	.7	39	144	3	19	.2	.7
WSWT	24	70	5	22	.2	.6	4	4					10	33	2	13	.1	.4
METRO TOTALS			779	2372		27.6			277	949		24.0			476	1575		25.7

Adults 25-49 / Adults 25-54 / Adults 35-64

STATION CALL LETTERS	25-49 TA AVG (00)	25-49 TA CUME (00)	25-49 MSA AVG (00)	25-49 MSA CUME (00)	25-49 RTG	25-49 SHR	25-54 TA AVG	25-54 TA CUME	25-54 MSA AVG	25-54 MSA CUME	25-54 RTG	25-54 SHR	35-64 TA AVG	35-64 TA CUME	35-64 MSA AVG	35-64 MSA CUME	35-64 RTG	35-64 SHR
KBQC	6	58	6	55	.4	1.7	6	58	6	55	.4	1.5	3	22	3	22	.2	.8
KFMH	12	55	11	55	.8	3.0	12	64	11	55	.7	2.7						
KIIK	219	820	116	474	8.4	32.0	228	852	123	495	7.9	29.9	95	368	64	228	5.2	17.5
KKZX	5	52	5	52	.4	1.4	5	55	5	55	.3	1.2	2	21	2	21	.2	.5
KRVR	28	109	23	82	1.7	6.4	34	135	28	95	1.8	6.8	36	193	33	137	2.7	9.0
WHBF	19	135	18	110	1.3	5.0	30	198	29	162	1.9	7.1	58	297	55	255	4.5	15.0
WHBF FM	32	254	22	181	1.6	6.1	33	273	23	190	1.5	5.6	18	154	13	94	1.1	3.6
WJRE	10	30	8	21	.6	2.2	3	15	3	15	.2	.7	6	58	6	19	.5	1.6
WKEI	13	44	13	27	.5	1.9	13	27	8	27	.5	1.9	19	41	14	41	1.1	3.8
WLLR	92	417	50	243	3.6	13.8	104	485	56	278	3.6	13.6	89	402	55	257	4.5	15.0
WMRZ	21	144	21	135	1.5	5.8	22	146	22	146	1.4	5.4	15	96	15	87	1.2	4.1
WOC	26	150	21	124	1.5	5.8	40	224	31	181	2.0	7.5	61	282	54	231	4.4	14.8
WXLP	32	203	16	133	1.2	4.4	36	207	16	133	1.0	3.9	6	31	2	27	.2	.5
KKRQ	2	8					2	8										
WGN	22	104	7	38	.5	1.9	33	127	10	44	.6	2.4	29	135	9	40	.7	2.5
WLS	22	147	6	59	.4	1.7	22	149	6	61	.4	1.5	11	49	2	23	.2	.5
WMT	39	136	3	19	.2	.8	47	153	3	22	.2	.7	39	103	2	14	.2	.5
WSWT	10	33	2	13	.1	.6	10	33	2	13	.1	.5	12	41	3	14	.2	.8
METRO TOTALS			362	1212		26.1			411	1362		26.4			366	1069		29.9

Footnote Symbols   (•) means audience estimates adjusted for actual broadcast schedule   ARBITRON RATINGS

PAGE 39

Source 10

Birch Radio Qualitative Report

Research Firm

Birch Radio, Inc.

Frequency

This report is published quarterly and is prepared for more than sixty markets in the forty-eight contiguous states.

Data Collection

Samples are drawn from listed telephone numbers in each market. The last digit of each number selected is then increased by "1" to cover unlisted numbers. Data are collected by telephone interview using a recall technique covering "yesterday's listening" in addition to product questioning.

Function/Purpose

Birch Radio Qualitative is an example of an audience study that goes beyond "head-counts." Birch combines media usage (station listenership) with product use. This combination provides the broadcast analyst a measure of station popularity directly related to consumer prospects. Thus, as in the example, a beer advertiser can select radio stations according to the number of beer drinkers who are listeners. This selection procedure is more specialized than selecting the station based on general demographic data alone.

Format Explanations

The Birch Qualitative marries audience data with some baseline measurement of popularity. In the example, the two far left columns labeled "AQH" and "Cume" establish the audience strength of each station.

AQH stands for average quarter hour or the average number of listeners estimated to be listening during a typical fifteen-minute segment, Monday through Sunday, from 6:00 A.M. to midnight. *Cume* indicates the different listeners measured over the same time frame (who heard the station for at least one segment within the period).

All the other columns listed refer to product use measurements (beer). It is characteristic in research based on use or consumption that segments be developed to indicate the amount or level of usage. It is more valuable to learn how much one uses than simply to be categorized as a user. Birch uses the standard definitions of "light," "medium," and "heavy" to clarify the limits of each level.

The columns titled "% Ind" and "% Pen" are comparative measures. These contrast each station's male cume audience (as beer drinkers) with the total number of male listeners (cume) regardless of beer use. Specifically, "% Ind" is an index and shows the likelihood of a listener being a beer drinker with some predetermined level of consumption. The higher the index the more likely a male listener to that station is a beer consumer. The "% Pen" provides a different perspective on the same question. It shows the size of the station's male beer-drinker audience. It is a form of specialized rating.

The Birch report also indicates the efficiency (low waste or nonprospect audience) of the station. This is shown in the last columns labeled "AQH Composition %" and "Cume Composition %." These columns tell us the relative percentage of each station's male audience that fits the product target. Although neither can suggest the size or magnitude, both indicate the proportion of desired audience within each station's total audience. Stations with the highest percentages are those with the least amount of wasted coverage. To a beer advertiser, a nondrinker is of little or no value. Because station rates are based on the size of the audience regardless of consumption patterns, the higher the percentage, the better the cost-per-thousand potential.

Illustration

If an audience that consumed a "medium level" of beer was the most desired, the logical questions from a time-buyer might be: Which station is the best in covering the target audience and which station has the highest proportion of beer drinkers in its audience?

Coverage is best reflected in the "% Pen" column and WFBQ-FM is clearly the first choice for size (44.3 percent of medium beer drinkers listen to WFBQ-FM). For efficiency, either the "AQH Composition %" or "Cume Composition" are worthwhile. In this case, it does not matter. WENS-FM (with 33.9 and 39.5 figures) is the choice for efficiency.

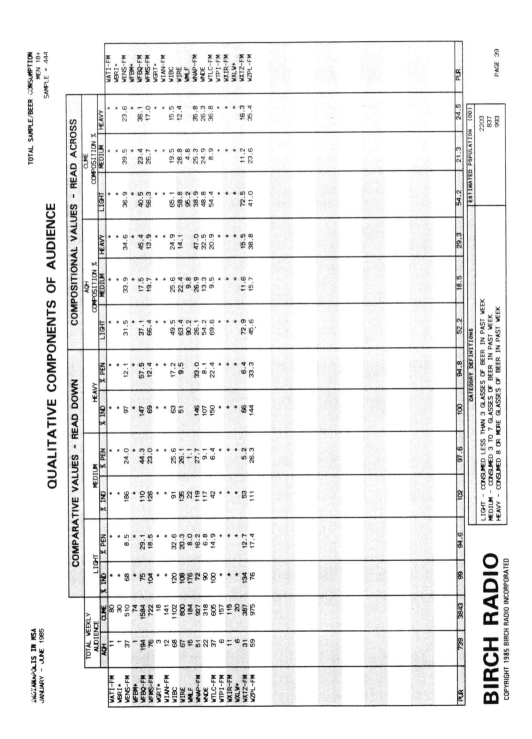

QUALITATIVE COMPONENTS OF AUDIENCE

INDIANAPOLIS IN MSA
JANUARY – JUNE 1985

TOTAL SAMPLE/BEER CONSUMPTION
MEN 18+
SAMPLE = 444

| | TOTAL WEEKLY AUDIENCE | | COMPARATIVE VALUES – READ DOWN | | | | | | | | COMPOSITIONAL VALUES – READ ACROSS | | | | | | | |
| | | | LIGHT | | MEDIUM | | HEAVY | | | AQH COMPOSITION % | | | CUME COMPOSITION % | | | |
	AQH	CUME	% IND	% PEN	% IND	% PEN	% IND	% PEN		LIGHT	MEDIUM	HEAVY	LIGHT	MEDIUM	HEAVY	
WATI-FM	11	80	*	*	*	*	*	*		*	*	*	*	*	*	WATI-FM
WBRI*	1	30	*	*	*	*	*	*		*	*	*	*	*	*	WBRI*
WENS-FM	37	510	68	8.5	186	24.0	97	12.1		31.5	33.9	34.6	36.9	39.5	23.6	WENS-FM
WFBM*	1	74	*	*	*	*	*	*		*	*	*	*	*	*	WFBM*
WFBQ-FM	194	1584	75	29.1	110	44.3	147	57.5		37.1	17.5	45.4	40.5	23.4	36.1	WFBQ-FM
WFMS-FM	76	722	104	18.5	126	23.0	69	12.4		66.4	19.7	13.9	56.3	26.7	17.0	WFMS-FM
WGRT*	3	18	*	*	*	*	*	*		*	*	*	*	*	*	WGRT*
WIAN-FM	12	141	*	*	*	*	*	*		*	*	*	*	*	*	WIAN-FM
WIBC	68	1102	120	32.6	91	25.6	63	17.2		49.5	25.6	24.9	65.1	19.5	15.5	WIBC
WIRE	67	800	108	20.3	135	26.1	51	9.5		63.4	22.4	14.1	58.8	28.8	12.4	WIRE
WMLF	15	184	176	8.0	22	1.1	*	*		90.2	9.8	*	95.2	4.8	*	WMLF
WNAP-FM	51	927	72	16.2	119	27.7	146	33.0		26.1	26.9	47.0	38.9	25.3	35.8	WNAP-FM
WNDE	22	318	90	6.8	117	9.1	107	8.1		54.2	13.3	32.5	48.8	24.9	26.3	WNDE
WTLC-FM	37	605	100	14.9	42	6.4	150	22.4		69.6	9.5	20.9	54.4	8.9	36.8	WTLC-FM
WTPI-FM	6	157	*	*	*	*	*	*		*	*	*	*	*	*	WTPI-FM
WXIR-FM	11	115	*	*	*	*	*	*		*	*	*	*	*	*	WXIR-FM
WXLW*	6	20	*	*	*	*	*	*		*	*	*	*	*	*	WXLW*
WXTZ-FM	31	387	134	12.7	53	5.2	66	6.4		72.9	11.6	15.5	72.5	11.2	16.3	WXTZ-FM
WZPL-FM	59	975	76	17.4	111	26.3	144	33.3		45.6	15.7	38.8	41.0	23.6	35.4	WZPL-FM
PLR	739	3843	99	94.6	102	97.6	100	94.8		52.2	18.5	29.3	54.2	21.3	24.5	PLR

ESTIMATED POPULATION (00)	
	2203
	837
	993

CATEGORY DEFINITIONS

LIGHT – CONSUMED LESS THAN 3 GLASSES OF BEER IN PAST WEEK
MEDIUM – CONSUMED 3 TO 7 GLASSES OF BEER IN PAST WEEK
HEAVY – CONSUMED 8 OR MORE GLASSES OF BEER IN PAST WEEK

BIRCH RADIO
COPYRIGHT 1985 BIRCH RADIO INCORPORATED

PAGE 39

Source 11

Survey of Adults and Markets of Affluence (SAMA)

Research Firm

Mendelsohn Media Research, Inc.

Frequency

This is an annual report conducted during the second and third calendar quarters and released late in the year of issue.

Data Collection

This is a purposive sample of United States households (forty-eight contiguous states) with household yearly incomes of $50,000 or more (approximately 15 percent of all U.S. households).

Because of the special segmentation, Mendelsohn uses great care in the sample preparation. The firm utilizes the facilities of Donnelley Marketing to preselect residences that have the highest probability of upper income status. The initial sample ranges from 20,000 to 25,000 households.

The survey is done by a mail questionnaire. From the original mailing and subsequent qualification of those returned, nearly 7,000 or 30+ percent of the questionnaires are used in the final tabulations.

Function/Purpose

This six-volume study is considered by many to be a specialized extension of the SMRB and MRI multimedia services. In concentrating its study among the affluent, Mendelsohn offers a special focus on what it terms "a prime market for many goods and services."

SAMA covers both product/service data and media audience estimations. Media covered are national magazines and newspapers and selected national television programs. The data are cross-referenced so that planners can see usage and buying patterns within media vehicles.

Format Explanations

In the excerpt shown on the facing page, SAMA audience data are reported in three ways: the projected number of adults, a proportion of the universe ("Percent Coverage"), and the proportion of the vehicle's total audience ("Percent Composition"). Note that to increase the value of a single-page excerpt, a *composite* of magazines, newspapers, and television programs is shown.

Coverage is a form of measurement reflecting the vehicle's coverage of the activity (in this case, purchase of a color television). Thus, an average issue of *Time* covers 25.7 percent of the affluent households that bought a color television set within the last year. Composition is an efficiency factor that tells us what percent of the magazine's total affluent readers participated in buying a color TV set. According to SAMA, 33 percent of *Time*'s affluent readers purchased color television sets.

The data shown refer to household expenditures on television sets during the past year. The top two rows, however, refer to the total audience of each vehicle (apart from television set expenditures). The remaining rows relate to expenditure and the degree of expenditure.

Illustration

Which vehicle on this page covers the most affluent adults who spent $500–$999 for a color television set in the past year? To answer use the $500–$999 segment and find the largest percentage listed. The answer is "CBS News" with a coverage of 28.6 percent.

Which vehicle has the *lowest* waste audience (percent of highest composition)? According to SAMA, *Town & Country Magazine,* with 12.6 percent of its readership involved in the segment, has the lowest percentage of "waste" coverage, 87.4% $(100.0 - 12.6 = 87.4)$.

TABLE 285
VOLUME II: TOTAL ADULTS WITH HOUSEHOLD INCOMES OF $50,000 OR MORE
EXPENDITURES IN PAST YEAR
AVERAGE ISSUE AUDIENCES
(IN THOUSANDS)

	TOTAL AFFLU- ENT ADULTS	SPORTS ILLUS- TRATED	SUNSET	TIME	TOWN & COUNTRY	TRAVEL & LEISURE	TRAVEL/ HOLIDAY	TV GUIDE	USA TODAY
TOTAL	32700	4891	2183	7864	2162	3522	1158	7908	3606
PERCENT COVERAGE	100.0	15.0	6.7	24.0	6.6	10.8	3.5	24.2	11.0
COLOR TELEVISION	10088	1623	699	2597	849	1244	412	2478	1266
PERCENT COMPOSITION	30.8	33.2	32.0	33.0	39.3	35.3	35.6	31.3	35.1
PERCENT COVERAGE	100.0	16.1	6.9	25.7	8.4	12.3	4.1	24.6	12.5
UNDER $250	1147	205	75	276	61	103	48	310	132
PERCENT COMPOSITION	3.5	4.2	3.4	3.5	2.8	2.9	4.1	3.9	3.6
PERCENT COVERAGE	100.0	17.9	6.5	24.1	5.3	9.0	4.2	27.0	11.5
$250 TO $499	4176	594	312	965	302	499	166	786	458
PERCENT COMPOSITION	12.8	12.1	14.3	12.3	14.0	14.2	14.4	9.9	12.7
PERCENT COVERAGE	100.0	14.2	7.5	23.1	7.2	11.9	4.0	18.8	11.0
$500 TO $999	3152	532	213	866	272	376	118	857	422
PERCENT COMPOSITION	9.6	10.9	9.7	11.0	12.6	10.7	10.2	10.8	11.7
PERCENT COVERAGE	100.0	16.9	6.7	27.5	8.6	11.9	3.8	27.2	13.4
$1,000 TO $1,999	1040	180	76	332	132	154	39	346	166
PERCENT COMPOSITION	3.2	3.7	3.5	4.2	6.1	4.4	3.4	4.4	4.6
PERCENT COVERAGE	100.0	17.3	7.3	31.9	12.6	14.8	3.8	33.3	15.9
$2,000 OR MORE	573	113	23	158	82	112	41	180	89
PERCENT COMPOSITION	1.8	2.3	1.1	2.0	3.8	3.2	3.5	2.3	2.5
PERCENT COVERAGE	100.0	19.6	4.0	27.6	14.3	19.5	7.1	31.4	15.5

TABLE 287
VOLUME II: TOTAL ADULTS WITH HOUSEHOLD INCOMES OF $50,000 OR MORE
EXPENDITURES IN PAST YEAR
AVERAGE ISSUE AUDIENCES
(IN THOUSANDS)

	NATIONAL NETWORK NEWS			THE TONIGHT SHOW
	ABC	CBS	NBC	
TOTAL	7958	7411	7782	4173
PERCENT COVERAGE	24.3	22.7	23.8	12.8
COLOR TELEVISION	2683	2381	2571	1526
PERCENT COMPOSITION	33.7	32.1	33.0	36.6
PERCENT COVERAGE	26.6	23.6	25.5	15.1
UNDER $250	220	215	346	195
PERCENT COMPOSITION	2.8	2.9	4.4	4.7
PERCENT COVERAGE	19.1	18.8	30.2	17.0
$250 TO $499	1109	909	1007	579
PERCENT COMPOSITION	13.9	12.3	12.9	13.9
PERCENT COVERAGE	26.6	21.8	24.1	13.9
$500 TO $999	858	901	876	493
PERCENT COMPOSITION	10.8	12.2	11.3	11.8
PERCENT COVERAGE	27.2	28.6	27.8	15.6
$1,000 TO $1,999	307	232	219	187
PERCENT COMPOSITION	3.9	3.1	2.8	4.5
PERCENT COVERAGE	29.5	22.3	21.1	18.0
$2,000 OR MORE	190	124	122	72
PERCENT COMPOSITION	2.4	1.7	1.6	1.7
PERCENT COVERAGE	33.1	21.6	21.3	12.5

Source 12

Publications: Total Audiences ("Demographic Status")

Research Firm

Simmons Market Research Bureau

Frequency

This is an annual report.

Data Collection

SMRB uses a personal interview of over 15,000 adults (one per household) in two waves, from six to eight weeks apart. The sample is disproportionally drawn to over-sample "high-income" households. Postmeasurement weighting then conforms the sample to representative population proportions.

The interview to measure readership of publications is done in person. Most of the more popular magazines are tested on the "through-the-book" method using a scaled-down version of the most current issue. Other publications are tested on the "recent reading" technique that uses an aided recall method. In this report, all locations of publication exposure are included (in or out-of-home reading) equally.

Function/Purpose

This report is a major component of magazine evaluation. Readership is reported through a wide variety of segmentations, both demographic and geographic. In this way, buyers and sellers of magazine placements have a significant amount of reader characteristics to match with the consumer profile of the advertiser.

Some media analysts argue that the audited sales of a publication (circulation) is the most reliable and current measure of reader interest. Circulation, however, tells the planner nothing about the readers. That is why sources such as this SMRB report are so central to planning and selection.

Format Explanations

Each page of this report examines two population groups: the readers of a publication and people with a particular characteristic. The SMRB format is designed to show these separately and in combination. In this way, we can learn how many read a magazine, how many people are in a particular gender segment, and most importantly, how many readers of a magazine are in that gender.

Report segments are divided by the particualr demographic to be reported. Each segmentation is separated into four columns of data. Each column gives a different perspective. For example, look at the last column heading titled "Female Homemakers":

Column A (000). This tells how many female homemakers are readers of a particular magazine.

Column B (% Down). This tells us the percentage of female homemakers who are readers of a particular magazine. The percentage is found by dividing the reader number in Column A by the figure at the very top of that column. That figure is the SMRB estimate of the total number of individuals that fit in the "Female Home-maker" category. Thus, if the top figure in Column A was the same as the figure in Column A for a particular magazine, the percentage in Column B would be 100 percent.

Column C (Across %). This tells us what percentage of the magazine's total read-ers fit into the category. The figure is found by dividing the magazine's figure in Column A by the figure on the far left row. The heading for that column labeled "Total U.S." indicates the total number of readers for the magazine regardless of gender category.

Column D (Indx). This figure, known as an index, compares two percentages—the average percentage of total U.S. adult population that is described as female homemakers and the magazine's percentage of female homemaker/readers shown in Column C. By dividing the magazine's percentage in Column C by the average percentage for the U.S. shown at the very top of Column C, an index is created for Column D. This index refers to chance. It reflects the probability that a reader of the magazine will also be a member of the gender segment. If the calculation produces a figure higher than 100, we have a better than average chance; if it is below 100, the odds are less than average.

These meanings become clearer when an illustration is involved.

Illustration

Assume the planner wanted to check *Vogue (VG)* readership in the female homemaker category:

The "Total U.S." indicates that *VG* has a total adult readership of an average issue of 4,583,000.

Column A, under the "Female Homemaker" heading, tells the planner that *VG* has a readership of 3,419,000 women who are identified as female homemakers.

Column B says that 4.2 percent of U.S. female homemakers are readers of an average issue of *VG* (82,273,000 [number at the very top of Column A] divided into 3,419,000).

Column C reports what percentage of all *VG* adult readers are in the desired female homemaker category (74.6 percent) (3,419,000/4,583,000 = 74.6).

Column D shows an index of 154 (74.6/48.6 = 1.54 × 100 = 154). You are 54 percent more likely to find an adult female homemaker in the *VG* audience than you would among all U.S. adults.

DEMOGRAPHIC STATUS
(ADULTS)

0005
M-1

	TOTAL U.S. '000	ADULTS A '000	B % DOWN	C ACROSS %	D INDX	MALES A '000	B % DOWN	C ACROSS %	D INDX	FEMALES A '000	B % DOWN	C ACROSS %	D INDX	FEMALE HOMEMAKERS A '000	B % DOWN	C ACROSS %	D INDX
TOTAL ADULTS	169460	169460	100.0	100.0	100	80052	100.0	47.2	100	89408	100.0	52.8	100	82273	100.0	48.6	100
SPORTS ILLUSTRATED	14467	14467	8.5	100.0	100	11602	14.5	80.2	170	2865	3.2	19.8	38	2561	3.1	17.7	36
STAR	9755	9755	5.8	100.0	100	3053	3.8	31.3	66	6702	7.5	68.7	130	5885	7.2	60.3	124
SUNDAY	49167	49167	29.0	100.0	100	23955	29.9	48.7	103	25212	28.2	51.3	97	23049	28.0	46.9	97
TV GUIDE	39279	39279	23.2	100.0	100	16852	21.1	42.9	91	22428	25.1	57.1	108	20155	24.5	51.3	106
TENNIS	1293	1293	0.8	100.0	100	795	1.0	61.5	130	498	0.6	38.5	73	413	0.5	31.9	66
TIME	23088	23088	13.6	100.0	100	13213	16.5	57.2	121	9875	11.0	42.8	81	8987	10.9	38.9	80
TOWN & COUNTRY	1356	1356	0.8	100.0	100	372	0.5	27.4	58	984	1.1	72.6	138	911	1.1	67.2	138
TRAVEL & LEISURE	2176	2176	1.3	100.0	100	1137	1.4	52.3	111	1040	1.2	47.8	91	996	1.2	45.8	94
TRUE STORY	3956	3956	2.3	100.0	100	670	0.8	16.9	36	3286	3.7	83.1	157	2970	3.6	75.1	155
USA TODAY	4192	4192	2.5	100.0	100	2973	3.7	70.9	150	1220	1.4	29.1	55	1151	1.4	27.5	57
USA WEEKEND	21399	21399	12.6	100.0	100	10065	12.6	47.0	100	11334	12.7	53.0	100	10550	12.8	49.3	102
U.S.NEWS & WORLD REPORT	10190	10190	6.0	100.0	100	6374	8.0	62.6	132	3817	4.3	37.5	71	3473	4.2	34.1	70
US	4486	4486	2.6	100.0	100	1753	2.2	39.1	83	2733	3.1	60.9	115	2191	2.7	48.8	101
VOGUE	4583	4583	2.7	100.0	100	455	0.6	9.9	21	4129	4.6	90.1	171	3419	4.2	74.6	154
WALL STREET JOURNAL	4843	4843	2.9	100.0	100	3323	4.2	68.6	145	1520	1.7	31.4	59	1494	1.8	30.8	64

0005
M-1

Source 13

Multi-Media Audiences: Adults "Buying Styles"

Research Firm

Simmons Market Research Bureau

Frequency

This is an annual report.

Data Collection

These data are derived from self-administered questionnaires completed by the base sample of the Simmons study. An extensive survey, it covers the use of, or purchase habits regarding, over 500 products and services. In addition, it covers personal motives and purchase behaviors. Simmons reports a completion rate of greater than 75% of the 15,000 adults interviewed.

The psychographic and life-style components of the sample are determined by responses to various position statements. A typical question might ask to what degree the person would agree that this statement fits them, "When in a store, I often will buy an item on the spur of the moment." Agreement would indicate an "impulsive" buying style.

Function/Purpose

The advertiser's marketing intelligence concerning the consumer needs more than social and economic segmentation. Measures of education, age, or income are helpful, but hardly infallible in identifying a brand prospect.

The psychographic or life-style profile gets "closer" to a person's motivation and behavior intentions. This is not a simple dimension to measure and reliability of "self-appraisal" is often questioned. Most agree, however, that adults are generally capable of accurately describing themselves.

This SMRB report makes an effort to expand marketing intelligence by providing some basic behavior profiles. They can be used to position marketing strategy or to assist in media vehicle selection (as in the example).

Format Explanations

The column and row explanations are the same as those already discussed in SMRB examples (see page 34).

Our excerpt of "Buying Styles" shows four categories that are appropriate for certain marketing and brand strategies:

Economy Minded. These are people who are likely to be interested in price reductions or in coupons or other means of efficiency. Although they will consider performance and reputation, these homemakers will not be inclined to pay a premium for such attributes. They are the best candidates for "push" or price promotions.

Experimenters. These are strong candidates for new brands or those that have made significant modifications. These homemakers are willing to change or to try something for the sake of variety or novelty.

Impulsive. This trait signifies a reactor—a person who will make fast and unplanned decisions while at the store. They are more susceptible to in-store displays and attractive packaging. Like experimenters, they will try the new and different.

Persuasible. An obvious description of those who rely, more than others, on advertising in making purchase decisions. These are above-average candidates for strong advertising campaigns.

These characteristics are used in conjunction with specific readership audiences for magazines. In this way, each magazine's readers can be evaluated for the desired psychographic buying style.

Illustration

Assume the planner for a media campaign that will involve on-page coupons is checking magazine candidates for some indication of coupon vitality. In such a situation, the buying style of the "economy minded" would be helpful. Use *Family Circle* as the illustration.

The first figure (A) shows the number of female homemakers of *Family Circle* who consider themselves economy minded. Column B indicates that of all female homemakers who are economy minded, an average issue of *Family Circle* will cover 20.9%. The next figure (C) tells what percentage of the total female homemaker readership of *Family Circle* is economy minded (47.9%). The figure in Column D gives the publication an above average index for economy minded readers (108). Planners could compare the performance of various magazines against one another either for selection or to help in deciding which magazine will receive the largest client investment.

0292 M-8

BUYING STYLE (FEMALE HOMEMAKERS)

0292 M-8

	TOTAL U.S. '000	ECONOMY MINDED A '000	B % DOWN	C % ACROSS	D INDX	EXPERIMENTER A '000	B % DOWN	C % ACROSS	D INDX	IMPULSIVE A '000	B % DOWN	C % ACROSS	D INDX	PERSUASIBLE A '000	B % DOWN	C % ACROSS	D INDX
TOTAL FEMALE HOMEMAKERS	79807	35396	100.0	44.4	100	22950	100.0	28.8	100	18733	100.0	23.5	100	20116	100.0	25.2	100
BARRON'S	*236	**136	0.4	57.6	130	**81	0.4	34.3	119	**36	0.2	15.3	65	**17	0.1	7.2	29
BETTER HOMES & GARDENS	15586	7240	20.5	46.5	105	4345	18.9	27.9	97	3760	20.1	24.1	103	3966	19.7	25.4	101
BON APPETIT	2194	880	2.5	40.1	90	447	1.9	20.4	71	528	2.8	24.1	103	452	2.2	20.6	82
BUSINESS WEEK	1313	584	1.6	44.5	100	372	1.6	28.3	99	239	1.3	18.2	78	271	1.3	20.6	82
CAR AND DRIVER	314	*214	0.6	68.2	154	**152	0.7	48.4	168	**80	0.4	25.5	109	**33	0.2	10.5	42
CBS MAGAZINE NETWORK (GROSS)	2463	1196	3.4	48.6	109	910	4.0	36.9	128	602	3.2	24.4	104	569	2.8	23.1	92
CHANGING TIMES	1087	433	1.2	39.8	90	285	1.2	26.2	91	260	1.4	23.9	102	235	1.2	21.6	86
COLONIAL HOMES	1233	546	1.5	44.3	100	384	1.7	31.1	108	*226	1.2	18.3	78	355	1.8	28.8	114
CONDE NAST MAG. PKG. (GROSS)	12548	5484	15.5	43.7	99	3824	16.7	30.5	106	3125	16.7	24.9	106	3396	16.9	27.1	107
CONSUMERS DIGEST	1138	525	1.5	46.1	104	257	1.1	22.6	79	339	1.8	29.8	127	270	1.3	23.7	94
COSMOPOLITAN	6885	2809	7.9	40.8	92	2210	9.6	32.1	112	1677	9.0	24.4	104	1687	8.4	24.5	97
COUNTRY LIVING	1904	750	2.1	39.4	89	608	2.6	31.9	111	418	2.2	22.0	94	377	1.9	19.8	79
CUISINE	1341	623	1.8	46.5	105	363	1.6	27.1	94	313	1.7	23.3	99	326	1.6	24.3	96
CYCLE WORLD	*206	**105	0.3	51.0	115	**152	0.7	73.8	257	**109	0.6	52.9	225	**35	0.2	17.0	67
DECORATING & CRAFT IDEAS	2244	1043	2.9	46.5	105	661	2.9	29.5	102	560	3.0	25.0	106	494	2.5	22.0	87
DEC CRFT ID/SOUTH LIV(GROSS)	6102	2916	8.2	47.8	108	1761	7.7	28.9	100	1458	7.8	23.9	102	1491	7.4	24.4	97
DISCOVER	775	329	0.9	42.5	96	241	1.1	31.1	108	*198	1.1	25.5	109	*161	0.8	20.8	82
EBONY	3579	1616	4.6	45.2	102	1068	4.7	29.8	104	749	4.0	20.9	89	961	4.8	26.9	107
ESQUIRE	744	319	0.9	42.9	97	*212	0.9	28.5	99	*120	0.6	16.1	69	*157	0.8	21.1	84
ESSENCE	1812	805	2.3	44.4	100	613	2.7	33.8	118	461	2.5	25.4	108	490	2.4	27.0	107
FAMILY CIRCLE	15476	7411	20.9	47.9	108	4537	19.8	29.3	102	3683	19.7	23.8	101	3914	19.5	25.3	100
THE FAMILY HANDYMAN	1038	515	1.5	49.6	112	282	1.2	27.2	94	292	1.6	28.1	120	351	1.7	33.8	134
FAMILY WEEKLY	12311	5789	16.4	47.0	106	3584	15.6	29.1	101	3276	17.5	26.6	113	3460	17.2	28.1	112
FIELD & STREAM	1750	871	2.5	49.8	112	529	2.3	30.2	105	507	2.7	29.0	123	556	2.8	31.8	126
FOOD & WINE	572	*160	0.5	28.0	63	*108	0.5	18.9	66	*165	0.9	28.8	123	**95	0.5	16.6	66
FORBES	855	344	1.0	40.2	91	*242	1.1	28.3	98	*175	0.9	20.5	87	**112	0.6	13.1	52
FORTUNE	820	271	0.8	33.0	75	*305	1.3	37.2	129	*165	0.9	20.1	86	*164	0.8	20.0	79
GENTLEMEN'S QUARTERLY	698	287	0.8	41.1	93	*204	0.9	29.2	102	*204	1.1	29.2	125	**98	0.5	14.0	56
GLAMOUR	4561	1848	5.2	40.5	91	1373	6.0	30.1	105	1190	6.4	26.1	111	1260	6.3	27.6	110
GOLF DIGEST	590	*216	0.6	36.6	83	*166	0.7	28.1	98	**105	0.6	17.8	76	*171	0.9	29.0	115
GOLF DIGEST/TENNIS (GROSS)	1113	459	1.3	41.2	93	380	1.7	34.1	119	*181	1.0	16.3	69	307	1.5	27.6	109
GOLF MAGAZINE	385	*148	0.4	38.4	87	**121	0.5	31.4	109	**91	0.5	23.6	101	**123	0.6	31.9	127
GOLF MAGAZINE/SKI (GROSS)	843	291	0.8	34.5	78	*241	1.1	28.6	99	*176	0.9	20.9	89	*206	1.0	24.4	97
GOOD HOUSEKEEPING	15927	7175	20.3	45.0	102	4926	21.5	30.9	108	3861	20.6	24.2	103	4266	21.2	26.8	106
GRIT	1505	914	2.6	60.7	137	546	2.4	36.3	126	427	2.3	28.4	121	386	1.9	25.6	102
HARPER'S BAZAAR	2218	847	2.4	38.2	86	672	2.9	30.3	105	484	2.6	21.8	93	514	2.6	23.2	92
HEALTH	1452	692	2.0	47.7	107	522	2.3	36.0	125	313	1.7	21.6	92	323	1.6	22.2	88
HEARST MAG CORP. BUY (GROSS)	41949	18420	52.0	43.9	99	12927	56.3	30.8	107	10171	54.3	24.2	103	10743	53.4	25.6	102
HEARST MAN POWER (GROSS)	1883	936	2.6	49.7	112	590	2.6	31.3	109	444	2.4	23.6	100	432	2.1	22.9	91
HEARST WOMAN POWER (GROSS)	29909	13302	37.6	44.5	100	9255	40.3	30.9	108	7629	40.7	25.5	109	7813	39.1	26.3	104
HOUSE BEAUTIFUL	3784	1575	4.4	41.6	94	1148	5.0	30.3	105	786	4.2	20.8	88	914	4.6	24.2	96
INC.	*207	**68	0.2	32.9	74	**59	0.3	28.5	99	**32	0.2	15.5	66	**15	0.1	7.2	29
JET	2697	1174	3.3	43.5	98	867	3.8	32.1	112	539	2.9	20.0	85	780	3.9	28.9	115
LADIES' HOME JOURNAL	11122	5196	14.7	46.7	105	3340	14.6	30.0	104	2862	15.3	25.7	110	3020	15.0	27.2	108
LHJ FAMILY GRP COMBO(GROSS)	14614	6814	19.3	46.6	105	4551	19.8	31.1	108	3684	19.7	25.2	107	3895	19.4	26.7	106
LIFE	3988	1821	5.1	45.7	103	1179	5.1	29.6	103	1013	5.4	25.4	108	951	4.7	23.8	95
L.A. TIMES HOME MAGAZINE	1120	422	1.2	37.7	85	191	0.8	17.1	59	253	1.4	22.6	96	206	1.0	18.4	73
MADEMOISELLE	2597	1276	3.6	49.1	111	886	3.9	34.1	119	693	3.7	26.7	114	756	3.8	29.1	115
MC CALL'S	13358	6297	17.8	47.1	106	4240	18.5	31.7	110	3278	17.5	24.5	105	3589	17.8	26.9	107
MC CALL'S/WRK MOTHER (GROSS)	14302	6753	19.1	47.2	106	4513	19.7	31.6	110	3555	19.0	24.9	106	3775	18.8	26.4	105
MECHANIX ILLUSTRATED	699	361	1.0	51.6	116	*201	0.9	28.8	100	**125	0.7	17.9	76	*197	1.0	28.2	112
METROPOLITAN HOME	821	284	0.8	34.6	78	231	1.0	28.1	98	*229	1.2	27.9	119	*152	0.8	18.5	73
MONEY	1568	725	2.0	46.2	104	532	2.3	33.9	118	262	1.4	16.7	71	311	1.5	19.8	79
MOTHER EARTH NEWS	1235	552	1.6	44.7	101	420	1.8	34.0	118	346	1.8	28.0	119	*246	1.2	19.9	79
MS.	852	349	1.0	41.0	92	*183	0.8	21.5	75	*140	0.7	16.4	70	*152	0.8	17.8	71
NATIONAL ENQUIRER	10228	4708	13.3	46.0	104	3108	13.5	30.4	106	2826	15.1	27.6	118	2791	13.9	27.3	108
NATIONAL GEOGRAPHIC	9123	3893	11.0	42.7	96	2476	10.8	27.1	94	2082	11.1	22.8	97	2078	10.3	22.8	90
NATIONAL SUNDAY MAGAZINE PKG	46735	20633	58.3	44.1	100	13614	59.3	29.1	101	11306	60.4	24.2	103	12261	61.0	26.2	104
NATURAL HISTORY	549	*209	0.6	38.1	86	*128	0.6	23.3	81	**82	0.4	14.9	64	**103	0.5	18.8	74
NEWSWEEK	6275	2504	7.1	39.9	90	1618	7.1	25.8	90	1574	8.4	25.1	107	1348	6.7	21.5	85
NEW YORK INCLUDING CUE	574	163	0.5	28.4	64	*131	0.6	22.8	79	*156	0.8	27.2	116	**91	0.5	15.9	63
THE N.Y. TIMES DAILY EDITION	1179	391	1.1	33.2	75	331	1.4	28.1	98	243	1.3	20.6	88	*138	0.7	11.7	46
THE N.Y. TIMES MAGAZINE	1720	591	1.7	34.4	77	435	1.9	25.3	88	311	1.7	18.1	77	230	1.1	13.4	53
THE NEW YORKER	1148	407	1.1	35.5	80	282	1.2	24.6	85	241	1.3	21.0	89	309	1.5	26.9	107
OMNI	652	247	0.7	37.9	85	*198	0.9	30.4	106	*207	1.1	31.7	135	*134	0.7	20.6	82
ON CABLE	834	380	1.1	45.6	103	280	1.2	33.6	117	252	1.3	30.2	129	*199	1.0	23.9	95
1001 HOME IDEAS	2040	926	2.6	45.4	102	689	3.0	33.8	117	509	2.7	25.0	106	552	2.7	27.1	107
ORGANIC GARDENING	1657	885	2.5	53.4	120	473	2.1	28.5	99	343	1.8	20.7	88	497	2.5	30.0	119
OUI	*176	**129	0.4	73.3	165	**90	0.4	51.1	178	**73	0.4	41.5	177	**57	0.3	32.4	128
OUTDOOR LIFE	1054	606	1.7	57.5	130	327	1.4	31.0	108	*240	1.3	22.8	97	*252	1.3	23.9	95
PARADE MAGAZINE	22500	10064	28.4	44.7	101	6676	29.1	29.7	103	5494	29.3	24.4	104	5843	29.0	26.0	103

Source 14

Newspaper Audience Ratings Study

Research Firm

Scarborough's Newspaper Ratings Company, Ltd.

Frequency

This is an annual study of newspaper readership in fifty-one ADI areas, seventy-four MSAs (metropolitan statistical areas) and twelve local newspaper markets.

Data Collection

Firm uses telephone interviews of adults (18+). Samples are selected with random digit process to retrieve unlisted directory numbers. Sample sizes vary by market, however, the current report used a national (in-tab) sample of over 61,000 interviews. Readership is reported by gender, age, education, and some selected consumer roles.

Function/Purpose

This study offers analysts qualitative or profile data that are absent in all circulation audits. This is an important measurement for many advertisers who have special target needs. Similarly, this study also estimates unduplicated readership on a two-issue and five-issue basis. Such estimates are not obtainable from any circulation study.

Format Explanations

Column headings cover one-, two-, and five-issue estimates for each newspaper. The number shown is the estimate of the number of readers who will read at least one of one, two, or five possible issues.

Rows express audience as whole numbers, as a percent of the whole market segment ("Coverage"), and as a percent of the total readers of the newspaper ("Composite"). "Index" refers to the comparison of the percent of the New York adults in each demographic category with the percent of each newspaper's readers in the demographic category. (Please note that all data are based on daily, Monday through Friday, readership patterns.)

Illustration

(The excerpt shown covers the major New York City metropolitan newspapers.) If a newspaper buyer was particularly interested in readers 25–49 years of age for an anticipated morning advertising schedule, here is a summary of the data that can be obtained from the report:

1. Competing Morning Papers: *Daily News* and the *Times*.
2. Single-Issue Coverage, Single Issue: *Daily News* 28.3; *Times* 20.9. This is the percentage of target adults exposed to one issue.
3. Single-Issue Composition: 45.7 percent of the *Daily News* readers are in the target, while 55.9 percent of the *Times* readers are 25–49.
4. Composite Index: *Daily News* has a below average index of 92, compared to an above average index of 112 for the *Times*.
5. Summary: The *Daily News* has a larger target readership but also a larger waste (nontarget) readership than the *Times*.

SCARBOROUGH'S 1987 NEWSPAPER AUDIENCE RATINGS STUDY

BASIC DEMOGRAPHIC CHARACTERISTICS
AND SELECTED NATIONAL PRODUCT USAGE
AMONG NEWSPAPER AUDIENCES

01-A1   PAGE   1

PROJECTED NUMBERS
IN HUNDREDS (00)

BASE: NEW YORK ADI

***************************** WEEKDAY NEWSPAPER AUDIENCE *****************************

	TOTAL	DAILY NEWS (M) AVG. ISSUE	2 ISSUE CUME	5 ISSUE CUME	TIMES (M) AVG. ISSUE	2 ISSUE CUME	5 ISSUE CUME	POST (A) AVG. ISSUE	2 ISSUE CUME	5 ISSUE CUME	NEWSDAY (E) AVG. ISSUE	2 ISSUE CUME	5 ISSUE CUME
TOTAL ADULTS	137023	42248	55015	70346	25528	34497	46203	21519	29912	41289	17973	22698	28632
COVERAGE 100%		30.8	40.2	51.3	18.6	25.2	33.7	15.7	21.8	30.1	13.1	16.6	20.9
COMPOSTN	100.0	100.0	100.0	100.0	100.0	100.0	100.0	100.0	100.0	100.0	100.0	100.0	100.0
SEX													
ADULT MEN	62945	19875	25968	33268	12828	16944	22180	11101	15121	20427	9200	12109	15874
COVERAGE 100%		31.6	41.3	52.9	20.4	26.9	35.2	17.6	24.0	32.5	14.6	19.2	25.2
COMPOSTN	45.9	47.0	47.2	47.3	50.2	49.1	48.0	51.6	50.6	49.5	51.2	53.3	55.4
INDEX	100	102	103	103	109	107	105	112	110	108	111	116	121
ADULT WOMEN	74078	22373	29047	37075	12701	17553	24056	10419	14791	20888	8773	10589	12797
COVERAGE 100%		30.2	39.2	50.0	17.1	23.7	32.5	14.1	20.0	28.2	11.8	14.3	17.3
COMPOSTN	54.1	53.0	52.8	52.7	49.8	50.9	52.1	48.4	49.4	50.6	48.8	46.7	44.7
INDEX	100	98	98	97	92	94	96	90	91	94	90	86	83
AGE													
18 - 24	17825	5431	7245	9458	2393	3264	4433	2808	4111	5977	2280	3333	4858
COVERAGE 100%		30.5	40.6	53.1	13.4	18.3	24.9	15.8	23.1	33.5	12.8	18.7	27.3
COMPOSTN	13.0	12.9	13.2	13.4	9.4	9.5	9.6	13.0	13.7	14.5	12.7	14.7	17.0
INDEX	100	99	101	103	72	73	74	100	106	111	98	113	130
25 - 34	30605	9127	11744	14883	6623	9153	12475	4904	6396	8304	4157	5145	6365
COVERAGE 100%		29.8	38.4	48.6	21.6	29.9	40.8	16.0	20.9	27.1	13.6	16.8	20.8
COMPOSTN	22.3	21.6	21.3	21.2	25.9	26.5	27.0	22.8	21.4	20.1	23.1	22.7	22.2
INDEX	100	97	96	95	116	119	121	102	96	90	104	101	100
35 - 44	27412	7276	10179	13927	5226	7175	9750	4156	6259	9382	3862	4632	5561
COVERAGE 100%		26.5	37.1	50.8	19.1	26.2	35.6	15.2	22.8	34.2	14.1	16.9	20.3
COMPOSTN	20.0	17.2	18.5	19.8	20.5	20.8	21.1	19.3	20.9	22.7	21.5	20.4	19.4
INDEX	100	86	92	99	102	104	105	97	105	114	107	102	97
45 - 54	19799	6271	8038	10133	3998	5840	8412	3302	4317	5615	3084	3892	4900
COVERAGE 100%		31.7	40.6	51.2	20.2	29.5	42.5	16.7	21.8	28.4	15.6	19.7	24.7
COMPOSTN	14.4	14.8	14.6	14.4	15.7	16.9	18.2	15.3	14.4	13.6	17.2	17.1	17.1
INDEX	100	103	101	100	108	117	126	106	100	94	119	119	118
55 - 64	17823	5518	6919	8569	4074	4929	5945	2399	3570	5297	2062	2646	3393
COVERAGE 100%		31.0	38.8	48.1	22.9	27.7	33.4	13.5	20.0	29.7	11.6	14.8	19.0
COMPOSTN	13.0	13.1	12.6	12.2	16.0	14.3	12.9	11.1	11.9	12.8	11.5	11.7	11.8
INDEX	100	100	97	94	123	110	99	86	92	99	88	90	91
65 AND OVER	23559	8627	10891	13489	3216	4137	5309	3954	5262	6959	2528	3049	3684
COVERAGE 100%		36.6	46.2	57.3	13.7	17.6	22.5	16.8	22.3	29.5	10.7	12.9	15.6
COMPOSTN	17.2	20.4	19.8	19.2	12.6	12.0	11.5	18.4	17.6	16.9	14.1	13.4	12.9
INDEX	100	119	115	112	73	70	67	107	102	98	82	78	75
(25 - 49)	68298	19319	25632	33402	14281	19859	27251	10416	14600	20330	9681	11839	14476
COVERAGE 100%		28.3	37.5	48.9	20.9	29.1	39.9	15.3	21.4	29.8	14.2	17.3	21.2
COMPOSTN	49.8	45.7	46.6	47.5	55.9	57.6	59.0	48.4	48.8	49.2	53.9	52.2	50.6
INDEX	100	92	93	95	112	115	118	97	98	99	108	105	101
(35 - 49)	37692	10192	13888	18552	7658	10706	14777	5513	8205	12155	5524	6693	8111
COVERAGE 100%		27.0	36.8	49.2	20.3	28.4	39.2	14.6	21.8	32.2	14.7	17.8	21.5
COMPOSTN	27.5	24.1	25.2	26.4	30.0	31.0	32.0	25.6	27.4	29.4	30.7	29.5	28.3
INDEX	100	88	92	96	109	113	116	93	100	107	112	107	103
MEDIAN AGE	42.1	43.9	43.2	42.5	41.7	41.3	41.0	41.5	41.0	40.6	41.1	40.3	39.6
EDUCATION													
COLLEGE GRADUATE OR MORE	29251	6281	8368	11030	11642	14907	18589	4127	5530	7378	3672	4538	5609
COVERAGE 100%		21.5	28.6	37.7	39.8	51.0	63.5	14.1	18.9	25.2	12.6	15.5	19.2
COMPOSTN	21.3	14.9	15.2	15.7	45.6	43.2	40.2	19.2	18.5	17.9	20.4	20.0	19.6
INDEX	100	70	71	73	214	202	188	90	87	84	96	94	92
SOME COLLEGE (1-3 YEARS)	23590	6854	8952	11500	4958	6442	8301	3242	4740	6902	3162	4133	5388
COVERAGE 100%		29.1	37.9	48.7	21.0	27.3	35.2	13.7	20.1	29.3	13.4	17.5	22.8
COMPOSTN	17.2	16.2	16.3	16.3	19.4	18.7	18.0	15.1	15.8	16.7	17.6	18.2	18.8
INDEX	100	94	95	95	113	108	104	87	92	97	102	106	109
HIGH SCHOOL GRADUATE	47900	16572	21288	26797	5800	8195	11543	7916	11453	16432	7533	8855	10422
COVERAGE 100%		34.6	44.4	55.9	12.1	17.1	24.1	16.5	23.9	34.3	15.7	18.5	21.8
COMPOSTN	35.0	39.2	38.7	38.1	22.7	23.8	25.0	36.8	38.3	39.8	41.9	39.0	36.4
INDEX	100	112	111	109	65	68	71	105	110	114	120	112	104
NOT HIGH SCHOOL GRADUATE	36283	12542	16407	20957	3130	4955	7951	6235	8190	10694	3607	5172	7414
COVERAGE 100%		34.6	45.2	57.8	8.6	13.7	21.9	17.2	22.6	29.5	9.9	14.3	20.4
COMPOSTN	26.5	29.7	29.8	29.8	12.3	14.4	17.2	29.0	27.4	25.9	20.1	22.8	25.9
INDEX	100	112	113	113	46	54	65	109	103	98	76	86	98
POSITION IN HOUSEHOLD													
CHIEF WAGE EARNER	69288	20873	27650	35900	13794	18774	25280	10423	14663	20495	8570	11531	15469
COVERAGE 100%		30.1	39.9	51.8	19.9	27.1	36.5	15.0	21.2	29.6	12.4	16.6	22.3
COMPOSTN	50.6	49.4	50.3	51.0	54.0	54.4	54.7	48.4	49.0	49.6	47.7	50.8	54.0
INDEX	100	98	99	101	107	108	108	96	97	98	94	100	107
PRINCIPAL FOOD SHOPPER	81275	24343	31755	40706	15474	20694	27436	11958	16734	23278	10764	13391	16650
COVERAGE 100%		30.0	39.1	50.1	19.0	25.5	33.8	14.7	20.6	28.6	13.2	16.5	20.5
COMPOSTN	59.3	57.6	57.7	57.9	60.6	60.0	59.4	55.6	55.9	56.4	59.9	59.0	58.2
INDEX	100	97	97	98	102	101	100	94	94	95	101	99	98

• PERCENTAGES RELATIVELY UNSTABLE BECAUSE OF SMALL BASE · USE WITH CAUTION
•• BASE TOO SMALL FOR RELIABLE PERCENTAGES · SHOWN FOR CONSISTENCY ONLY

Source 15

Newspaper Circulation Analysis ("Section II—ADI Market Areas")

Research Firm

Standard Rate and Data Service

Frequency

This is an annual edition that has been produced by the company for more than thirty years.

Data Collection

Most of the newspaper and magazine circulation reports are compiled from *Audit Reports* by the Audit Bureau of Circulations. Other circulation figures are from sworn statements from the publisher.

The geographic areas are defined by Arbitron in its county-by-county analysis of television viewing patterns. Its designation, known as the Area of Dominant Influence (ADI), is a standard for advertising purposes. The market demographic data are provided by National Decision Systems, a leading market data supplier.

Function/Purpose

NCA provides planners with a unique view of publication coverage. Conforming newspaper and magazine circulation to a television market description allows analysis of multimedia scheduling opportunities.

Format Explanations

These market summaries are too comprehensive for a complete explanation of each term or code designation, but here are some of the most significant highlights:

Metro Area. These are the county areas found within the government's MSA description for each market.

Non-Metro Area. These are counties within the ADI but not fitting the MSA definition.

Total ADI. Covers all counties that have been identified with a "home market" television signal.

Spillover. Newspapers that originate outside of the ADI, but still provide some coverage within it.

"% Circ to HH." This is the coverage percentage (generally referred to as GRP). It is found by dividing the circulation of the publication by the households in the market or market area.

Illustration

Assume a planner wanted 100 rating points (GRP) in the San Antonio market ADI. If the plan called for newspaper, there are two major competitors: The *Express* generates a daily GRP of 28.9; the *Light* delivers 24.3 daily GRP. Four insertions (issues) in the *Express* would give more than 100 GRPs (4×28.9). It would take five insertions in the *Light* to achieve the goal (5×24.3). If the cost was not prohibitive, a combination of the newspapers could also achieve the goal.

NEWSPAPER CIRCULATION/MARKET DATA APPLIED TO TV MARKET AREAS
(Newspaper Group Circulation is not included in any total.)

SAN ANTONIO, TX

Market Data & Demographic Summary

		Hshlds	Percent of ADI	Gr HH Inc (000)	Percent of ADI	HH Expend (000)	Percent of ADI	Women 18+ (000)	Men 18+ (000)	Teens 12-17 (000)	Child 0-11 (000)
SAN ANTONIO, TX	MSA	431,800	78.0	13,399,987	82.1	6,693,797	79.8	470	426	129	253
BALANCE NON-MSA COUNTIES		122,130	22.0	2,913,234	17.9	1,695,236	20.2	133	121	38	76
TOTAL FOR MARKET AREA		553,930	100.0	16,313,221	100.0	8,389,033	100.0	603	547	167	329
RANKINGS		44		42		45					

Daily Circulation And Coverage / Sunday Or Weekend

SAN ANTONIO, TX METRO AREA	Daily Inch Rate ($)	Total Circ (000)	Morning Circ (000)	Morning % Circ To HH	Evening Circ (000)	Evening % Circ To HH	Group Circ (000)	Group % Circ To HH	Total ADI Circ (000)	Total ADI Percent %	Sunday Inch Rate ($)	Total ADI Circ (000)	Total ADI Percent %
NEW BR/SEG HZ GE =	12.63	12.5	.0	.0.	12.0	2.2	.0	.0	12.0	2.2	12.63	14.4	2.6
SAN ANTONIO EX ▲	69.52	166.9	.0	.0	160.2	28.9	.0	.0	160.2	28.9	76.75	223.1	40.3
SAN ANTONIO LIG ▲	63.98	139.9	.0	.0	134.5	24.3	.0	.0	134.5	24.3	71.60	197.4	35.6
SANANTONIO USSPW +	N/A	202.2	.0	.0	.0	.0	201.6	36.4	201.6	36.4	N/A	.0	.0
METRO TOTAL			.0	.0	306.7	55.4	.0	.0	306.7	55.4		434.9	78.5
NON-METRO													
DEL RIO NEWS-HER =	10.32	6.2	.0	.0	6.1	1.1	.0	.0	6.1	1.1	10.32	6.5	1.2
GONZALES INQUIRE +	3.22	2.5	.0	.0	2.3	.4	.0	.0	2.3	.4	N/A	.0	.0
KERRVILLE TIMES =	4.57	8.6	.0	.0	8.1	1.5	.0	.0	8.1	1.5	4.57	9.6	1.7
NON METRO TOTAL			.0	.0	16.5	3.0	.0	.0	16.5	3.0		16.1	2.9
METRO/NON METRO TOTAL			.0	.0	323.2	58.3	.0	.0	323.2	58.3		451.0	81.4
SPILLOVER													
HARTE-HANKS NWSD			.0	.0	.0	.0	6.4	1.1	6.4	1.1		6.6	1.2
HARTE-HANKS NWSW			.0	.0	.0	.0	7.5	1.4	7.5	1.4		.0	.0
HARTE-HANKS NWSC			.0	.0	.0	.0	13.9	2.5	13.9	2.5		6.6	1.2
SO WEST TX NTW D			.0	.0	.0	.0	26.3	4.7	26.3	4.7		30.5	5.5
SO WEST TX NTW W			.0	.0	.0	.0	7.5	1.4	7.5	1.4		.0	.0
SO WEST TX NTW C			.0	.0	.0	.0	33.8	6.1	33.8	6.1		30.5	5.5
VICTORIA ADVOCAT			7.8	1.4	.0	.0	.0	.0	7.8	1.4		8.1	1.5
** SPILLOVER TOTAL			10.1	1.8	1.4	.2	.0	.0	11.4	2.1		12.5	2.3
TOTAL MARKET AREA			10.1	1.8	324.5	58.6	.0	.0	334.6	60.4		463.4	83.7

Magazine Circulation Data

Magazine	Circ.	%	Magazine	Circ.	%	Magazine	Circ.	%	Magazine	Circ.	%	Magazine	Circ.	%	Magazine	Circ.	%
Bet H&G	41,739	8	Fam Hndy	6,631	1	Lds Hm J	27,486	5	Newsweek	16,525	3	Pop Scnc	9,180	2	Sprt III	12,126	2
Bon Appt	5,995	1	Fld Strm	10,309	2	Life	9,452	2	1001 H I	9,532	2	Prvntion	12,977	2	Teen	5,511	1
Boys Lif	7,112	1	Glamour	13,063	2	McCalls	28,179	5	Outdr Lf	7,021	1	Read Dig	92,957	17	Time	28,238	5
Cosmo	15,567	3	Globe	9,100	2	Mademsle	6,262	1	Parents	8,435	2	Redbook	19,942	4	True Str	8,290	1
Cntry Lv	4,948	1	Golf Dig	5,811	1	Mod Mat	72,798	13	Penthse	14,983	3	Rod Org	5,604	1	TV Guide	23,653	4
Discover	8,731	2	Gd Food	6,942	1	Money	8,201	1	People	14,807	3	Sevnteen	10,800	2	Us News	16,459	3
Ebony	6,821	1	Gd House	21,565	4	Natl Exm	8,054	1	Playboy	20,864	4	Smthsnin	12,477	2	Vogue	5,818	1
Fam Circ	32,178	6	Home Mec	6,862	1	Natl Geo	50,292	9	Pop Mech	7,660	1	South Lv	31,261	6	Womns Dy	26,789	5

Source 16

Network Television Cost Estimator

Research Firm

Compiled from agency/network negotiations.

Frequency

There is no cost structure more volatile than network television. Fixed pricing (published rates for shows) is almost nonexistent. A series of unique factors has prompted networks to sell participations and sponsorships on a negotiated basis. Because, technically, each program finds its own price level depending on popularity and demand, agency cost advisories are under constant revision. (The compilations, such as the example on the next page, are for general reference only and are *not used* for actual negotiation.)

Data Collection

Experience from negotiation is the only way to approximate anticipated costs for programming in each daypart. Projection (future) is based on estimated demand by advertisers and by viewership forecasting. Much of the foundation for the projections is based on recent history.

Format Explanations

Most agency compilations are arranged by television daypart rather than by program title. Because program titles change nearly every month, it would be unwise to use them as a reference.

Costs are usually projected by calendar quarter. This allows pricing to reflect advertiser patterns and to also reflect seasonal changes in sets in use (SIU) or the homes using television (HUT). The price projections shown per quarter are high averages and are based on rating estimations that reflected very little of the people meter rating technology. Household ratings currently show a 10 percent decrease in prime time from the new methodology. If this trend continues into the middle of 1988, prices for the 1988–89 fall season will be forced downward.

Further, the single price noted for prime-time program costs may be misleading to those not familiar with the range of pricing available. Depending on how the position is bought ("upfront" vs. "scatter"), the range could be very wide (from $50,000 to $350,000 per thirty-second participation). The figure of $199,700 is a compromise figure that suggests a price in the "better" performing programs.

In addition to base unit costs, the table also shows the base CPRP (households) for each daypart. This format allows estimates to be made either on participations desired (where the daypart rating range is narrow) or on a cost per gross rating point basis. The latter cost frame is preferred when planners work with budget goals (working back from dollars available) or from reach and frequency objectives (working forward from GRP needs).

Illustration

Assume that an agency planner for network is estimating the cost of yearly schedule in daytime. In the past, the client has used approximately eighty participations spread throughout the year, and the expectation is the same for the coming year. To compute the estimated cost for the coming year, the planner would begin by dividing the participations evenly by quarter. That would mean each quarter would receive twenty participations (80/4 quarters). The calculation would then be to multiply the number of participations by the quarterly price as follows:

First Quarter	20 × $14,000 ea. = $ 280,000
Second Quarter	20 × $16,500 ea. = $ 330,000
Third Quarter	20 × $14,000 ea. = $ 280,000
Fourth Quarter	20 × $15,400 ea. = $ 308,000
Totals	80 $1,198,000

To illustrate the cost-per-rating-point (CPRP) method of estimation, the same agency planner wants to know what a fourth-quarter allocation of $750,000 will deliver in prime evening. The table shows a prime fourth-quarter CPRP of $12,481. By dividing the CPRP into the allocation ($750,000/$12,481), about 60 GRPs could be purchased. At an average household rating of 16.0, this would be from three to four prime thirty-second positions in the quarter.

1988–89 Projected Network
Television Prices for Select Dayparts

	First Quarter	Second Quarter	Third Quarter	Fourth Quarter
1. Daytime				
Avg. Cost/30*	$14,000	$16,500	$14,000	$15,400
Avg. HH Rat.	6.1	5.4	5.8	5.7
CPRP	$2,295	$3,056	$2,414	$2,702
2. Evening News				
Avg. Cost/30	$44,200	$53,700	$39,900	$52,300
Avg. HH Rat.	13.5	10.8	9.8	13.1
CPRP	$3,274	$4,972	4,071	$3,932
3. Prime Evening				
Avg. Cost/30	$103,600	$110,000	$80,200	$199,700
Avg. HH Rat.	16.5	13.8	11.5	16.0
CPRP	$6,279	$7,971	$6,974	$12,481

*All costs based on thirty-second units.

Source 17

Cable Television Network/"Superstation" Cost Estimator

Research Firm

Data are based on composite agency sources.

Frequency

Agency planning departments publish these unit costs on a yearly basis. Actual negotiated costs are quite fluid. This estimator is designed for advertiser reference and does not necessarily reflect current pricing.

Function/Purpose

Estimators based exclusively on unit prices are unusual in broadcast media. Until cable networks and the so-called superstations (e.g., WTBS, WGN, WWOR, and WPIX) regularly appear in national rating reports, unit cost estimation will be used. For specific negotiations, Nielsen's *Cable TV Status Report* data are available.

Format Explanations

Because of the diversity of programming within a daypart, and the use of an open pricing system, unit cost ranges are necessary. Advertiser demand, program popularity, and other factors all will affect the actual program charge.

Illustration

Use of the estimator is self-explanatory. The planner designates the number of participations needed, judges which part of the cost range is most applicable, and multiplies to learn the total cost.

Cable Network/Superstation Cost Estimator
Thirty-Second Length–Selected Dayparts
(Yearly Ranges)

	Thirty-Second Cost Ranges		
Cable Network	**Daytime**	**Prime Evening**	**Late Evening**
A & E	$250–500	$300–1,500	$500–850
CBN	450–650	2,000–2,800	1,000–1,750
CNN	200–300	1,500–3,500	500–2,500
ESPN	1,500–3,500	5,500–7,500	1,000–2,000
Lifetime	400–800	900–2,000	500–900
MTV	800–1,200	1,500–2,000	1,500–2,000
USA	500–1,200	1,200–2,500	1,000–2,000
WTBS	2,500–5,500	4,500–9,000	300–1,500

Source: Agency sources.

Note: Costs do *not* necessarily reflect special events or other programs of unusual audience interest.

Source 18

Spot Television Cost Estimator

Research Firm

Compilations from advertising agency spot market buying experience.

Frequency

Major agencies issue such data on an annual basis to provide general guidelines for spot television costs. Agency media departments do not use annual estimates, however, relying instead on the most current cost projections reflecting current experience.

Data Collection

The estimator sources for spot television are compilations for tracking market-by-market costs and GRP experiences. Costs from all buys going into the market are programmed in as soon as the contracts are finalized. Rating reports are also programmed as they become available.

Function/Purpose

Agency planners use these estimators for allocation of dollars according to desired reach and frequency levels. The "true" costs and gross-rating-point levels will not be known until the buyers negotiate station contracts. Rates for each market (and station) are very fluid and vary from purchase to purchase. The cost of announcements are set in the negotiation between the station's representative and the agency buyer. However, a pattern that can lead to a reasonably accurate estimate for future plans can be established from a series of "buys." These market "rates" are what planners use to forecast expected costs.

Format Explanations

The costs shown in the example are not actual prices for an announcement. What is shown is a common denominator used extensively in TV planning known as cost per rating point (CPRP). This is a price factor derived from the household ratings and the unit price. The cost of the thirty-second spot (average for the daypart) is divided by the rating (average for the daypart). Thus, if the average rating for the daypart were 10.0 and the cost average for a thirty-second spot were $500, the CPRP would be $50.

The time periods or dayparts use particular names instead of an hour range. The hours become confusing because of time zones:

> DA = Daytime—follows the early morning news/information shows and runs until late afternoon.
>
> EF = Early Fringe—follows daytime and runs until the beginning of the evening network schedules.
>
> PR = Prime Time—evening hours runs until network service ends and the local news begins.
>
> LF = Late Fringe—begins with the late evening local news and runs until sign-off or about 1:00 A.M. E.S.T.

The "seasonal indicies" are included to modify the CPRP for calendar rate and audience changes. The adjusted price per point for any quarter (other than the first which is calculated) is found by mutiplying the first-quarter rate by the index for another quarter. The product is the adjusted CPRP for the new quarter.

Illustration

Estimators can be used in two ways: to estimate the cost of a desired number of rating points, or to estimate the number of rating points that can be obtained from a fixed budget or allocation.

The first illustration assumes a planner wants to find out how many rating points or GRPs can be estimated in San Antonio, Texas for an allocation of $10,000. The plan calls for the late fringe daypart to be scheduled equally between the third and fourth quarters.

To begin the planner will adjust the CPRP for the third and fourth quarters. The base rate in San Antonio for Late Fringe is $35. The third quarter index for Late Fringe is 110; 120 for the fourth quarter. The multiplication gives an adjusted rate for the third quarter of $38.50 ($35 × 110 or 35 × 1.10). The fourth-quarter adjusted rate is $42 ($35 × 120 or 35 × 1.20).

The planner then decides that the allocation will be split evenly between quarters ($5,000 to each). After that split, it is just a matter of dividing the allocation by the adjusted CPRP ($5,000/$38.50 = 129 GRPs and $5,000/$42.00 = 119 GRPs). The total late fringe rating points available for the allocation is 248 (129 + 119).

To illustrate how a campaign can be estimated *for cost* assume the similar situation except the goal is to purchase 200 GRPs in each of the third and fourth quarters (total 400). Once the adjusted CPRP are known, then it is a matter of multiplying the GRPs needed by the CPRP and adding the two quarters together. In this case it is (200 × $38.50) + (200 × $42.00) = $16,100.

Spot Television Market Summaries
Cost per :30 Rating Point

DMAs by Rank	% U.S. TV Households	DA ($)	EF ($)	LF ($)	PR ($)	DMAs by Rank	% U.S. TV Households	DA ($)	EF ($)	LF ($)	PR ($)
1. New York	7.77	175	160	185	538	61. Knoxville	.48	19	26	29	40
2. Los Angeles	5.07	180	168	232	539	62. Toledo	.47	11	15	17	29
3. Chicago	3.49	97	101	142	283	63. Fresno-Visalia	.46	16	16	15	35
4. Philadelphia	2.91	78	90	125	234	64. Jacksonville	.46	21	22	34	54
5. San Francisco	2.39	97	111	155	275	65. Albuquerque	.45	18	17	27	46
6. Boston	2.27	70	86	148	245	66. Syracuse	.43	17	20	23	39
7. Detroit	1.92	47	53	78	165	67. Green Bay	.42	11	13	18	25
8. Washington, DC	1.79	49	62	77	155	68. Des Moines	.41	12	13	16	29
9. Dallas-Ft. Worth	1.78	77	81	122	253	69. Omaha	.40	12	17	22	31
10. Cleveland	1.65	36	37	53	110	70. Rochester	.40	19	18	24	38
Total Top 10	31.10	906	949	1,317	2,797*	Total Top 70	75.17	2,476	2,790	3,742	6,970
11. Houston	1.61	61	66	118	231	71. Roanoke-Lynchburg	.39	12	14	17	34
12. Pittsburgh	1.42	40	42	65	110	72. Portland-Poland Spring	.38	11	17	14	34
13. Atlanta	1.37	45	65	108	148	73. Davenport-Rock Island	.38	10	11	23	15
14. Seattle/Tacoma	1.36	48	58	87	158	74. Cedar Rapids-Waterloo	.37	11	11	26	14
15. Tampa-St. Petersburg	1.34	38	46	59	137	75. Honolulu	.37	11	13	18	26
16. Miami	1.34	47	74	95	191	76. Champaign-Springfield-Decatur	.37	12	13	15	26
17. Minneapolis-St. Paul	1.34	64	65	88	149	77. Paducah-Cape Girard	.37	12	12	9	29
18. St. Louis	1.21	42	42	53	110	78. Spokane	.37	10	13	22	13
19. Denver	1.15	46	67	96	107	79. Austin	.34	13	15	21	40
20. Sacramento-Stockton	1.03	32	44	49	110	80. Lexington	.34	10	11	12	29
Total Top 20	44.31	1,369	1,518	2,135	4,248	Total Top 80	78.90	2,588	2,920	3,919	7,230
21. Baltimore	1.01	33	44	64	115	81. Johnstown-Altoona	.33	8	17	24	27
22. Indianapolis	1.00	30	29	45	93	82. Chattanooga	.33	9	11	16	35
23. Phoenix	.97	44	48	65	103	83. Jackson, MS	.32	12	14	16	29
24. Hartford-New Haven	.93	51	63	82	127	84. South Bend-Elkhart	.32	12	12	15	28
25. Portland, OR	.90	35	42	48	100	85. Tucson	.32	11	12	12	24
26. San Diego	.88	69	74	82	127	86. Springfield, MO	.32	10	11	11	21
27. Orlando-Daytona Beach	.82	36	39	46	94	87. Tri-Cities	.31	9	12	16	24
28. Cincinnati	.82	24	31	38	53	88. Huntsville-Decatur	.30	9	10	17	27
29. Kansas City	.81	24	24	37	70	89. Lincoln-Hastings-Kearney	.29	13	11	15	31
30. Milwaukee	.80	26	29	39	66	90. Baton Rouge	.29	15	14	18	30
Total Top 30	52.37	1,741	1,941	2,681	5,196	Total Top 90	82.07	2,696	3,044	4,079	7,506
31. Nashville	.77	27	28	33	56	91. Columbia, SC	.29	13	15	17	31
32. Charlotte	.74	28	32	39	74	92. Evansville	.29	8	10	12	20
33. New Orleans	.73	21	23	37	51	93. Greenville-New Bern-Wshngtn	.27	10	13	14	21
34. Buffalo	.71	25	29	33	83	94. Youngstown	.27	11	10	14	28
35. Greenville-Spartanburg-Asheville	.71	26	24	39	48	95. Springfield-Holyoke, MA	.27	10	13	20	34
36. Columbus, OH	.69	21	32	35	56	96. Burlington-Plattsburg	.27	12	15	19	34
37. Oklahoma City	.69	19	21	26	54	97. Fort Wayne	.26	9	9	12	22
38. Birmingham	.68	17	20	24	46	98. Las Vegas	.26	8	12	13	26
39. Raleigh-Durham	.67	24	31	45	58	99. El Paso	.25	9	10	12	27
40. Salt Lake City	.67	23	31	38	58	100. Sioux Falls-Mitchell	.25	9	11	11	22
Total Top 40	59.48	1,972	2,212	3,030	5,780	Total Top 100	84.80	2,795	3,162	4,223	7,771
41. Grand Rapids-Kalamazoo	.66	21	23	34	43						
42. Providence-New Bedford	.66	17	24	33	50						
43. Memphis	.64	18	17	22	35						
44. Harrisburg-York-Lncstr-Lbnon	.60	15	19	27	42						
45. San Antonio	.60	26	33	35	55						
46. Wilkes Barre-Scranton	.59	13	15	22	35						
47. Louisville	.59	17	18	25	41						
48. Norfolk-Portsmouth-Nwprt News	.58	16	21	28	46						
49. Charleston-Huntington	.57	13	17	21	29						
50. Albany-Schenectady-Troy	.55	23	26	29	50						
Total Top 50	65.60	2,151	2,425	3,306	6,206						
51. Dayton	.55	24	24	28	45						
52. Greensboro-W. Salem-H. Point	.55	19	21	23	42						
53. Tulsa	.53	17	19	20	46						
54. Little Rock	.51	12	14	14	28						
55. Flint-Saginaw-Bay City	.51	15	15	18	35						
56. Richmond	.51	15	17	21	48						
57. Shreveport-Texarkana	.50	12	12	14	33						
58. West Palm Beach	.49	23	28	30	49						
59. Mobile-Pensacola	.48	17	20	25	37						
60. Wichita-Hutchinson	.48	15	18	18	34						
Total Top 60	70.76	2,320	2,613	3,517	6,604						

Sources: Ketchum Estimates and NSI U.S. Television Households by County Size —
1985-1986

Cost-Per-Point Seasonal Indices By Daypart

	1st Quarter	2nd Quarter	3rd Quarter	4th Quarter
Daytime	100	127	111	122
Early Fringe	100	127	110	120
Late Fringe	100	122	110	120
Prime	100	126	112	118

Source 19

Network Radio Cost Estimator

Research Firm

Data are based on composite agency sources.

Frequency

Agency planning departments publish these unit costs on a yearly basis. Actual negotiated costs are quite fluid. This estimator is designed for advertiser reference and does not necessarily reflect current pricing.

Function/Purpose

See "Frequency" (earlier). The rates used in this estimator are standard prices released by the networks.

Format Explanations

This estimator includes an interesting cross-section of pertinent data for the major radio networks. What follows is a brief description of the major elements:

Affiliates. This is the estimated number of markets that carry some portion of this network's programming. Actual markets carrying a specific program will vary.

ROS Cost. Run of schedule unit costs are usually the lowest available at fixed price levels. Officially, the ROS price allows the network to select the days and times (programs) for the advertiser's commercials. In actuality, some advertiser control can be negotiated.

Average Quarter Hour Rating (Adult). Percentage of U.S. adults listening to an average fifteen-minute segment. Average shown is based on all quarter hours from 6:00 A.M. to 10:00 P.M., Monday through Friday. Selected program ratings may vary substantially from this average.

Adult CPRP. Cost equivalent of exposing one percent of U.S. adults to the advertiser's message.

Illustration

During a campaign planning meeting the brand manager for the client is curious about the cost of 100 GRPs on the ABC Information Network. She also wants to know how many announcements would be needed for 100 GRPs.

To estimate the cost, she multiplies the ABC (Info) CPRP $3,500 by 100 to learn that it would be $350,000. To estimate the number of announcements needed for 100 GRPs she divides the average adult rating 0.8 into 100 to learn an estimated 125 announcements would be needed.

Network Radio Cost Estimator
Adult CPRP of Selected Networks
(Yearly Averages, Thirty-Second Length)

Network	No. Affl.	ROS Thirty-Sec. Cost	Average Rating[2] Adults 6:00 A.M.–10:00 P.M.	Adult CPRP[3]
ABC				
Contemporary	260	$2,800	0.4	$7,000
Entertainment	573	2,700	0.9	3,000
Information	624	2,800	0.8	3,500
CBS	400	2,950	0.5	5,900
Mutual	800	1,650	0.8	2,063
NBC	379	1,900[1]	0.6	3,177
Source	118	3,600	0.5	7,200
TalkNet	284	850	0.4	2,125

Source: Composite of agency compilations.

[1]Rate shown is weighted average. Range = $1,600–$2,700.
[2]The only popularity source for network radio is RADAR®.
[3]Projected. Actual CPRP for each network may be more or less than shown here.

Source 20

Spot Market Radio Cost Estimator

Research Firm

Agency compilations based on Arbitron (ADI) areas and costs provided by current buying experience. Because many radio stations in major markets no longer publish rates, accurate estimates must come from recent schedules.

Frequency

Radio costs are quite fluid. Estimates are continuously monitored to reflect current negotiations and the latest rating reports.

Function/Purpose

The primary function of this data is for planning reference. It is a fast and convenient way to compare multiple market use of radio to other possibilities. Agencies with active radio clients will also provide individual market estimators based on station format and dayparts. For general use, however, an estimator of market groups is sufficient.

Format Explanations

Costs shown are based on the cost of one male or female rating point in all of the markets within the market group (e.g., one point in each of ten markets). The unit (sixty-second announcement) price is divided by the average quarter hour rating for each of the selected audiences. Each market's contribution is figured from the top three stations in popularity.

Dayparts are composed of announcement rates and ratings for the period of 6:00 A.M. to 7:00 P.M. Rates assume that the buy will need a minimum of 400 GRPs per month in each market (about 100 rating points per week). Plans with different parameters should not use this estimator.

Illustration

A planner wants to estimate the cost of 1,200 male GRPs in the top twenty markets. What is the estimated cost?

1. Calculate male CPRP (cost per rating point) for the twenty markets
   (1–10 = $1,985 + 11–20 = $911 or $1,985 + $911 = $2,896 CPRP).
2. Multiply the CPRP by the needed GRP level ($2,896 × 1,200 = $3,475,200, the cost of 1,200 male GRPs in each of the top twenty markets).

Spot Market Radio Estimator
Cost per Rating Points/Top Fifty Market Areas
(Sixty-Second Units)

ADI Market Group	Adult Men (18+) CPRP	Adult Women (18+) CPRP
1–10	$1,985	$1,992
11–20	911	986
21–30	647	698
31–40	606	421
41–50	469	719

Source: Agency compilations.

Source 21

Daily Newspaper Cost/Coverage Estimator

Research Firm

Data are provided from numerous media research sources and compiled by agency buyers.

Frequency

Cost data are updated as changes are available. Coverage figures are reviewed with current Audit Bureau of Circulation reports and with each successive report from Scarborough.

Data Collection

Newspaper cost data are supplied by publishers directly or through SRDS. (See page 54.) The geographic projections are provided by the ARBITRON service. Scarborough data are generated from telephone interviews.

Function/Purpose

Estimators are used, almost exclusively, for general planning purposes. They provide quick reference for budgeting and allocation. With frequency or reach goals, planners simply want a convenient format to see how newspaper cost and coverage fit with other alternatives. Any serious attempt at cost estimation requires checking the rate cards of individual papers, but this would follow the "groundwork" done with the estimator.

Format Explanations

Formats of estimators can vary widely as they are customized to the needs of the planner. In this version, markets are arrayed (set in size order) by ADI households. (See pages 40 and 110 for ADI discussion.) MSA (metropolitan statistical area) is a governmental description of population concentrations of cities 50,000 and above with contiguous suburban areas that qualify (substantial social and economic dependence on the metro). The data shown are based on a single leading (largest ADI circulation) newspaper in each market.

Newspaper audience projections are derived from per-copy readership factors applied to the current circulation figures. For example, if the Scarborough study estimated that an average of 1.5 adult readers saw an issue and the circulation of the newspaper was 100,000, the estimated adult readership would be 150,000. The readership figure is then divided by either the ADI or MSA estimated adults to express the percentage.

Because newspaper widths are variable, the common space unit used is the standard advertising unit (SAU) for a column inch. This is a common (across newspapers) unit of space generally accepted by many publishers. Finding a common size helps alleviate unusual production arrangements by the advertiser. The SAU width is the same for all cooperating newspapers regardless of individual page sizes.

Illustration

Assume that a plan for the top Sunbelt ADIs (Los Angeles, Dallas-Ft. Worth, Houston, Miami, Atlanta, and Tampa-St. Petersburg) calls for the cost estimate on 2,000 SAU column inches.

The first step for convenience would be to add up the markets for a single column inch rate ($235 + 105 + 105 + 163 + 108 + 70 = 786 per column inch). To find the estimated cost, the planner then multiplies the space need (2,000 inches) by the combined cost ($786 \times 2,000 = $1,572,000$).

Daily Newspaper
Rates and Coverage of Top Twenty ADI/MSA Areas
(Selected Newspapers with Highest Circulation)

Market Area	Percent Daily Adult Coverage		$ SAU/Col. Inch**
	ADI	MSA*	
New York	33	46	306
Los Angeles	31	36	235
Chicago	37	41	224
Philadelphia	28	39	233
San Francisco	26	44	205
Boston	36	44	168
Detroit	40	40	203
Dallas-Ft. Worth	23	34	105
Washington, D.C.	57	64	235
Houston	34	37	105
Cleveland	36	65	110
Pittsburgh	30	40	95
Seattle	22	26	100
Miami	41	53	163
Atlanta	30	34	108
Minneapolis-St. Paul	39	44	110
Tampa-St. Petersburg	24	29	70
St. Louis	38	47	75
Denver	30	40	80
Sacramento	28	51	67

Source: Agency compilations.

*Some markets do not use counties in MSA definition.
**Rounded to nearest dollar.

Source 22

Newspaper Rates and Data

Research Firm

Standard Rate and Data Service

Frequency

This service is continuously updated and is published monthly.

Data Collection

The basic information for each newspaper is supplied by the publisher to SRDS. The circulation figures originate from ABC audits, other audit groups, or publishers' sworn statements. The market data on market/state population and other economic indicators are gathered from various governmental sources and analyzed and processed by National Decision Systems, Inc.

Function/Purpose

For planners/buyers outside of the newspaper's home market, this is the most reliable source for space costs and mechanical and production information presented in a concise and simplified manner.

SRDS may be used to evaluate market areas and to evaluate newspapers. Its primary function, however, is to provide current space rates for budgeting and estimation. Because this edition includes national newspapers, daily newspapers, national newspaper magazines, national comics, and college newspapers in one volume, it is a most complete source for these purposes.

Format Explanations

Each type of newspaper activity appears in a separate section. The order is set on an alpha system. For example, daily newspapers are listed alphabetically by state (Alabama to Wyoming) and by market.

Each listing follows a strict SRDS order of twenty possible titled segments. Segments are numbered consecutively for simple access (e.g., Category 14 covers closing times for each publication). Because this source is primarily designed for advertising agency planners/buyers, all space rates include agency commission.

Space units or sizes are now reported under an industry-wide system known as standard advertising units (SAU). The SAU system was created because of serious format problems in newspaper advertising. Since the 1960s, newspapers had used many different newsprint sizes with little regard for consistency. This lack of consistency created serious problems for advertisers who use multiple newspapers in their campaigns. The same advertisement was too large for some formats and too small for others. In 1984, responding to complaints over the chaos created by so many different page sizes, publishers adopted the SAU system. The goal of SAU was to insure that individual advertising layouts would appear the way the advertiser intended (without distortions). The SAU system is not compulsory, but most newspapers participate, making national and regional newspaper campaigns easier to manage.

The rate unit quoted in SRDS may be per line, per column inch, and in page units. The standard unit of measure for newspaper, however, is the column inch (column wide by one inch in depth). Discounts vary but generally are based on volume (inches or lines contracted for within a year) or on frequency (number of pages contracted for).

Illustration

Assume a planner wants to learn the cost of a proposed year-long campaign in Rochester, New York. Schedules will use morning newspapers; the total planned insertions (ad sizes vary) are 1,200 column inches in black and white.

In the sample listing, the morning paper's (*Democrat & Chronicle*) rates for black and white are listed in Category 5. The planner notes the "open rate" at $80.96. An open rate is the cost for an inch of space that is not eligible for discounts. The more accurate rate, in this case, is a volume discount because the advertiser will commit to a contract for 1,200 inches. The planner notes that the newspaper does not have a 1,200 discount, but does show a 1,000-inch rate. In a bulk discount situation, the correct rate is the lowest one for which the schedule is eligible. Therefore, the 1,000-column-inch rate ($58.75) is the correct rate and all inches contracted for will be billed at that rate. The estimated campaign cost in Rochester is $70,500 (1,200 × 58.75).

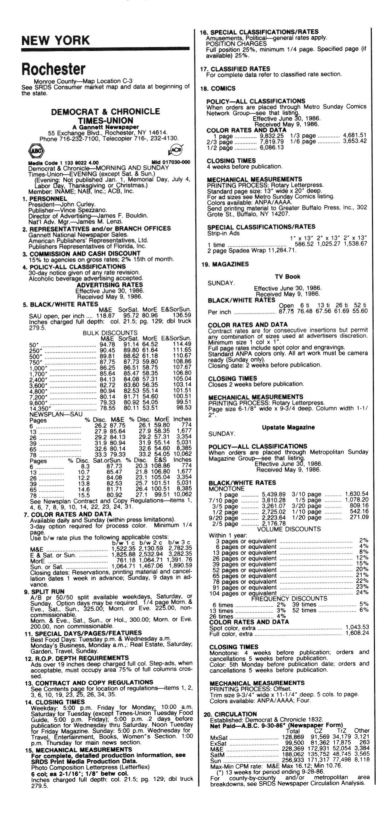

NEW YORK

Rochester

Monroe County—Map Location C-3
See SRDS Consumer market map and data at beginning of the state.

DEMOCRAT & CHRONICLE
TIMES-UNION
A Gannett Newspaper
55 Exchange Blvd., Rochester, NY 14614.
Phone 716-232-7100, Telecopier 716-, 232-4130.

Media Code 1 133 8022 4.00   Mid 017030-000
Democrat & Chronicle—MORNING AND SUNDAY
Times-Union—EVENING (except Sat. & Sun.)
(Evening: Not published Jan. 1, Memorial Day, July 4, Labor Day, Thanksgiving or Christmas.)
Member: INAME; NAB, Inc.; ACB, Inc.

1. PERSONNEL
President—John Curley.
Publisher—Vince Spezzano.
Director of Advertising—James F. Bouldin.
Nat'l Adv. Mgr.—James M. Lenzi.

2. REPRESENTATIVES and/or BRANCH OFFICES
Gannett National Newspaper Sales.
American Publishers' Representatives.
Publishers Representatives of Florida, Inc.

3. COMMISSION AND CASH DISCOUNT
15% to agencies on gross rates; 2% 15th of month.

4. POLICY-ALL CLASSIFICATIONS
30-day notice given of any rate revision.
Alcoholic beverage advertising accepted.
ADVERTISING RATES
Effective June 30, 1986.
Received May 9, 1986.

5. BLACK/WHITE RATES

	M&E	SorSat.	MorE	E&SorSun.
SAU open, per inch	118.87	95.72	80.96	136.59

Inches charged full depth: col. 21.5; pg. 129; dbl truck 279.5.

BULK DISCOUNTS

	M&E	SorSat.	MorE	E&SorSun.
50"	94.78	91.14	64.52	114.49
250"	90.45	89.80	61.64	111.65
500"	89.81	88.62	61.18	110.67
750"	87.75	87.73	59.80	108.86
1,000"	86.25	86.51	58.75	107.67
1,700"	85.64	85.47	58.35	106.80
2,400"	84.13	84.08	57.31	105.04
3,600"	82.72	83.60	56.35	103.14
4,800"	80.94	82.53	55.14	101.51
7,200"	80.14	81.71	54.60	100.51
9,600"	79.33	80.92	54.05	99.51
14,350"	78.55	80.11	53.51	98.53

NEWSPLAN—SAU

Pages	% Disc.	M&E	% Disc.	MorE	Inches
6	26.2	87.75	26.1	59.80	774
13	27.9	85.64	27.9	58.35	1,677
26	29.2	84.13	29.2	57.31	3,354
39	31.9	80.94	31.9	55.14	5,031
65	32.6	80.14	32.6	54.60	8,385
78	33.3	79.33	33.2	54.05	10,062

Pages	% Disc.	Sat.orSun.	% Disc.	E&S	Inches
6	8.3	87.73	20.3	108.86	774
13	10.7	85.47	21.8	106.80	1,677
26	12.2	84.08	23.1	105.04	3,354
39	13.8	82.53	25.7	101.51	5,031
65	14.6	81.71	26.4	100.51	8,385
78	15.5	80.92	27.1	99.51	10,062

See Newsplan Contract and Copy Regulations—items 1, 4, 6, 7, 8, 9, 10, 14, 22, 23, 24, 31.

7. COLOR RATES AND DATA
Available daily and Sunday (within press limitations).
3-day option required for process color. Minimum 1/4 page.
Use b/w rate plus the following applicable costs:

	b/w 1 c	b/w 2 c	b/w 3 c
M&E	1,522.35	2,130.59	2,782.35
E & Sat. or Sun.	1,825.88	2,532.94	3,282.35
MorE	761.18	1,064.71	1,391. 76
Sun. or Sat.	1,064.71	1,467.06	1,890.59

Closing dates: Reservations, printing material and cancellation dates 1 week in advance; Sunday, 9 days in advance.

9. SPLIT RUN
A/B pr 50/50 split available weekdays, Saturday, or Sunday. Option days may be required. 1/4 page Morn. & Eve., Sat., Sun., 325.00; Morn. or Eve. 225.00, noncommissionable.
Morn. & Eve., Sat., Sun., or Hol., 300.00; Morn. or Eve. 200.00, non commissionable.

11. SPECIAL DAYS/PAGES/FEATURES
Best Food Days: Tuesday p.m. & Wednesday a.m.
Monday's Business, Monday a.m.,: Real Estate, Saturday; Garden, Travel, Sunday.

12. R.O.P. DEPTH REQUIREMENTS
Ads over 19 inches deep charged full col. Step-ads, when acceptable, must occupy area 75% of full columns crossed.

13. CONTRACT AND COPY REGULATIONS
See Contents page for location of regulations—items 1, 2, 3, 6, 10, 19, 23, 25, 26, 34, 35.

14. CLOSING TIMES
Weekday: 5:00 p.m. Friday for Monday; 10:00 a.m. Saturday for Tuesday (except Times-Union Tuesday Food Guide, 5:00 p.m. Friday); 5:00 p.m. 2 days before publication for Wednesday thru Saturday. Noon Tuesday for Friday Magazine. Sunday: 5:00 p.m. Wednesday for Travel, Entertainment, Books, Women's Section. 1:00 p.m. Thursday for main news section.

15. MECHANICAL MEASUREMENTS
For complete, detailed production information, see SRDS Print Media Production Data.
Photo Composition Letterpress (Letterflex)
6 col; ea 2-1/16"; 1/8" betw col.
Inches charged full depth: col. 21.5; pg. 129; dbl truck 279.5.

16. SPECIAL CLASSIFICATIONS/RATES
Amusements, Political—general rates apply.
POSITION CHARGES
Full position 25%, minimum 1/4 page. Specified page (if available) 25%.

17. CLASSIFIED RATES
For complete data refer to classified rate section.

18. COMICS

POLICY—ALL CLASSIFICATIONS
When orders are placed through Metro Sunday Comics Network Group—see that listing.
Effective June 30, 1986.
Received May 9, 1986.
COLOR RATES AND DATA

1 page	9,832.25	1/3 page	4,681.51
2/3 page	7,819.79	1/6 page	3,653.42
1/2 page	6,086.13		

CLOSING TIMES
4 weeks before publication.

MECHANICAL MEASUREMENTS
PRINTING PROCESS: Rotary Letterpress.
Standard page size: 13" wide x 20" deep.
For ad sizes see Metro Sunday Comics listing.
Colors available: ANPA/AAAA.
Send printing material to Greater Buffalo Press, Inc., 302 Grote St., Buffalo, NY 14207.

SPECIAL CLASSIFICATIONS/RATES
Strip-in Ads

	1" x 13"	2" x 13"	2" x 13"
1 time	586.52	1,025.27	1,538.67

2 page Spadea Wrap 11,284.71.

19. MAGAZINES

TV Book
SUNDAY.
Effective June 30, 1986.
Received May 9, 1986.
BLACK/WHITE RATES

	Open	6 ti	13 ti	26 ti	52 ti
Per inch	87.75	76.48	67.56	61.69	55.60

COLOR RATES AND DATA
Contract rates are for consecutive insertions but permit any combination of sizes used at advertisers discretion.
Minimum size 1 col x 1".
Full page rates include spot color and engravings.
Standard ANPA colors only. All art work must be camera ready (Sunday only).
Closing date: 2 weeks before publication.

CLOSING TIMES
Closes 2 weeks before publication.

MECHANICAL MEASUREMENTS
PRINTING PROCESS: Rotary Letterpress.
Page size 6-1/8" wide x 9-3/4 deep. Column width 1-1/2".

Upstate Magazine
SUNDAY.

POLICY—ALL CLASSIFICATIONS
When orders are placed through Metropolitan Sunday Magazine Group—see that listing.
Effective June 30, 1986.
Received May 9, 1986.

BLACK/WHITE RATES
MONOTONE

1 page	5,439.89	3/10 page	1,630.54
7/10 page	3,810.28	1/5 page	1,078.20
3/5 page	3,261.07	3/20 page	809.16
1/2 page	2,725.02	1/10 page	542.16
9/20 page	2,223.64	1/20 page	271.09
2/5 page	2,176.78		

VOLUME DISCOUNTS
Within 1 year:

3 pages or equivalent	2%
6 pages or equivalent	4%
13 pages or equivalent	8%
26 pages or equivalent	12%
39 pages or equivalent	15%
52 pages or equivalent	20%
65 pages or equivalent	21%
78 pages or equivalent	22%
91 pages or equivalent	23%
104 pages or equivalent	24%

FREQUENCY DISCOUNTS

6 times	2%	39 times	5%
13 times	3%	52 times	6%
26 times	4%		

COLOR RATES AND DATA

Spot color, extra	1,043.53
Full color, extra	1,608.24

CLOSING TIMES
Monotone: 4 weeks before publication; orders and cancellations 4 weeks before publication.
Color: 5th Monday before publication date; orders and cancellations 5 weeks before publication.

MECHANICAL MEASUREMENTS
PRINTING PROCESS: Offset.
Trim size 9-3/4" wide x 11-1/4" deep. 5 cols. to page.
Colors available: ANPA/AAAA; Four.

20. CIRCULATION
Established: Democrat & Chronicle 1832.
Net Paid—A.B.C. 9-30-86* (Newspaper Form)

	Total	CZ	TrZ	Other
MxSat	128,869	91,569	34,179	3,121
ExSat	99,500	81,362	17,875	263
M&E	228,369	172,931	52,054	3,384
SatM	188,062	135,752	48,745	3,565
Sun	256,933	171,317	77,498	8,118

Max-Min CPM rate: M&E Max 16.12; Min 10.76.
(*) 13 weeks for period ending 9-28-86.
For county-by-county and/or metropolitan area breakdowns, see SRDS Newspaper Circulation Analysis.

Source 23

Consumer Magazine and Agri-Media Rates and Data

Research Firm

Standard Rate and Data Service

Frequency

This service is published monthly.

Data Collection

The primary source for magazine information comes from the publishers and is included by SRDS at no cost. The circulation data are from audited services (ABC, VAC) or from sworn publishers' statements. See page 40 for more details.

Function/Purpose

As is true for other SRDS editions, this report is primarily intended as a cost reference for media planners and others who need current information for campaign planning. Although the eventual, contracted cost may be different due to negotiation, SRDS is still the recognized basis for estimating magazine space costs for planning purposes.

Format Explanations

SRDS uses a systematic classification system to organize all the information in the listings. Rate card (cost) information is compiled for eighteen categories. Each numbered category covers the identical subject across all magazines to enable planners to use the SRDS source efficiently.

Magazines are arranged under an alpha system by editorial title (e.g., "general editorial" or "home service" or "sports"). If the planner is unsure of the magazine's editorial class, an index (by title) is included in each issue.

Unlike newspapers' use of a common unit of space, magazine rates are based on the page or page-fraction. Rates are shown for black and white and for the various color options available. To estimate magazine costs for a campaign, a planner must know the frequency of insertion for each size to be used.

The discount structures vary for each publication, but most use either a frequency discount or a dollar-volume discount. The frequency discount rewards those advertisers using the greatest number of separate insertions. The greater the number used, the greater the discount. Further, many magazines allow advertisers to combine smaller sizes with the larger units for discounts—if a brand used six pages and three half-pages in a campaign, the frequency rate would be nine times for all units.

The dollar-volume discount is based on the total expenditure of the advertiser; the more dollars committed, the greater the discount. Costs are summed for the space planned and then the planner refers to an expenditure table to find the applicable percentage of discount.

Geographic divisions of circulation are important parts of magazine listings, particularly those magazines with large national circulations. These magazines sell portions of circulation (regions, states, or metropolitan areas). Regional estimates take additional calculation because the costs are charged on a per-thousand-copies of circulation used basis.

Illustration

Assume a planner is considering the use of *Video Review* for a campaign. The insertion plan calls for advertisements in two-color with this schedule: five pages, two half-pages, and three one-third pages.

The color rates for all magazines listed in SRDS are found in Category 6. *Video Review* uses the frequency discount system. The combined number of yearly insertions for this campaign, is ten $(5+2+3)$. The highest "earned" frequency rate will be the nine-time rate ("9ti"). Because ten insertions qualifies, all units are entitled to use the "9ti" rate schedule. The estimate then is five pages at $15,250 each ($76,250) + two half-pages at $9,570 each ($19,140) + three one-third pages at $6,730 each ($20,190). The total estimation for the space cost on this schedule is $115,580.

Video Review

(ABC)   MPA

Media Code 8 702 6798 6.00   **Mid 001232-000**
Published monthly by Viare Publishing, 902 Broadway, New York, NY 10010. Phone 212-477-2200.

PUBLISHER'S EDITORIAL PROFILE
VIDEO REVIEW, is edited for consumers who want news on home video technology, programming, and events, with reviews of videodiscs, tapes, TV programs, by reviewers in different topic areas. There are also "how to" articles on videotaping, editing, camera use, lighting, etc. Also included are investigative reports on controversies of interest to video consumers, shoppers' guides to new equipment, and news coverage of coming technologies, including teletext, direct satellite broadcasts, and low-power TV. Departments include: Q&A, New Products, Previews, Coming on TV. Rec'd 8/20/85.

1. PERSONNEL
Publisher/Editor-in-Chief—Richard Ekstract.
Editor—Maury Z. Levy.
Associate Publisher—Jeffrey Zink.

2. REPRESENTATIVES and/or BRANCH OFFICES
New York 10010—Barbara Nalley, Lisa Naugle, Adv. Sales Reps., 902 Broadway. Phone 212-477-2200.
Los Angeles 90036—Paul Turcotte, Western Sales Managers, 5900 Wilshire Blvd. Phone 213-933-3984.

3. COMMISSION AND CASH DISCOUNT
15% to recognized agencies, 2% 10 days, net 30 days.

ADVERTISING RATES
Rates effective January 1987 issue.
Rates received September 17, 1986.

5. BLACK/WHITE RATES

	1 ti	6 ti	9 ti	12 ti	16 ti
1 page	14,770.	13,290.	12,925.	12,550.	12,185.
2/3 page	11,330.	10,190.	9,915.	9,630.	9,345.
1/2 page	9,275.	8,350.	8,115.	7,880.	7,650.
1/3 page	6,520.	5,865.	5,705.	5,540.	5,380.
1/6 page	4,060.	3,650.	3,550.	3,450.	3,350.
Spread	29,540.	26,580.	25,850.	25,100.	24,370.

	24 ti	36 ti
1 page	11,815.	11,220.
2/3 page	9,065.	8,610.
1/2 page	7,420.	7,050.
1/3 page	5,215.	4,950.
1/6 page	3,245.	3,085.
Spread	23,630.	22,440.

CONTINUITY DISCOUNTS
Minimum 1 full page per issue.

	12 pgs	18 pgs	24 pgs	36 pgs
1 page	11,920.	11,575.	11,225.	10,660.

6. COLOR RATES
2 color:

	1 ti	6 ti	9 ti	12 ti	16 ti
1 page	17,430.	15,680.	15,250.	14,805.	14,380.
2/3 page	13,370.	12,030.	11,700.	11,365.	11,030.
1/2 page	10,940.	9,845.	9,570.	9,295.	9,025.
1/3 page	7,690.	6,925.	6,730.	6,535.	6,345.
Spread	34,860.	31,360.	30,500.	29,610.	28,760.

	24 ti	36 ti
1 page	13,945.	13,245.
2/3 page	10,700.	10,160.
1/2 page	8,750.	8,315.
1/3 page	6,155.	5,840.
Spread	27,890.	26,490.

4 color:

	1 ti	6 ti	9 ti	12 ti	16 ti
1 page	19,780.	17,805.	17,310.	16,810.	16,320.
2/3 page	15,395.	13,850.	13,470.	13,085.	12,700.
1/2 page	12,605.	11,340.	11,030.	10,710.	10,400.
1/3 page	9,170.	8,250.	8,025.	7,795.	7,565.
Spread	39,560.	35,610.	34,615.	33,620.	32,640.

	24 ti	36 ti
1 page	15,825.	15,035.
2/3 page	12,315.	11,700.
1/2 page	10,085.	9,580.
1/3 page	7,335.	6,970.
Spread	31,650.	30,070.

CONTINUITY DISCOUNTS
Minimum 1 full page per issue.

	12 pgs	18 pgs	24 pgs	36 pgs
2 color	14,065.	13,660.	13,245.	12,585.
4 color	15,970.	15,505.	15,035.	14,285.

7. COVERS
4 color only.

	1 ti	6 ti	12 ti	18 ti	24 ti
2nd or 3rd cover	22,750.	20,470.	19,335.	18,770.	18,195.
4th cover	26,585.	23,930.	22,600.	21,930.	21,275.

	36 ti
2nd or 3rd cover	17,290.
4th cover	20,205.

8. INSERTS
Available.

9. BLEED
No charge.

10. SPECIAL POSITION
Extra 10%
Non-cancellable.

11. CLASSIFIED/MAIL ORDER
Classified:
3.90 per word. Minimum 10 words. 299.70 per column inch.
Prepayment and camera-ready material required.
No agency commissions or discounts allowed.
DISPLAY CLASSIFICATIONS:

MAIL ORDER
BLACK AND WHITE RATES:

	1 ti	6 ti	12 ti	18 ti	24 ti
1 page	11,430.	10,290.	9,715.	9,430.	9,145.
2/3 page	8,765.	7,890.	7,450.	7,230.	7,010.
1/2 page	7,200.	6,485.	6,120.	5,940.	5,760.
1/3 page	5,030.	4,530.	4,275.	4,150.	4,025.
1/6 page	3,145.	2,830.	2,670.	2,595.	2,515.
Spread	22,860.	20,580.	19,430.	18,860.	18,295.

COLOR RATES:
2 color:

	1 ti	6 ti	12 ti	18 ti	24 ti
1 page	13,485.	12,145.	11,460.	11,125.	10,790.
2/3 page	10,340.	9,310.	8,785.	8,530.	8,270.

---

	1 ti	6 ti	12 ti	18 ti	24 ti
1/2 page	8,500.	7,655.	7,220.	7,010.	6,800.
1/3 page	5,935.	5,345.	5,045.	4,895.	4,750.
Spread	26,970.	24,290.	22,920.	22,250.	21,580.

4 color:

	1 ti	6 ti	12 ti	18 ti	24 ti
1 page	15,310.	13,785.	13,010.	12,630.	12,250.
2/3 page	11,910.	10,725.	10,120.	9,825.	9,530.
1/2 page	9,720.	8,755.	8,260.	8,020.	7,780.
1/3 page	7,095.	6,390.	6,030.	5,850.	5,675.
Spread	30,620.	27,570.	26,020.	25,260.	24,500.

PUBLISHERS RATES
BLACK AND WHITE RATES:

	1 ti	6 ti	12 ti	18 ti	24 ti
1 page	12,545.	11,285.	10,660.	10,350.	10,030.
2/3 page	9,620.	8,650.	8,170.	7,935.	7,690.
1/2 page	7,900.	7,110.	6,715.	6,520.	6,320.
1/3 page	5,520.	4,965.	4,690.	4,555.	4,415.
1/6 page	3,455.	3,105.	2,930.	2,850.	2,765.
Spread	25,090.	22,570.	21,320.	20,700.	20,060.

	36 ti	48 ti
1 page	9,780.	8,155.
2/3 page	7,500.	6,250.
1/2 page	6,160.	5,140.
1/3 page	4,305.	3,590.
1/6 page	2,690.	2,245.
Spread	19,560.	16,310.

CONTINUITY DISCOUNTS

	12 pgs	18 pgs	24 pgs	36 pgs
1 page (Minimum 1 full page per issue)	10,340.	10,040.	9,730.	9,485.

COLOR RATES:
2 color:

	1 ti	6 ti	12 ti	18 ti	24 ti
1 page	14,800.	13,320.	12,585.	12,210.	11,840.
2/3 page	11,345.	10,210.	9,650.	9,360.	9,080.
1/2 page	9,325.	8,390.	7,930.	7,695.	7,460.
1/3 page	6,510.	5,860.	5,540.	5,375.	5,210.
Spread	29,600.	26,640.	25,170.	24,420.	23,660.

	36 ti	48 ti
1 page	11,545.	9,620.
2/3 page	8,850.	7,375.
1/2 page	7,275.	6,060.
1/3 page	5,080.	4,235.
Spread	23,090.	19,240.

CONTINUITY DISCOUNT

	12 pgs	18 pgs	24 pgs	36 pgs
1 page (Minimum 1 full page per issue)	12,210.	11,845.	11,485.	11,200.

4 color:

	1 ti	6 ti	12 ti	18 ti	24 ti
1 page	16,795.	15,115.	14,280.	13,855.	13,435.
2/3 page	13,080.	11,770.	11,120.	10,790.	10,460.
1/2 page	10,665.	9,600.	9,070.	8,800.	8,530.
1/3 page	7,780.	7,005.	6,615.	6,420.	6,225.
Spread	33,590.	30,230.	28,560.	27,710.	26,870.

	36 ti	48 ti
1 page	13,100.	10,915.
2/3 page	10,200.	8,500.
1/2 page	8,320.	6,930.
1/3 page	6,070.	5,060.
Spread	26,200.	21,830.

CONTINUITY DISCOUNT

	12 pgs	18 pgs	24 pgs	36 pgs
1 page (Minimum 1 full page per issue)	13,850.	13,440.	13,030.	12,705.

RENEWAL DISCOUNT
An Extra 5% discount is earned by any advertiser who, in any 12-month period, runs an amount of space equal to or greater than the amount run at least 6 insertions, in the previous 12-month period.

10% GROWTH DISCOUNT
An advertiser placing more space in their present contract year than in the previous 12-month period will be eligible for an additional 25% discount on all such incremental advertising space. To qualify there must be a written contract in advance of the 1st insertion, specifying at least 4 insertions of 1/3 page or more, with at least 2 more insertions of same or larger size than in the previous 12-month period.

MULTI-PAGE IMPACT DISCOUNT
Earns up to 8%. Not applicable to fewer than 4 pages per issue. Frequency, Renewal and Growth discounts applicable if qualify under terms previously stated. Covers earn or contribute to Multi-Page Impact Discount.

	Discount:
4-5 pages per issue	4%
6-7 pages per issue	6%
8 or more pages per issue	8%

15. MECH. REQUIREMENTS
For complete, detailed production information, see SRDS Print Media Production Data.
Printing Process: Web Offset.
Trim size: 8 x 10-1/2; No./Cols. 3&4.
Binding method: Saddle-stitched.
Colors available: AAAA/ABP; Matched; 4-Color Process (AAAA/MPA): Simulated Metallic.
Cover colors available: Publisher's Choice; Publisher's Standard; AAAA/ABP; Matched; 4-Color Process (AAAA/MPA); 5-Color Process: Metallic; Simulated Metallic.

DIMENSIONS-AD PAGE

1	7 x 10	1/3	7 x 3-1/8
2/3	7 x 6-1/8	1/3	4-1/2 x 5
2/3	4-1/2 x 10	1/3	2-1/8 x 10
1/2	7 x 5	1/6	2-1/8 x 4-7/8
(*)	4-1/2 x 7-1/2	1/6	4-1/2 x 2-1/4

(*) 1/2 page island.

16. ISSUE AND CLOSING DATES
Published monthly. Issued mid month prior to cover date. Last forms close 60 days prior to cover date. Copy and art or negatives requiring proofs, 4 days earlier. Cancellations will only be accepted prior to published closing dates.

17. SPECIAL SERVICES
A.B.C. Supplemental Data Report released October 1986 issue.

18. CIRCULATION
Established 1980. Single copy 1.95; per year 12.00.
Summary data—for detail see Publisher's Statement.
A.B.C. 12-31-86 (6 mos. aver.—Magazine Form)

Tot. Pd. (Subs.)	(Single)	(Assoc.)
443,147 359,641	83,506	

Average Total Non-Pd Distribution (not incl. above):
Total 11,348
TERRITORIAL DISTRIBUTION 10/86—461,120

N.Eng.	Mid.Atl.	E.N.Cen.	W.N.Cen.	S.Atl.	E.S.Cen.
27,110	88,200	74,298	25,885	70,684	19,588
W.S.Cen.	Mtn.St.	Pac.St.	Canada	Foreign	Other
38,337	20,370	75,156	12,542	2,519	6,431

Publisher states: "Effective with January, 1987 issue, circulation rate base 450,000."

Source 24

Spot Television Rates and Data

Research Firm

Standard Rate and Data Service

Frequency

This catalog service is published monthly.

Data Collection

All rates and contract guidelines are provided by each commercial station in the United States. Each station chooses whether or not to provide rate information.

Function/Purpose

Through no fault of SRDS, this source is not the same reference authority it once was. SRDS must rely on published rates (those available to every qualified advertiser) alone. In today's media marketplace, television stations have been increasingly reluctant to publish a series of prices for spot inventory. The stations' reasons for using negotiated prices instead of published rates are complex. Suffice it to say, station management believes that to compensate for changing program popularity and shifting advertiser demand pricing should be very fluid.

Though an issue of SRDS does not contain many rate cards, it still has a value for the purposes of this text, that is, to demonstrate the unique nature of spot television pricing. Spot television rates differ so greatly from newspaper and most magazine rate cards that only an example could illustrate these differences.

Format Explanations

Spot television inventory (availabilities) is produced from announcements adjacent to programs (preceding and following) and by announcements within programs (participations). Nearly all published rate cards use the thirty-second announcement rate for reference even though most stations also sell ten-second and sixty-second announcements.

Many of the published rate cards use multiple prices for the same program position. This arrangement allows some flexibility in the face of varying market conditions. Although each station can be unique in its pricing strategy, a tested method adopted by many stations uses a system of pricing known as *fixed* and *preemptible* rates. The fixed price is the highest price an advertiser can pay for a given position. (See prices under "F-1" in the example.) Such prices may be paid when it is strategically valuable to be guaranteed a specific program situation. Most advertisers, however, are willing to risk the chance of losing the position in return for a lower unit cost. The lower cost placements are called preemptibles. (See prices under "P-1 to P-8" columns in the example.) In this case, the station reserves the right to move the advertiser's position should another advertiser be willing to pay a higher price for the same position. A further "discounting" is possible under the ROS rate (run of schedule). This is the lowest available rate; with ROS rates the station has complete control over where and when the announcements run within the time period. Skilled buyers are able to negotiate the lowest rates with an acceptable degree of schedule stability using this or other systems.

Illustration

Note the "Prime Time" rate listings at the bottom of Section 7 for WDIV-TV. The price range for one thirty-second announcement is from $13,500 (F-1) to $1,150 (P-8 ROS). Thus, it is possible (but not probable) to have as many as eighteen different rates for the same position. This might be confusing to outsiders but it is a practice that skilled negotiators expect to encounter.

Cheboygan

Cheboygan County—Map Location E-4
See SRDS Consumer market map and data at beginning of the state.

See Traverse City-Cadillac-Sault Ste. Marie-Cheboygan Area

Detroit

Wayne County—Map Location F-8
See SRDS Consumer market map and data at beginning of the state.

WDIV
(Airdate June 3, 1947)
DETROIT

NBC Television Network

NAB BROADCASTERS

Media Code 6 223 0062 2.00   Mid 007506-000
Post-Newsweek Stations
550 Lafayette Blvd., Detroit, MI 48231. Phone 313-222-0444, TWX, 810-221-1623.

1. PERSONNEL
Pres. & Gen'l Mgr.—Amy McCombs.
Vice-Pres. & Gen'l Sls. Mgr.—Christopher J. Rohrs.
National Sales Manager—Keith Simmons.
Local Sales Manager—Bill Burke.

2. REPRESENTATIVES
Petry Television.

3. FACILITIES
Video 97,700 w.; audio 9,770 w.; ch 4.
Antenna ht.: 1,010 ft. above average terrain.
Operating schedule: 6:30-1:30 am. EST.

4. AGENCY COMMISSION
15% to recognized agencies; no cash discount.

5. GENERAL ADVERTISING See coded regulations
General: 2a, 2b, 3a, 3b, 3c, 4a, 5, 6b, 7b, 8.
Rate Protection: 10f, 12f, 13f, 14f, 16b.
Contracts: 20c, 21, 22a, 22c, 23, 24b, 25, 26, 27a, 27c, 31a, 31c, 32b, 33, 34a.
Basic Rates: 40a, 40b, 41b, 41c, 42, 43a, 44b, 45a, 49, 50, 51a, 52, 52a.
Comb; Cont. Discounts: 60a, 60d, 60e, 60f, 61c, 62a, 62d.
Cancellation: 70a, 70i, 71, 72, 73a, 73b, *73c, 73d.
Prod. Services: 80, 83, 84, 87a, 87b, 87c.
(*) The conditions of termination set forth herein may be modified or eliminated when in station's sole judgment an extreme hardship would result to station or advertiser due to force majeure, acts of God or rare and unusual events.
Station shall not be liable to Agency or Advertiser for any special consequential damages arising out of any breach by Station of any term hereof. Station shall not be liable for damages in the event of failure of Station to broadcast any announcement in accordance with a contract, or in accordance with any makegood arrangement accepted by Agency.
Station shall bill Agency monthly, or weekly whenever Station shall so elect, for the charges due hereunder for such period. Agency shall pay Station, in accordance with such billing, within seven calendar days after receipt thereof. Upon reasonable belief of Station that Agency's credit has been impaired, Station shall have the right to change the terms of payment for further broadcasts. Any failure whatsoever by Agency to make timely payment of any charges, or any other breach whatsoever by Agency shall give Station the right, in addition to its other rights, to cease performance of the affected orders and to so notify Advertiser. The foregoing shall govern in the event of a failure of timely payment by Agency, and articles 1(b) and 1(e) of the Standard Conditions approved by AAA shall have no applicability to Station. If any discounts allowed in any billing to Agency are not actually earned in accordance with Station's applicable Rate Card, Agency shall promptly pay Station at its request the difference between the payments due calculated on the basis of discounts as allowed and those due calculated on the basis of discounts as earned.
Rate Protection
Station reserves the right to revise any of the rates or terms and conditions set forth herein by publication of a new or revised rate card. Spots covered by a contract at the time of publication of an increase in rates or change in terms or conditions will be protected against such increases or change in terms and/or conditions for a period up to 90 days from the starting date of the spot schedule, provided that the spot schedule in the contract has a starting date less than 28 days from the effective date of the rate increase and provided that there is no lapse in consecutive weekly telecasting pursuant to the contract. In all other cases, including renewals, a rate increase or change in terms and conditions is applicable to spots telecast on or after the effective date of the increase or change in terms and conditions. Station is not obligated to notify advertiser of changes in rates or terms and conditions except with respect to rate increases or changes in terms and conditions applicable to spots covered by a contract with advertiser. Advertiser may purchase telecasts of spots and/or programs based on rates and terms and conditions of only one rate card during protection periods in which more than one rate card may be in effect.
Affiliated with NBC Television Network.

6. TIME RATES
Eff———Rec'd 12/11/87.

---

7. SPOT ANNOUNCEMENTS

DAYTIME/FRINGE/ACCESS
Stand-By

	F1	P1	P2	P3	P4	P5	P6	P7	P8
MON THRU FRI, AM:									
6-7, NBC Sunrise/News 4 Today									
	560	420	360	310	265	225	190	160	135
7-9, Today Show									
	560	420	360	310	265	225	190	160	135
9-noon, Morning Rotation									
	560	420	360	310	265	225	190	160	135
PM:									
Noon-12:30, 12 O'Clock Live									
	560	420	360	310	265	225	190	160	135
Noon-4, Afternoon Rotation									
	560	420	360	310	265	225	190	160	135
4-5, Magnum P.I.									
	875	700	600	530	460	400	345	300	250
5-6/6-6:30 Mon thru Sun, News 4									
	1150	925	800	700	600	530	460	400	350
7-7:30, Jeopardy									
	3000	2600	2300	2000	1725	1500	1300	1150	1000
7:30-8 Mon thru Fri, 7-7:30 Sat, Wheel of Fortune									
	3000	2600	2300	2000	1725	1500	1300	1150	1000
7:30-8 Sat, Dom Deluise Show									
	3000	2600	2300	2000	1725	1500	1300	1150	1000
11-11:30 Mon thru Sun, News 4									
	3500	3000	2600	2300	2000	1850	1700	1500	1250
11:30 pm-12:30 am, Tonight Show									
	1330	1065	925	800	700	600	530	450	400
12:30-1 am, Hollywood Squares									
	575	460	400	350	300	275	230	200	175
1-1:05 am, News 4 Update									
	575	460	400	350	300	275	230	200	175
1:05-2:05 am, David Letterman									
	375	300	275	230	200	175	155	135	120
2:05-3 am, Ironside									
	375	300	275	230	200	175	155	135	120
11:30 pm-1 am Sat, Saturday Night Live									
	1330	1065	925	800	700	600	530	450	400
1-1:30 am Sat, The Laugh Machine									
	575	460	400	350	300	275	230	200	175
1:30-2:30 am Sat, At The Movies									
	575	460	400	350	300	275	230	200	175
11:30-midnight Sun, Sports Final Edition									
	2750	2300	2000	1750	1525	1325	1150	1000	875
Midnight-1 am Sun, Magnum, P.I.									
	1250	1000	800	700	600	530	460	400	350
1-2 am Sun, The Next President									
	375	300	275	230	200	175	155	135	120
2-3:30 am Sun, Mystery Classics									
	375	300	275	230	200	175	155	135	120
1-6 am Mon thru Sun, Night Shift									
	75	60	50	45	40	35	30	25	20
Noon-6 pm/8 am-6 pm Sat/Sun, ROS Non-Sports									
	330	275	230	200	175	150	130	115	100
Noon-12:30 pm Sat, America's Top Ten									
	450	350	300	275	230	200	175	150	125
12:30-1:30 pm Sat, New American Bandstand									
	620	515	430	360	300	250	215	180	150
7:30-8 am Sun, Health Talks/Due Process (alt weeks)									
	330	275	230	200	175	150	130	115	100
8-9:30 am Sun, Sunday Today									
	450	350	300	275	230	200	175	150	125
9:30-10 am Sun, Little Rascals									
	450	350	300	275	230	200	175	150	125
10-11:30 am, Sunday Morning Movie									
	620	515	430	360	300	250	215	180	150
11:30 am-noon/noon-12:30 pm Sun, Agronsky/Meet The Press									
	450	350	300	275	230	200	175	150	125
Various Sat/Sun, Sportsworld									
	1500	1200	1050	925	800	700	600	525	450
Various, Various, NCAA Basketball									
	1500	1200	1050	925	800	700	600	525	450
Various, Various, NFL Football									
	3500	3000	2750	2500	2250	2000	1750	1500	1250
Various, Various, NBC/NFL Vs. CBS/Lions									
	1500	1200	1050	925	800	700	600	525	450
Various Sat/Sun, Professional Golf									
	1500	1200	1050	925	800	700	600	525	450
KIDS									
7 am-noon Sat, Kids Rotation									
	685	550	465	395	335	285	240	205	175

PRIME TIME

	F1	P1	P2	P3	P4
8-11 Mon thru Sat; 7-11 Sun					
		13500	11150	9700	8400	7300
8-11 Mon thru Sun,					
Prime ROS		3500	3000	2600	2300	2000

	P5	P6	P7	P8
8-11 Mon thru Sat; 7-11 Sun	6300	5500	4800	4200
8-11 Mon thru Sun, Prime ROS	1725	1500	1300	1150

Preemptibility
All 10 sec spots are preemptible. All other spots purchased at a rate below the applicable F-1 rate are subject to preemption at the sole discretion of station without notice.
10 Second: When available, 10 sec spots take 60% of the 30 sec in all day parts.
60 Second: When available and where rates are not shown, 60 sec spots take twice the applicable 30 sec.

11. SPECIAL FEATURES

COLOR
Schedules network color, film slides, tape and live.
Equipped with high and low band VTR.

13. CLOSING TIME
72 hours prior film, slides, programs or announcements; 48 hours artwork. At least fourteen (14) calendar days prior to the scheduled time of broadcast of each program, Agency shall deliver to Station all Agency material therefore together with a list of the names of all creative and artistic personnel used or to be used on or in connection therewith and a list of the titles of all musical compositions to be used and the names of the authors, composers and publishers of such compositions. If Agency does not furnish required Agency material, or any part thereof, or any list as provided for herein, or if any of the same is at any time not approved by Station, then Station shall have no obligation with respect to the concerned program but Agency shall remain obligated to make payment in connection therewith and Agency shall, in addition, be obligated to pay Station for all unrecouped costs incurred by it in arranging for the broadcast of a substitute program, it being specifically understood that such substitute program, need not advertise or promote Advertiser or any product or service of Advertiser.

Source 25

Outdoor Billboard (Thirty-Sheet) Cost Estimator

Research Firm

Agency compilations based on Arbitron (ADI) areas and costs provided by *Buyer's Guide to Outdoor Advertising*. Cost data is now provided by the Institute of Outdoor Advertising.

Frequency

Estimators are updated at periodic intervals with poster and cost changes.

Data Collection

Costs per market often involve several poster companies; these have been combined for estimation convenience.

Function/Purpose

The primary function of this data is planning reference. It is a fast and easy way to allocate dollars for outdoor purposes. Actual cost and locations are subject to individual negotiation.

Format Explanations

Outdoor locations are usually packaged by each poster company. This means the outdoor company preselects where each advertiser's posting will be unless the client's sales strategy restricts locations.

The number of locations is dependent on the reach and frequency desired. Traditionally, outdoor called these levels "showings." Today, the industry has replaced showing with the GRP level. Rates shown in the example are based on 50 daily GRPs. According to SMRB estimates, this should deliver a reach of 80–85 percent and a frequency of repeat exposure of from twelve to seventeen times per month.

Billboard locations are either illuminated (for night viewing) or not. The exposure advantages are obvious, but clients usually have to accept nonilluminated locations as part of the board schedule.

Illustration

Media planning uses this data in a very straightforward manner. Markets are selected and the rental costs summed for the desired markets. Total cost is a function of market rental multiplied by the number of scheduled months. Cost schedules are also available for 25, 75, and 100 GRP.

Thirty-Sheet Outdoor Rentals
(Fifty GRPs/Day for the Top Twenty ADI Areas)

	Poster Numbers		Monthly
ADI Market	**Nonilluminated**	**Illuminated**	**Cost**
New York	188	387	$289,150
Los Angeles	62	458	248,615
Chicago	70	225	113,000
Philadelphia	128	136	82,930
San Francisco	35	208	111,500
Boston	55	115	71,800
Detroit	—	92	48,800
Dallas-Ft. Worth	44	92	41,150
Washington, D.C.	8	94	45,400
Houston	12	106	39,520
Cleveland	23	138	60,711
Pittsburgh	37	63	38,725
Minneapolis-St. Paul	34	76	44,460
Miami-Ft. Lauderdale	6	100	44,950
Atlanta	45	93	50,140
Seattle-Tacoma	5	75	34,100
St. Louis	16	64	37,800
Tampa-St. Petersburg	3	72	25,620
Denver	8	31	15,808
Sacramento-Stockton	25	48	31,580

Source: *Buyer's Guide to Outdoor Advertising.*

Source 26

Buyer's Guide to Outdoor Advertising

Research Firm

Rate and plant directory information are supplied by the Institute of Outdoor Advertising. The source is published by Leading National Advertisers, Inc. (LNA).

Frequency

Published monthly.

Data Collection

Compilation is organized by IOA. Data are supplied by each operating plant in the area.

Function/Purpose

This is the official rate reference for thirty-sheet and rotary bulletin costs. It is the most up-to-date source for such information. Actual location availabilities must be negotiated with the outdoor plant directly.

Illustration

The source needs little explanation. Note that showing sizes are organized by estimated GRP level. Individual coverages (reach) for markets are rare; most plants use the estimates from national syndicated research. The SMRB (1986) monthly reach and frequency levels for various GRP showings are as follows:

$$25\text{-GRP showing/month} = 77.3 \text{ R} \qquad 8.2 \text{ F}$$
$$50\text{-GRP showing/month} = 83.9 \text{ R} \qquad 15.2 \text{ F}$$
$$100\text{-GRP showing/month} = 88.1 \text{ R} \qquad 28.9 \text{ F}$$

Costs shown are for space only and do not include poster costs.

An outdoor schedule of 100 GRPs per month in Monmouth County costs $13,800 and uses twelve nonilluminated and twenty-eight illuminated posters. Thus, a three-month schedule would cost $41,400.

PLANT NO.	MARKET NO.	MARKET NAME	COUNTY NAME	POP.	EFF. DATE	GRP/ SHOW	POSTERS NON ILL.	POSTERS ILL	COST PER MONTH	DIS.
4990.0 RCMAX	00600	ATLANTIC CITY METRO PHL	ATLANTIC	202.1	01/01/86	* 100 * 75 * 50 * 25	20 15 10 5	24 18 12 6	15404.00 11553.00 7702.00 3851.00	14 14 14 14
		—Sub Markets (Sold Separately) ATLANTIC CITY URBAN, NJ ATLANTIC COUNTY-MAINLAND, NJ								
4990.0 RCMAX	00650	ATLANTIC CITY URBAN PHL SEE MARKET NO. 34-00600**	ATLANTIC	134.3	01/01/86	* 100 * 75 * 50 * 25	4 3 2 1	20 15 10 5	8720.00 6540.00 4360.00 2160.00	14 14 14 14
4990.0 RCMAX	00700	ATLANTIC COUNTY-MAINLAND PHL SEE MARKET NO. 34-00600**	ATLANTIC	67.8	01/01/86	* 100 * 75 * 50 * 25	48 36 24 12		15600.00 11700.00 7800.00 3900.00	14 14 14 14
5005.0 RCMAX	02800	BURLINGTON COUNTY MKT PHL	BURLINGTON	371.4	01/01/86	100 75 50 25	12 9 6 3	24 18 12 6	12060.00 9045.00 6030.00 3015.00	14 14 14 14
4990.0 RCMAX	03150	CAPE MAY COUNTY PHL	CAPE MAY	87.2	01/01/86	* 100 * 75 * 50 * 25	24 18 12 6		7800.00 5850.00 3900.00 1950.00	14 14 14 14
6490.0 ROL:NS	04800	CUMBERLAND CO METRO MKT PHL	CUMBERLAND	137.6	07/01/86	100 75 50 25	18 14 9 4	10 7 5 3	5720.00 4270.00 2860.00 1450.00	27 27 27 27
6535.0 ROLINS	08475	CHESTER CITY MARKET PHL	DELAWARE	43.8	07/01/86	100 75 50 25	4 3 2 1	4 3 2 1	3800.00 2850.00 1900.00 950.00	27 27 27 27
7840.0 JCWILL	10550	LONG BRANCH-ASBURY PARK-EATONTOWN M NYC SEE MARKET NO. 34-12860**	MONMOUTH	339.1	01/01/86	* 100 * 75 * 50 * 25	12 9 6 3	28 21 14 7	13800.00 10350.00 6900.00 3450.00	
7840.0 JCWILL	12400	MIDDLESEX COUNTY-SOUTH MKT NYC SEE MARKET NO. 34-12860**	MIDDLESEX	115.0	01/01/86	* 100 * 75 * 50 * 25	2 2 2 1	4 3 2 2	2070.00 1725.00 1380.00 1035.00	
7840.0 JCWILL	12450	MONMOUTH COUNTY MKT NYC SEE MARKET NO. 34-12860**	MONMOUTH	539.1	01/01/86	* 100 * 75 * 50 * 25	12 9 6 3	28 21 14 7	13800.00 10350.00 6900.00 3450.00	
7840.0 JCWILL	12860	MONMOUTH-OCEAN METRO MKT NYC	MIDDLESEX-MONMOUTH-OCEAN	1024.1	01/01/86	* 100 * 75 * 50 * 25	24 18 12 7	53 40 27 14	26565.00 20010.00 13455.00 7245.00	
		SINGLE PANEL RATE NON ILL 370- ILL 425-								
		—Sub Markets (Sold Separately) LONG BRANCH-ASBURY PARK-EATONTOWN M, NJ MIDDLESEX COUNTY-SOUTH MKT, NJ MONMOUTH COUNTY MKT, NJ OCEAN COUNTY, NJ								
3715.0 GANNET	13820	NEW JERSEY METRO, NJ NYC	ESSEX-BERGEN-HUDSON-MIDDLESEX MONMOUTH-MORRIS-PASSAIC SOMERSET-UNION-HUNTERDON SUSSEX-WARREN	5239.7	09/30/86	100 75 50 25		320 240 160 80	138560.00 103920.00 69280.00 34640.00	32 32 32 32
		ABOVE MKT. ALLOT. EQUALS COMBO NON ILL & ILL								
6535.0 ROLINS	13840	NEW JERSEY TRI-COUNTY ,PHL SEE MARKET NO. 34-15890** SEE MARKET NO. 42-45300**	BURLINGTON-CAMDEN-GLOUCESTER	1086.4	07/01/86	100 75 50 25	20 15 10 5	60 45 30 15	36300.00 29250.00 19500.00 9750.00	27 27 27 27
4990.0 RCMAX	14800	OCEAN-BURLINGTON COUNTIES SOUTH PHL	BURLINGTON-OCEAN	14.6	01/01/86	* 100 * 75 * 50 * 25	10 8 5 3		3250.00 2600.00 1625.00 975.00	14 14 14 14
7840.0 JCWILL	14900	OCEAN COUNTY NYC SEE MARKET NO. 34-12860**	OCEAN	370.0	01/01/86	* 100 * 75 * 50 * 25	10 7 4 3	21 16 11 5	10695.00 7935.00 5175.00 2760.00	
		SINGLE PANEL RATE NON ILL 370- ILL 425-								

Media Audience Reach Estimators

Source 27

Nielsen Television Index (NTI) Brand Cumulative Audience Report

Research Firm

Nielsen Media Research Company

Frequency

These are compiled reports from the data gathered during the October, February, and June NTI Pocketpiece surveys and are released three times yearly.

Data Collection

See the description of the Pocketpiece method on page 22. Example schedules are based on actual schedules of Nielsen advertiser clients. Selected brand competitors are also included.

Function/Purpose

Most network advertising schedules use multiple programs and dayparts. Advertisers and their agencies are vitally interested in the cumulative effects of scheduling—reach and frequency. Although reach and frequency can be estimated from mathematical models (probability), the BCA report is more reliable because it is based on "observed" panel data.

The BCA is of particular value to those whose schedules are analyzed, but there is also research value to others. The reported schedule dynamics are used as prototype experiences or models for other advertisers' future planning. This is particularly true in message distribution. *Message distribution* is the calculation of each level of reach for a specific frequency of exposure, that is, percent seeing one, two, three, and so forth, programs of the total scheduled.

Many research experts believe that an advertiser's message must be exposed a minimum number of times in order for any communication value to take place. Similarly, there is belief that repeated exposure past a certain level is wasteful (the audience has learned all it can from the commercial). The concept of using these levels of "effective reach or frequency" is dependent upon the availability of the data from BCA estimates.

Format Explanations

Each schedule report is divided into two portions. The top portion (A) reports the program-by-program schedule. The average rating, cost, and cost per thousand is shown, as well as the individual program reach and frequency. The (B) portion is a message distribution summary that combines all programs within a daypart ("Prime Time") and also combines dayparts. This portion reports the households reached by each frequency level possible.

Illustration

Assume that a frequency strategy has been designated for an advertiser that states maximum reach values are found within a three-time to seven-time range. This means that households having an opportunity for exposure less than three times within a 4-week period, or more than seven times, are not considered to be effectively reached. The client asks for an analysis of its current schedule as it is now running. The objective would be to have as high a proportion of schedule reach fall within the three to seven range. Here is an illustration of how the report might look:

Schedule reach (1+)	75.7 percent Households Reached
Average frequency	7.3 Times
Schedule reach (3–7 times)	27.8 percent Households Reached (Computed: 6.9+6.4+5.8+4.8+3.9)
Proportion of total reach within effective frequency range: 36.7 percent (computed: 27.8/75.7)	

NTi

**SEARS ROEBUCK & CO
INSURANCE**

**ALLSTATE INSURANCE
REF CODE: 15**

OCT 1987

TABLE A – ESTIMATES OF REACH, AVERAGE FREQUENCY AND COST EFFICIENCY

NETWORK & PROGRAM NAME	NO COMLS USED MSGS	30'S	AVG MSG %	HH REACHED IN 4 WEEKS %	(MILLS)	AVG COML FREQUENCY MSGS	30'S	COMMERCIALS DELIVERED GR RTG PTS MSGS	30'S	COMMERCIALS DELIVERED MILLIONS MSGS	30'S	TIME & TALENT EXPEND $(000) PER 30	4 WKS	COST/1000 MSGS	30'S
ABC MON. NIGHT MOVIE SPEC	2	2.0	12.4	14.2	12.58	1.7	1.7	24.8	24.8	22	21.9	140.3	280.6	12.77	12.77
NBC AMER. LEAGUE CHAMP GM 1	3	3.0	15.2	25.1	22.24	1.8	1.8	45.6	45.6	40	40.4	115.0	345.0	8.54	8.54
NBC AMER. LEAGUE CHAMP GM 1	2	2.0	17.4	26.5	23.48	1.3	1.3	34.7	34.7	31	30.7	115.0	230.0	7.48	7.48
NBC NAT'L LEAGUE CHAMP GM 1	2	2.0	14.2	21.2	18.78	1.3	1.3	28.5	28.5	25	25.2	115.0	230.0	9.11	9.11
NBC NAT'L LEAGUE CHAMP GM 4	2	2.0	14.2	19.9	17.63	1.4	1.4	28.3	28.3	25	25.0	115.0	230.0	9.17	9.17
ABC NFL MONDAY NIGHT FOOTBALL	4	4.0	15.1	29.0	25.69	2.1	2.1	60.3	60.3	53	53.4	171.4	685.6	12.83	12.83
ABC WORLD SERIES GAME #2	1	1.0	21.2	21.2	18.78	1.0	1.0	21.2	21.2	19	18.7	267.5	267.5	14.24	14.24
ABC WORLD SERIES GAME #4	2	2.0	22.0	29.8	26.40	1.5	1.5	44.0	44.0	39	38.9	267.5	535.0	13.72	13.72
ABC PRIME TIME	18	18.0	16.0	63.1	55.91	4.6	4.6	287.5	287.5	255	254.7	155.8	2803.7	11.01	11.01
NBC NAT'L LEAGUE CHAMP GM 2	2	2.0	8.4	12.9	11.43	1.3	1.3	16.8	16.8	15	14.8	19.0	38.0	2.55	2.55
ABC COLLEGE FOOTBALL-GAME	4	4.0	3.2	9.5	8.42	1.3	1.3	12.9	12.9	11	11.4	39.4	157.6	13.79	13.79
ABC SUNDAY AFTERNOON BSBL	1	1.0	4.3	4.3	3.81	1.0	1.0	4.3	4.3	4	3.8	26.3	26.3	6.90	6.90
NBC AMER. LEAGUE CHAMP GM 3	2	2.0	9.0	14.3	12.67	1.3	1.3	17.9	17.9	16	15.8	59.5	119.0	7.50	7.50
CBS NFL FOOTBALL GAME 1	4	4.0	10.1	24.6	21.80	1.6	1.6	40.4	40.4	36	35.7	80.1	320.4	8.95	8.95
CBS NFL FOOTBALL GAME 2	3	3.0	7.0	13.8	12.23	1.5	1.5	20.9	20.9	19	18.5	41.6	124.8	6.74	6.74
ABC MCDONALD'S BSKTBALL OPEN	4	4.0	2.0	4.9	4.34	1.6	1.6	7.9	7.9	7	7.0	25.0	100.0	14.29	14.29
NBC NAT'L LEAGUE CHAMP GM 5	1	1.0	6.3	10.3	9.13	1.0	1.0	10.3	10.3	9	9.1	59.5	59.5	6.52	6.52
NBC NBC MAJOR LEAGUE BASEBALL	4	4.0	9.3	12.2	10.81	2.1	2.1	25.1	25.1	22	22.2	24.0	96.0	4.32	4.32
NBC NFL GAME 2	1	1.0	9.3	9.3	8.24	1.0	1.0	9.3	9.3	8	8.2	92.0	92.0	11.17	11.17
NBC NFL SINGLE	3	3.0	7.2	14.4	12.76	1.5	1.5	21.5	21.5	19	19.0	68.0	204.0	10.71	10.71
ABC WORLD SERIES PRE GAME #6	1	1.0	8.2	8.2	7.27	1.0	1.0	8.2	8.2	7	7.2	121.6	121.6	16.73	16.73
ABC WORLD SERIES GAME #6	3	3.0	22.2	30.4	26.93	2.2	2.2	66.5	66.5	59	58.9	267.5	802.5	13.62	13.62
ABC WEEKEND DAYTIME ADULT	31	31.0	7.9	61.4	54.40	4.0	4.0	245.2	245.2	217	217.2	71.7	2223.7	10.24	10.24
BRAND TOTAL	51	51.0	10.8	75.7	67.07	7.3	7.3	549.5	549.5	487	486.8	99.3	5065.4	10.40	10.40

TABLE B – ESTIMATES OF FREQUENCY DISTRIBUTION OF COMMERCIAL MESSAGES RECEIVED

DAYPART	NO OF MSGS USED	AVG MSG %	4-WK REACH %	AVG NO MSGS	MM CML MSGS DLVD	% DIST. OF TOTAL TV HSHLDS BY NO. OF CML MSGS RECEIVED 1	2	3	4	5	6	7	8	9-10	11-12	13-16	17+
P-PRIME TIME	18	16.0	63.1	4.6	255	11.2	12.1	7.7	6.3	4.7	4.8	4.1	3.3	4.8	2.6	1.5	
D-WEEKDAY DAYTIME	2	8.4	12.9	1.3	15	9.0	3.9										
A-WEEKEND DAYTIME ADULT	31	7.9	61.4	4.0	217	14.4	10.4										
P-D	20	15.2	64.0	4.8	270	11.2	12.1	7.6	6.0	4.8	4.3	4.0	3.7	4.8	3.3	2.0	.2
P-A	49	10.9	75.2	7.1	472	10.7	8.4	7.1	6.2	5.9	4.8	3.9	3.6	6.3	4.9	7.1	6.2
D-A	33	7.9	62.5	4.2	232	14.1	9.7	9.8	7.2	5.0	3.9	3.7	2.1	3.0	2.3	1.6	.1
BRAND TOTAL	51	10.8	75.7	7.3	487	10.8	8.4	6.9	6.4	5.8	4.8	3.9	3.0	6.4	5.6	6.7	7.0

Source 28

Spot Market Television Reach Table

Research Firm

Formerly, reach projections were developed exclusively from agency experiences in spot schedules that conformed to empirical (Nielsen) estimates from network television. For the most part these projections have been replaced by statistical probability formulas developed by researchers and employed by media software firms such as Telmar. Until such time that primary viewing data is available on a *continuous* basis for many markets, reach and frequency projection will be driven by math models.

Data Collection

See "Research Firm" (this source). Currently, the market-by-market measures are primarily done by diary. Whether the development of individual recording meters will change this remains to be seen.

Function/Purpose

Reach or unduplicated exposure opportunity is not quite the standard of schedule performance it once was. Today, many planners qualify reach levels by desired frequency levels. If someone was not exposed often enough, they might not be counted in the "exposed" category. Despite this, reach is still a very important measure for advertising schedules running a month or more. Though it is understood that specific schedules may deviate substantially from a table figure, the reference is still valuable.

Format Explanations

Reach projections are based on the number of programs in which the advertiser's message appears, and the number of viewers available for each of the programs. This intensity is measured as the total rating values of all the programs, expressed as gross rating points (GRPs).

Reach levels reflect GRP levels, but much of the dynamic potential for exposing *different* viewers is actually determined by the dispersion of programs. Planners who project these levels trust that the buying schedules will include different stations, times, and programs. Only in this "spread" can the reach potential be found.

Illustration

The table can be used in two ways. The planner can select the desired reach level and use the table to identify how many GRPs in the daypart are needed to achieve the reach. This is a budgeting function. An alternative involves situations where the allocation is known and the planner uses the affordable GRP figure to see how many reach level options there are.

It is worth emphasizing that the estimates shown are not absolute. Prudent use of such tables would express possible reach as a range. To illustrate, the first row shows a reach of "33" for 50 GRPs monthly in early evening programming. A more realistic expression might show the reach as low as 30 and as high as 36. So much depends on how the GRPs are finally scheduled.

Spot Market Telvision Reach Table
Adult Viewers/Selected Dayparts
(Assumes Maximum Dispersion)

	Percent Adult Viewers		
Four-Week Total GRPs	**Early Evening**	**Prime Evening**	**Late Evening**
50	33	41	28
100	41	57	36
150	53	68	43
200	64	74	52
300	68	81	59
400	72	86	65

Source: Agency estimates.

Source 29

Network Radio Reach and Frequency Table

Research Firm

Compiled from agency and network sales sources. Presumed basis is the sole network measurement firm, Statistical Research, Inc., from its RADAR® report.

Data Collection

As with other reach and frequency projections, the data reflect application of probability statistics on basic survey measurements. Sample schedules used are from agency experience.

Function/Purpose

Though radio is often thought of as a frequency medium (suitable for heavy message repetition), many planners are interested in ways to use network advertising that will maximize reach. Building tables based on maximum dispersion (spreading) of programs and use of multiple networks is clear evidence that reach is still considered an important parameter.

Format Explanations

The organization of this table allows planners to estimate how GRPs should be distributed between networks. Depending on needs of optimum reach or frequency, some idea of how many networks to use is possible.

Illustration

Assume a planner seeks a minimum average frequency of 3.0 times per month for an adult target audience. The table indicates these frequency opportunities:

    One network—must use above 30 GRPs per month.

    Two networks—must use above 60 GRPs (spread between the two) per month.

    Three networks—must use above 80 GRPs (spread) per month.

    Four networks—minimum requirement is 100 GRPs.

Planners can also use this table when working from allocations of dollars (i.e., dollars are fixed). In this case, the dollars control the GRPs to be purchased. Once the planner knows the affordable GRPs, the various combinations of reach and frequency can be compared, especially at higher GRP levels.

**Network Radio Reach and Frequency Projections
(By Networks Used in ROS Dispersion—Mon.–Sun.
6:00 A.M. to 12:00 M.; Adults 25+ Years)**

| Four-Week Total | Number of Networks Used | | | | | | | |
| | One | | Two | | Three | | Four | |
GRP	R	F	R	F	R	F	R	F
30	10	3.0	—*	—	—	—	—	—
40	11	3.6	—	—	—	—	—	—
50	12	4.2	19	2.6	—	—	—	—
60	13	4.6	20	3.0	—	—	—	—
70	14	5.0	21	3.3	—	—	—	—
80	15	5.3	22	3.6	28	2.9	—	—
90	16	5.6	23	3.9	29	3.1	—	—
100	16	6.3	25	4.0	30	3.3	34	2.9

Source: Agency estimates based on RADAR®, Statistical Research, Inc.

*Presence of "—" indicates GRP level too low for multiple net use.

Source 30

Spot Market Radio Reach Table

Research Firm

Most market-by-market radio reach projections were developed by advertising agencies with the cooperation of the Radio Advertising Bureau (RAB). Many of the early reach curves have been replaced by statistical probability formulas developed by researchers and employed by media software firms.

Data Collection

See "Research Firm" (this source). Currently, the market-by-market measures are primarily done by diary and telephone interviews (Arbitron and Birch respectively).

Function/Purpose

Radio does not command the large individual audiences that television can, but, with so many station and programming options available in the top 100 markets, the potential for unduplicated audiences has expanded.

Format Explanations

Reach projections for radio are oriented more to quarter-hour segments than to specific shows. Although music and information formats are reasonably consistent on a given station, different listeners are available at different times of the day. This means that the more dayparts (quarter-hour segments) used the greater the reach potential. The table shown uses two of the daypart options often considered.

Drive time periods are historically the most popular for radio listening. The hours vary but most will run between 6:00 A.M. and 10:00 A.M. in the morning and 4:00 P.M. and 7:00 P.M. in the afternoon. The incidence of a mobile workforce ensures a relatively constant turnover from automobile listening. ROS (run-of-schedule) patterns use nearly the complete broadcast day. Advertisers not limited to key demographics stand a better chance of higher reach with this type of dispersion.

Note that both one-week and four-week levels are shown. As discussed earlier, the one-week figures are available in individual market reports. The four-week projections are based upon statistical probability.

Illustration

As explained in the spot television reach estimates, the table can be used in two ways. The planner can select the desired reach level and use the table to identify how many GRPs in the daypart are needed to achieve the reach. This is a budgeting function. An alternative use involves situations in which the allocation is known and the planner uses the affordable GRP figure to see how many reach level options there are between dayparts. Remember, to expect to achieve these levels, the schedules should contain a number of stations.

Spot Market Radio Reach Table
Adult Listeners/Selected Dayparts
(Assumes Maximum Station Dispersion)

Weekly Total GRPs	Percent Adult Listeners			
	Morning and Evening Drive		ROS 6:00 A.M.–12:00 M.	
	One Week	Four Weeks	One Week	Four Weeks
50	23	44	27	50
100	34	58	39	63
150	41	63	50	70
200	48	69	53	73
250	51	73	55	75
300	53	75	62	79

Source: Agency estimates.

Source 31

Daily Newspaper Reach Table

Research Firm

Agency compilations from Scarborough data.

Frequency

There are infrequent changes once the table is developed due to the relative stability of newspaper readership patterns. Agency media researchers, however, can review the annual Scarborough to ascertain if the table figures are still appropriate.

Function/Purpose

Though most consider newspaper readership to be relatively static (low opportunity for new exposure), multiple insertions do increase the probability of gaining nonsubscriber readers. Reach projections give the more serious users of newspaper advertising an accurate estimate of unduplicated coverage.

Format Explanations

The table shown here is a two-stage projection. Before the reach levels can be ascertained, the coverage must be calculated. This is done by dividing the circulation within the ADI by ADI total households to provide a coverage percentage. The coverage figure then determines the base potential for reach. The reach estimate is then developed from the number of insertions used within a month's time.

Illustration

Assume a planner has an anticipated schedule of four monthly insertions in a newspaper that has a base household coverage of the ADI of 51 percent. In consulting the table, the planner would use the most appropriate coverage row. In this case, that is the 50 coverage. Because four insertions are planned, that is the correct column to use. The intersect of column and row indicates that a 63 percent reach of ADI adults can be expected.

Daily Newspaper
Adult Reader/Reach Table
(At Selected Insertion Levels per Month)

Daily ADI	Reach of Adult Readers			
HH Coverage	One Insertion	Two Insertions	Four Insertions	Eight Insertions
30	27	35	43	49
35	32	39	52	53
40	36	44	57	57
45	39	47	62	63
50	42	51	63	64
55	45	54	64	67
60	48	57	65	69
65	51	61	70	73
70	56	66	75	79

Source: Scarborough data compiled.

Source 32

Publications: Twelve-Issue Reach and Frequency ("Adults")

Research Firm

Simmons Market Research Bureau

Frequency

This is an annual report.

Data Collection

The information in this report is derived from the interviews described in other SMRB report discussions (see page 34 or 36 for details). Those interviews cover reading patterns for two consecutive issues of each publication (current and one preceding). These data are considered "empirical" because they come directly from the respondents.

To estimate the readership dynamics beyond two issues, SMRB must resort to mathematical projections based on a probability formula. This is an estimation based on statistical "laws" and not observation. The formula currently used by SMRB is the beta binomial. Through its application, estimates of unduplicated readership are made for up to twelve issues of the same magazine. As an estimate, the projection may or may not reflect the "true" pattern.

Function/Purpose

Because many advertisers use multiple issues of a magazine within a campaign year, there is interest in learning how many different target readers might be exposed to the multiple issues used in the campaign. There is also an interest in the comparative patterns between magazines. For example, which magazine reaches the most different readers in a six-issue schedule? This SMRB report can assist with these questions.

Format Explanations and Illustration

The format for this report is done in a straight (linear) projection from the first issue through the twelfth.

The rows indicate three levels of estimate: "Net Reach," "Average Frequency," and "Rating." The explanations of each are illustrated by the first magazine listed, *New Woman (NW)*.

Net Reach (Adults). This is the estimated number of different readers that are exposed to each number of issues. Under "1" is the average reader audience for a single issue of *NW* (2,630,000). If five issues were used, *NW* would reach 6,289,000 adult readers. This would be called the net reach for five issues. Note that for purposes of the beta binomial formula, issues need not be consecutive.

Rating (Adults). This is a percentage expression of the net reach figure. For five issues of *NW*, 3.6 percent of U.S. Adults would be exposed (6,289,000/173,681,000). Note that the single-issue rating is 1.5. With five issues the *NW* rating would more than double.

Average Frequency (Adults). This is the average number of issues read by the different readers. Logically, most subscribers to a magazine would likely see each issue, but a newsstand or pass-along reader might only see one of the twelve. This figure only reflects the mean or average. For *NW*, the five-issue frequency is 2.09 or an average of two of the five issues are seen by the readership.

How is it calculated? We know that the single or individual issue is read by 2,630,000. If we used five issues the *gross reader impressions* would be 13,150,000 (5 × 2,630,000). The gross readers divided by the net readers (five issues) gives the average frequency (13,150,000/6,289,000 = 2.09).

0166
M-3

0166
M-3

TWELVE ISSUE REACH AND AVERAGE FREQUENCY
TOTAL ADULT AUDIENCE
U.S. POPULATION 173,681 (IN THOUSANDS)

		NUMBER OF ISSUES											
		1	2	3	4	5	6	7	8	9	10	11	12
NEW WOMAN	NET REACH	2630	4033	4987	5709	6289	6774	7189	7553	7877	8168	8433	8676
	AVERAGE FREQUENCY	1.00	1.30	1.58	1.84	2.09	2.33	2.56	2.79	3.01	3.22	3.43	3.64
	RATING	1.5	2.3	2.9	3.3	3.6	3.9	4.1	4.3	4.5	4.7	4.9	5.0
NEW YORK	NET REACH	1598	2090	2380	2586	2745	2875	2985	3080	3164	3239	3306	3368
	AVERAGE FREQUENCY	1.00	1.53	2.01	2.47	2.91	3.33	3.75	4.15	4.54	4.93	5.32	5.69
	RATING	0.9	1.2	1.4	1.5	1.6	1.7	1.7	1.8	1.8	1.9	1.9	1.9
THE NEW YORKER	NET REACH	2551	3683	4409	4942	5363	5712	6008	6266	6494	6699	6885	7055
	AVERAGE FREQUENCY	1.00	1.39	1.74	2.06	2.38	2.68	2.97	3.26	3.54	3.81	4.08	4.34
	RATING	1.5	2.1	2.5	2.8	3.1	3.3	3.5	3.6	3.7	3.9	4.0	4.1
NEWSWEEK	NET REACH	17278	25013	29905	33451	36215	38473	40376	42017	43457	44740	45894	46942
	AVERAGE FREQUENCY	1.00	1.38	1.73	2.07	2.39	2.69	3.00	3.29	3.58	3.86	4.14	4.42
	RATING	9.9	14.4	17.2	19.3	20.9	22.2	23.2	24.2	25.0	25.8	26.4	27.0
THE N.Y. TIMES DAILY EDITION	NET REACH	2840	4121	4946	5553	6033	6430	6769	7063	7324	7558	7770	7964
	AVERAGE FREQUENCY	1.00	1.38	1.72	2.05	2.35	2.65	2.94	3.22	3.49	3.76	4.02	4.28
	RATING	1.6	2.4	2.8	3.2	3.5	3.7	3.9	4.1	4.2	4.4	4.5	4.6
THE N.Y. TIMES MAGAZINE	NET REACH	3991	5584	6576	7295	7858	8321	8713	9054	9354	9623	9867	10090
	AVERAGE FREQUENCY	1.00	1.43	1.82	2.19	2.54	2.88	3.21	3.53	3.84	4.15	4.45	4.75
	RATING	2.3	3.2	3.8	4.2	4.5	4.8	5.0	5.2	5.4	5.5	5.7	5.8
OMNI	NET REACH	2677	4194	5249	6058	6712	7262	7735	8150	8520	8853	9157	9435
	AVERAGE FREQUENCY	1.00	1.28	1.53	1.77	1.99	2.21	2.42	2.63	2.83	3.02	3.22	3.40
	RATING	1.5	2.4	3.0	3.5	3.9	4.2	4.5	4.7	4.9	5.1	5.3	5.4
1,001 HOME IDEAS	NET REACH	3704	5666	6996	7999	8804	9476	10052	10555	11002	11405	11770	12105
	AVERAGE FREQUENCY	1.00	1.31	1.59	1.85	2.10	2.35	2.58	2.81	3.03	3.25	3.46	3.67
	RATING	2.1	3.3	4.0	4.6	5.1	5.5	5.8	6.1	6.3	6.6	6.8	7.0
OUTDOOR LIFE	NET REACH	8341	12120	14543	16319	17717	18868	19846	20694	21443	22113	22719	23272
	AVERAGE FREQUENCY	1.00	1.38	1.72	2.04	2.35	2.65	2.94	3.22	3.50	3.77	4.04	4.30
	RATING	4.8	7.0	8.4	9.4	10.2	10.9	11.4	11.9	12.3	12.7	13.1	13.4
PARADE MAGAZINE	NET REACH	63287	76352	83228	87782	91142	93781	95942	97763	99332	100707	101927	103023
	AVERAGE FREQUENCY	1.00	1.66	2.28	2.88	3.47	4.05	4.62	5.18	5.73	6.28	6.83	7.37
	RATING	36.4	44.0	47.9	50.5	52.5	54.0	55.2	56.3	57.2	58.0	58.7	59.3
PARENTS	NET REACH	6467	9292	11088	12400	13433	14283	15005	15632	16185	16681	17129	17538
	AVERAGE FREQUENCY	1.00	1.39	1.75	2.09	2.41	2.72	3.02	3.31	3.60	3.88	4.15	4.42
	RATING	3.7	5.3	6.4	7.1	7.7	8.2	8.6	9.0	9.3	9.6	9.9	10.1
PEOPLE	NET REACH	24627	36844	44731	50463	54920	58542	61576	64178	66448	68457	70254	71878
	AVERAGE FREQUENCY	1.00	1.34	1.65	1.95	2.24	2.52	2.80	3.07	3.34	3.60	3.86	4.11
	RATING	14.2	21.2	25.8	29.1	31.6	33.7	35.5	37.0	38.3	39.4	40.5	41.4
PLAYBOY	NET REACH	9433	13257	15635	17352	18694	19792	20721	21526	22234	22868	23439	23961
	AVERAGE FREQUENCY	1.00	1.42	1.81	2.17	2.52	2.86	3.19	3.51	3.82	4.12	4.43	4.72
	RATING	5.4	7.6	9.0	10.0	10.8	11.4	11.9	12.4	12.8	13.2	13.5	13.8
POPULAR HOT RODDING	NET REACH	2107	3250	4032	4626	5104	5505	5849	6150	6418	6660	6880	7082
	AVERAGE FREQUENCY	1.00	1.30	1.57	1.82	2.06	2.30	2.52	2.74	2.95	3.16	3.37	3.57
	RATING	1.2	1.9	2.3	2.7	2.9	3.2	3.4	3.5	3.7	3.8	4.0	4.1
POPULAR MECHANICS	NET REACH	6191	9079	10950	12330	13421	14322	15089	15756	16346	16875	17354	17791
	AVERAGE FREQUENCY	1.00	1.36	1.70	2.01	2.31	2.59	2.87	3.14	3.41	3.67	3.92	4.18
	RATING	3.6	5.2	6.3	7.1	7.7	8.2	8.7	9.1	9.4	9.7	10.0	10.2
POPULAR SCIENCE	NET REACH	4500	6780	8299	9436	10342	11096	11740	12302	12801	13249	13655	14027
	AVERAGE FREQUENCY	1.00	1.33	1.63	1.91	2.18	2.43	2.68	2.93	3.16	3.40	3.63	3.85
	RATING	2.6	3.9	4.8	5.4	6.0	6.4	6.8	7.1	7.4	7.6	7.9	8.1
PREVENTION	NET REACH	6665	9470	11236	12520	13528	14356	15058	15667	16205	16686	17121	17518
	AVERAGE FREQUENCY	1.00	1.41	1.78	2.13	2.46	2.79	3.10	3.40	3.70	3.99	4.28	4.57
	RATING	3.8	5.5	6.5	7.2	7.8	8.3	8.7	9.0	9.3	9.6	9.9	10.1
PSYCHOLOGY TODAY	NET REACH	3311	4852	5853	6593	7179	7665	8079	8440	8759	9046	9306	9543
	AVERAGE FREQUENCY	1.00	1.36	1.70	2.01	2.31	2.59	2.87	3.14	3.40	3.66	3.91	4.16
	RATING	1.9	2.8	3.4	3.8	4.1	4.4	4.7	4.9	5.0	5.2	5.4	5.5
READER'S DIGEST	NET REACH	37532	49651	56604	61393	65009	67894	70284	72317	74080	75635	77022	78272
	AVERAGE FREQUENCY	1.00	1.51	1.99	2.45	2.89	3.32	3.74	4.15	4.56	4.96	5.36	5.75
	RATING	21.6	28.6	32.6	35.3	37.4	39.1	40.5	41.6	42.7	43.5	44.3	45.1
REDBOOK	NET REACH	8442	12526	15197	17172	18736	20027	21125	22080	22924	23679	24363	24987
	AVERAGE FREQUENCY	1.00	1.35	1.67	1.97	2.25	2.53	2.80	3.06	3.31	3.57	3.81	4.05
	RATING	4.9	7.2	8.7	9.9	10.8	11.5	12.2	12.7	13.2	13.6	14.0	14.4
ROAD & TRACK	NET REACH	2864	4149	4975	5583	6064	6461	6800	7094	7355	7589	7801	7995
	AVERAGE FREQUENCY	1.00	1.38	1.73	2.05	2.36	2.66	2.95	3.23	3.50	3.77	4.04	4.30
	RATING	1.6	2.4	2.9	3.2	3.5	3.7	3.9	4.1	4.2	4.4	4.5	4.6

Source 33

Publications: Duplication of Audiences

Research Firm

Simmons Market Research Bureau

Frequency

This is an annual report.

Data Collection

The data for this report are gathered from a two-wave set of personal interviews of approximately 15,000 adults. The sample is randomly drawn and is purposely designed to be initially composed of "upscale" households. The survey is later conformed to national norms for income, education, and so forth.

The interview process involves one of two methods used by Simmons: "recent reading," a sequential recall process; or "through-the-book," a reader validation process using a current issue of the publication. Each interview involves multiple publications, allowing Simmons to estimate the duplication of readers between publications.

The two-wave procedure allows measurement of each publication over two consecutive issues. This enables Simmons to estimate if the publication attracts different readers over multiple issues (if readers read one issue but not both).

Function/Purpose

People who regularly are exposed to magazines and newspapers generally read in multiples—they read more than one publication and/or read more than one issue of any one publication. One result of such a pattern is that exposure changes or is dynamic. Certain magazines, if scheduled by advertisers for a series of issues, will duplicate some readers but will also capture new or unduplicated readers. In this case, a planner wants to know how many *different* readers may come in contact with two or more issues.

Media plans may also use more than one magazine at a time. In these situations, planners need to know how many different readers would be exposed from a combination of magazines.

Planning for magazines must have some basis for estimating the degree of overlap "within" and "between" publications. In some situations, a high degree of overlap or duplication may be desired. In others, the different reader or unduplicated readership is desired. Regardless of the strategy, planning needs the measurement of these reader patterns.

The Simmons report covers both of the measurements previously described. It reports the "within audience" over two issues (different readers from two issues of the same magazine), and it reports the "between audience" for every possible pair of publications it measures. Specifically, Simmons gives us estimates on how many readers read one or two issues of each publication individually, as well as estimates of how many readers read one or both publications in each possible pair (based on a single issue of each).

Why doesn't Simmons measure more than two issues for each publication or measure the duplication for more than pairs? Simply stated, there isn't the time or the dollars available to do this on a regular schedule. Where would the limit on the number of weekly publications be drawn? And even if the cost could be underwritten, would the sample respondents cooperate for a year? Although Simmons provides only the "baseline" measurements of duplication, other methods (covered later) have been developed to extend the Simmons data.

Format Explanations

The duplication data are displayed in a two-way matrix. The top portion reports the different readers for each pair of publications ("Net Unduplicated") and the "Single" and "Two-Issue" estimates for each *individual* publication. The bottom portion reports the number of readers seeing both publications ("Duplicated").

To find the figures for each pair, locate a desired publication by its top column heading (listed alphabetically) and trace down that column until the other desired publication is located on the horizontal row (also listed alphabetically). The intersect figure is the value for that pair.

Illustration

Assume a planner wished to see how *Vogue* performed with an audience of adult females. The "Single-Issue" figures tell how many of the target read an average issue (4,536,000). The "Rating" is the percentage coverage or 5.2 percent of the total target. The "Two-Issue" figures are the extension to the next issue.

Now assume that the planner wants to pair *Vogue* with *Woman's Day* magazine. To learn the combined audience of the pair, add the "Single-Issue" figures for each (4,536,000 + 16,508,000 = 21,044,000). This is known as the total reader impressions of the pair. To learn the number of different readers (read one of the pair) the first intersect (column = *Vogue* and row = *Woman's Day*) of the top portion called "Unduplicated," shows 19,487,000. To learn the duplicated readers, find the intersect in the lower portion ("Duplicated") and the figure is 1,558,000 (read both). To verify, subtract the duplicated (1,558,000) from the total reader impressions of the pair (21,044,000) and the answer is the unduplicated readers of the pair (19,487,000). Difference of 1000 is due to rounding.

If the planner is interested in combining the audience of more than two publications, there are a number of accumulation (statistical) models that have been developed to extend this base Simmons data. These models incorporate the observed measurement from Simmons or other similar sources and then utilize mathematical probability to continue the estimation process. Using models such as the Hofmans's example on page 78, a planner can combine as many publications as desired.

0210
M-4
PAGE 30

DUPLICATION OF AVERAGE ISSUE AUDIENCES

SUMMARY / ADULT FEMALES

0210
M-4
PAGE 30

ROWS - SEVENTEEN
TO
WKEND/SUN NEWSPAPERS-ANY

(IN THOUSANDS)

COLUMNS - VOGUE
TO
WKEND/SUN NEWSPAPERS-ANY

	U.S.TOTAL	VOGUE	WALL STREET JOURNAL	WOMAN'S DAY	WORKING MOTHER	WORKING WOMAN	ZIFF-DAVIS MAG NTWK (NET)	DAILY NEWS-PAPERS READ ANY	WKND/SUN NEWS-PAPERS READ ANY
SINGLE ISSUE	86771	4536	2035	16508	993	1235	2131	56430	56226
RATING	100.0	5.2	2.3	19.0	1.1	1.4	2.4	65.0	64.7
TWO ISSUE	86771	6580	3261	22665	1549	1915	3165	65619	64410
RATING	100.0	7.5	3.7	26.1	1.7	2.2	3.6	75.6	74.2
NET UNDUPLICATED									
VOGUE	6580	6580	6327	19487	5415	5517	6284	57705	57326
WALL STREET JOURNAL	3261	6327	3261	18084	2996	3193	4028	56826	56566
WOMAN'S DAY	22665	19487	18084	22665	17143	17156	17905	60498	60171
WORKING MOTHER	1549	5415	2996	17143	1549	2088	3012	56692	56478
WORKING WOMAN	1915	5517	3193	17156	2088	1915	3219	56754	56470
ZIFF-DAVIS MAG NTWK(NET)	3165	6284	4028	17905	3012	3219	3165	57064	56786
DAILY NEWSPAPER READ ANY	65619	57705	56826	60498	56692	56754	57064	65619	68229
WKEND/SUN NEWSPAPERS-ANY	64410	57326	56566	60171	56478	56470	56786	68229	64410
DUPLICATED									
VOGUE	2493	2493	244	1558	114	254	383	3262	3437
WALL STREET JOURNAL	809	244	809	459	31	77	138	1639	1695
WOMAN'S DAY	10351	1558	459	10351	358	587	735	12441	12564
WORKING MOTHER	436	114	31	358	436	140	111	731	741
WORKING WOMAN	555	254	77	587	140	555	147	911	991
ZIFF-DAVIS MAG NTWK(NET)	1097	383	138	735	111	147	1097	1497	1571
DAILY NEWSPAPER READ ANY	47241	3262	1639	12441	731	911	1497	47241	44427
WKEND/SUN NEWSPAPERS-ANY	48042	3437	1695	12564	741	991	1571	44427	48042

Source 34

Hofmans's Model for Estimating the Reach of Three or More Publications (Single Insertion)

Research Firm

This model, designed by Pierre Hofmans in 1966, utilizes the readership duplication factors for pairs of publications provided by Simmons and Mediamark Research.

Frequency

Because the model uses base data from syndicated services, it can be updated whenever new pair information is available.

Data Process

The development of the pair data is described elsewhere (see page 76). Hofmans's model was designed to best describe the specific condition of magazine audience duplication. It is not theoretical, nor was it intended to estimate any other exposure probability. No probability model is as accurate as actual observation and measurement, but Hofmans's model has been simulated against known outcomes and has performed well. There are a number of generally similar models—some of which are felt to be more reliable, especially with smaller schedules. This model was selected because it is a good compromise between accuracy and simplified operation.

Function/Purpose

The calculation of duplication and unduplication between different publications is limited in Simmons and Mediamark to pairs. Many schedules, however, use more than two publications. If planners wish to determine the estimated different readers to schedules with more than two publications running advertisements, some model projection is necessary. The estimation of multiple publications is termed *between vehicle reach*.

This model operates only on a single-insertion condition. For schedules using more than one insertion and multiple publications, other models are available.

Model Description/ Illustration

Here is the formulation of the Hofmans's model:

$$\text{Unduplicated Readers} = \frac{A^2}{A + KD}$$

Where
A = Gross reader impressions of the magazine
KD = Hofmans's Constant (calculated later)

Situation. Three magazines are proposed: (X) has 500 readers, (Y) has 300 readers, and (Z) has 100 readers. We want to know how many *different* people will read at least one of the magazines.

Step 1. Find the gross reader impressions by adding the readerships of each magazine $(500 + 300 + 100)$, thus, $A = 900$. Squaring $(900 \times 900) = A^2 = 810,000$. Note that many magazine reader levels are in millions of readers. Most hand calculators do not display more than ten digits. To compute A^2 a decimal should be used. If $A = 10,200,000$, calculate A^2 as 10.2×10.2 or 104.04. Remember, the final answer will be in millions.

Step 2. To find the KD constant, set up a table with these headings:

Col.1 (Pair)	Col. 2 (Gross Pair)	Col. 3 (Pair Dup.)	Col. 4 (Pair Undup.)	Col. 5 (Col. 2/Col. 4)	Col. 6 (Col. 3 × Col.5)
X+Y	800*	200	600	1.333	266.6
X+Z	600	100	500	1.200	120.0
Y+Z	400	100	300	1.333	133.3
				KD =	519.9

*The numbers shown in the table are found through Steps 3 to 9.

Step 3. List all possible pairs in Column 1 vertically (X+Y, etc.).

Step 4. Add the readers for each magazine in the pair. Put in Column 2, "Gross Pair."

Step 5. Column 3 and Column 4 in this example use numbers that have supposedly come from a magazine audience research source. For situations using actual magazine reader audiences, use either Simmons or Mediamark. Look up each pair and post the answers for duplicated and unduplicated in Columns 3 and 4. Please see page 77 for the SMRB format for pair duplication and unduplication.

Step 6. Divide the figures in Column 2 ("Gross Pair") by Column 4 ("Pair Undup."). Place the answers in Column 5.

Step 7. Multiply the figures from Column 3 ("Pair Dup.") by Column 5 ("Col.2/Col. 4") for each pair and put the answers in Column 6.

Step 8. Add all the figures in Column 6. This sum = KD.

Step 9. Place the appropriate values in the formula and solve:

$$\frac{810,000}{900 + 519.9}$$

or 810,000/1419.9 = 570 unduplicated readers of XYZ.

Source 35

Outdoor Reach and Frequency Table

Research Firm

Simmons Market Research Bureau

Data Collection

Because actual observation of audience exposure to outdoor locations is practically impossible, researchers must use indirect methods to estimate exposure and the frequency of exposure.

The Study of Media and Markets by SMRB employs a survey to estimate automobile usage on a daily basis. Reach projections are estimated from the degree of auto use. The table shown is based on a national sample, and may vary substantially from market-to-market estimates.

Function/Purpose

As an impact medium, outdoor can expose large audiences in a relatively short time. Exposure is "controlled" by the incremental levels of locations purchased each month. Planners use these projections to understand and gauge the impact of various levels on target audience demographics.

Format Explanations

The reach and frequency data on the table reflect the two most popular levels of outdoor scheduling—50 daily GRPs and 100 daily GRPs.

These levels were recently known as "showings." But, the outdoor industry now finds the "GRP" description more worthwhile. As in other media, a gross rating point is 1 percent of the demographic population potentially exposed to the advertiser's message.

Illustration

The table indicates that reach levels in outdoor operate with a fairly narrow range (83–91 percent). Frequency fluctuates more dramatically (15–34 times per month).

The GRP levels are indicated as daily increments but do not actually achieve this. To verify compare the thirty-day figure for adults at 50 daily GRPs. This should mean 1,500 GRPs for a month (50×30), but the actual GRP is 1,277 based on the table figures ($GRP = Reach \times Frequency$ or $84 \times 15.2 = 1276.8$). The difference is likely due to changes in driving habits on Saturday and Sunday.

Outdoor Reach and Frequency Table
Thirty-Day Projections for 50 and 100 Schedules
(Selected Demographics)

Target Market	50 Daily GRPs		100 Daily GRPs	
	R	F	R	F
Adults	84	15.2	88	28.9
Men	85	15.7	89	30.1
Women	83	14.7	88	27.8
Age				
18–24	85	16.4	89	31.5
18–34	88	17.5	91	33.8
18–49	87	16.3	90	31.3
College Grads	86	15.8	90	30.2
Income $40K+	87	16.0	91	30.6

Source: Simmons Market Research Bureau *Study of Media and Markets.*

S·E·C·T·I·O·N T·W·O

Exercises

Practice is the only way to master a skillful use of the data sources and references covered in the preceding section. If you are to gain familiarity you must use these resources consistently.

This section has two purposes. First, it identifies the capabilities of the data by illustrating the sorts of inquiries that can be answered. Second, the exercises demonstrate a step process to help lead you through solutions.

Many of the exercises make use of only a single source of media information. These exercises aid in finding and interpreting the data that are provided by the sources.

Other exercises utilize two or more sources in combination, to demonstrate the interrelationships of multiple sources and to permit comparisons of data.

Single-Source Exercises

Exercise 1

Reference

SAMI® Market Resume (Source 1)

Application

Many national advertisers do market-by-market advertising. The decision of how to divide the advertising dollars fairly usually reflects market sales activity. Planners will work with sales reports to use in the allocation plan.

Situation

The media planning group for Kellogg's Sugar Frosted Flakes brand (KSFF) is preparing advertising recommendations for four Eastern seaboard markets: Baltimore-Washington, Boston-Providence, New York, and Philadelphia. A special fund will be allocated between these markets.

1. What is the current twelve-week dollar volume of KSFF for all four seaboard markets? Answer in full dollars.
2. What is the current four-week dollar volume of KSFF for all four seaboard markets? Answer in full dollars.
3. What is the current twelve-week dollar volume of all brands (category) in these four markets? Answer in full dollars.
4. What share of four-week dollar volume is held by these four markets against four-week U.S. sales of the cereal category? Round the answer to two decimal places.
5. What is Philadelphia's share of KSFF seaboard market sales for the current twelve weeks? Round the answer to two places.

Exercise 2

Reference

Media Records Newspaper Spending (Source 5)

Application

Selection of local media can be dependent upon how much space is used by competing brands.

Situation

A planner for a major beer brand is considering a first-time schedule of newspaper advertising in San Antonio, Texas. Part of the decision depends on how active major competitors (Budweiser brands and Busch brands) have been in the local newspapers.

1. What is total newspaper expenditure to date (nine months) for the *Budweiser* brands?
2. What is the total newspaper expenditure to date (nine months) for the *Busch* brands?
3. What percentage of *Budweiser*'s total expenditures was done in July? Round to one decimal place.
4. What percentage of *Busch*'s total expenditures was done in July? Round to one decimal place.

Exercise 3

Reference

Leading National Advertisers (LNA) Six-Media Competitive Spending Report (Source 4)

Application

This report is used to track competitor activity and intensity. It allows tabulation of share of voice. Share of voice is the proportion of competitive expenditures done by various brands.

Situation

The account coordinator is assisting the media planner in finding the advertising intensities of competitive nasal sprays. The client wants the following five brands analyzed: Dristan Long-Lasting Nasal Mist, Dristan Nasal Mist, 4-Way Nasal Spray, Vick Sinex (Long-Acting), and Duration Nasal Spray.

1. What is the combined spending of all considered brands?
2. Which brand of the five is the top spender (all media)? What is its share of voice (based on total spending)?
3. Which (of the five) is the leading spender in network television? What is its share of voice in network television?
4. Which brand is the leading spender in magazine? What is its share of voice?

Exercise 4

Reference

Nielsen Television Index (NTI) Pocketpiece (Network Television Ratings) (Source 6)

Application

Network planners and buyers verify the monthly performance of network television programs (household and selected demographics performance).

Situation

The network buyer is checking the performance of a client participation that ran in ABC's "Hooperman" (9:00 P.M.–9:30 P.M.).

1. What is the average household rating for the half hour?
2. According to the household audience pattern, is the first quarter hour or the second quarter hour preferable for client commercial positions? Show figures to support.
3. What is the share of audience rank (all programming) for "Hooperman" within its time slot? Show the rank (1st, 2nd, etc.) and also the actual share figure.

Exercise 5

Reference

Arbitron Spot Television Report (Source 8)

Application

This is a key source for making station and spot location decisions.

Situation

The time buyer for a household cleanser is checking Utica, New York, spot availabilities for a target audience of women 18–49 years of age.

1. How many target viewers in the total survey area are available *within* the "Wheel of Fortune" program? Use the "Time Period Average" section.
2. How many target viewers in the total survey area are available on the break position preceding the "Bill Cosby Show"? Use the "Station Break Average" section.
3. What is the ADI target audience rating for the break preceding the "Cosby Show"? Note that this answer must be calculated. In your opinion, is the answer a reasonable estimate of the audience available on the break?

Exercise 6

Reference

Arbitron Spot Radio Ratings Report (Source 9)

Application

These reports have two functions for advertising: to assist in the selection of radio stations and to assist in postcampaign evaluation of performance.

Situation

The radio buyer is selecting stations for a pain reliever brand. The target audience is adults 35–64 years of age living in metropolitan areas of the Quad Cities market area.

1. How many stations would have to be scheduled to achieve at least a 50 percent share of the target audience? Show the stations and the individual shares for each.
2. Which station has the highest average rating of the target audience? Show the figure.
3. Which station has the highest cumulative target audience? Show the figure.
4. If the buyer used three commercials per day (Monday–Friday), how many target audience impressions would be generated by KIIK each week?

Exercise 7

Reference

Birch Radio Audience (Beer Consumption) (Source 10)

Application

Qualitative measures of consumption by station listenership are not a substitute for listener ratings, but they do sharpen the selection when used in conjunction with the most current radio ratings.

Situation

A time buyer for a major brewing firm is finalizing selection of stations by checking audiences of "Heavy" and "Medium" beer use by station listeners.

1. Which station shows the highest penetration of the adult 18+ medium beer drinker? Show the percentage.
2. Which station shows the highest composition of medium beer drinkers on a cumulative basis? Show the percentage.
3. Under the "Comparative Values" section and "Heavy" beer drinkers column look at the figures for WTLC-FM. This station is rated fourth in penetration (22.4) but has the highest index ("% Ind"). Explain why this isn't a contradiction.

Exercise 8

Reference

Mendelsohn Media Research—Affluent Adult Purchasing of Television Sets (Source 11)

Application

This is a supplementary source for evaluating media audiences. Along with reader characteristics, a media audience's buying habits will indicate interest in the product category.

Situation

A planner for a television set manufacturer is checking network evening news show audiences. The client markets high-end sets at $500+ per unit.

1. How many adults (total) were involved in set expenditures at and above $500? What percent is that of all affluent adults?
2. What is the average rating of CBS for the target audience? Note that the answer must be calculated.
3. Which network has the highest combined audience in the target segment? Show the figure.
4. Which network has the largest waste (non-TV-set purchasing) audience? Show the figure.

Exercise 9

Reference

SMRB Magazine Demographics (Source 12)

Application

This reference provides a fast comparison of basic demographic characteristics of magazine readers.

Situation

The advertiser is a manufacturer of cereal aimed at the adult market. A planner is checking the adult male profiles on magazines and Sunday supplements.

1. What is the percent coverage of the target by a typical issue of *TV Guide* magazine? What percentage of *TV Guide* readers are males?
2. What is the percent coverage of the target by a typical issue of *Sports Illustrated* magazine? What percentage of *Sports Illustrated* readers are males?
3. Which publication (of those shown) offers the highest coverage of males?
4. What is the probability index of the magazine that is most likely to have a target reader in its audience?

Exercise 10

Reference

SMRB Buying Styles (Psychographics) (Source 13)

Application

Often used in conjunction with reader demographics or usage profiles to identify special characteristics.

Situation

A magazine buyer has narrowed the choice of magazine to *Money* or the *New York Times Magazine*. The product is a new car model with unique engine development. The plan calls for adult targets who would be willing to innovate. SMRB's "experimenter" tabulation is appropriate.

1. Which magazine has the highest coverage of experimenters? Show the percentage of single-issue coverage.
2. What percentage of *Money* readers consider themselves experimenters?
3. Which magazine gives us the highest probability of exposing a reader that fits the target? Show the figure used in making a selection.

Exercise 11

Reference

Scarborough Newspaper Readership Profiles (Source 14)

Application

For those advertisers who have key audience targets, this source is essential for selection in competitive newspaper markets.

Situation

A space buyer must decide which New York newspaper to use. The target audience is senior adults (65+ years). The client is a medical insurance underwriter.

1. Which newspaper has the highest percentage of its readers in the target age (average issue basis)? Show the figure.
2. Which newspaper has the highest average issue coverage (reach) of the target segment? Show the figure.
3. What is the pecentage of increase in coverage between the average issue and five issues for the *Post*? Note that the percentage of increase is determined by finding the difference in audience between the issue frequency and dividing by the average issue audience.
4. What is the percentage of increase in coverage between the average issue and five issues for the *Times*? See Question 3 for instruction.

Exercise 12

Reference

Newspaper Circulation Analysis (NCS-II) (Source 15)

Application

This analysis compares newspaper and magazine circulation coverage of predefined metropolitan and market areas.

Situation

A brewing company media planner is evaluating print alternatives for coverage in the San Antonio, Texas, area. Because the brand has wide distribution, the area of dominant influence (ADI) will be used as the market parameter.

1. Which *daily* newspaper has the highest coverage of the ADI? Show the figure.
2. Which *Sunday* newspaper has the highest coverage of the ADI? Show the figure.
3. Using the column inch prices listed in NCS, which San Antonio daily newspaper has the lowest cost per coverage point in the ADI? Show the figure.
4. Using the column inch prices listed in NCS, which San Antonio Sunday newspaper has the lowest cost per coverage point in the ADI? Show the figure.
5. Using the ADI coverage percentage as a rating (GRP), how may GRPs would be delivered from four daily insertions (issues) in the *San Antonio Light* ("Lig") and one insertion in *Time*?

Exercise 13

Reference

Network Television Cost Estimator (Selected Dayparts) (Source 16)

Application

This source allows rough approximation of unit costs (thirty-second participations) and per program household ratings. For target audience rating estimates, the household rating must be converted to a target demographic. The data for conversion are available from other audience sources.

Situation

A network planning supervisor is about to give a "basics" presentation to a new network client. He/she will review cost forecasts for different seasons and dayparts.

1. In dollars, what is the total cost difference (prime evening) for 100 GRPs between the first and fourth quarters? What is the percentage difference?
   Note that to calculate percent difference subtract the two dollar figures and divide the difference by the smaller of the original numbers. Multiply the division answer by 100 to find the correct place for the decimal.
2. In dollars, what is the total cost difference (evening news) for 50 GRPs between the first and fourth quarters? What is the percentage difference? See Question 1 for calculation procedure for percent difference.
3. For an allocation of $400,000 in September, how many evening news GRPs could be purchased?
4. For an allocation of $450,000 in May, how many prime evening GRPs could be purchased?

Exercise 14

Reference

Cable Network/"Superstation" Cost Estimator (Source 17)

Application

This source is used for rough approximations on cost and scheduling alternatives.

Situation

In a media orientation meeting, a planner is reviewing various options that might be of interest for discussion with the client.

1. Based on the highest unit cost, what is the cost for 125 daytime thirty-second participations for each of the USA Network and the Lifetime Network? Would the cost be less or more if the late evening period were used instead? Show the calculations.
2. Based on the highest unit cost, what is the cost for 100 prime evening participations for each of WTBS and ESPN? For the total cost of prime evening on ESPN, how many *more* units could be bought if *late evening* were used instead? Again, use the highest unit price between the two.
3. For an allocation of $180,000, how many prime (minimum cost) participations could be purchased from ESPN?
4. For an allocation of $120,000, how many late evening (minimum cost) participations could be purchased on WTBS?

Exercise 15

Reference

Spot Television Cost Estimator (Source 18)

Application

Nothing is more changeable in advertising media than the costs and rating performance of local market television stations. Clients committed to considerable television investment need accurate (and continually updated) cost-per-rating-point projections.

Situation

The plan for a greeting card company recommends 400 GRPs in prime evening programming in each of the following markets: Chicago, Atlanta, Phoenix, and New Orleans. The GRPs are to be scheduled in late winter (January/February).

1. What is the combined cost per GRP for all markets based on first quarter rates?
2. What is the percentage of adjustment for scheduling in the second quarter?
3. What is the combined estimated cost of the campaign (if it runs in the second quarter)?

Exercise 16

Reference

Network Radio Cost Estimator (Source 19)

Application

Because of wide variation in listener formats and demographics, network specific cost estimates are preferred in radio. Costs shown are for reference only and do not reflect what the negotiated price may be.

Situation

A national car stereo manufacturer is considering various cost options for a third-quarter campaign.

1. Based on adult CPRP figures, what is the cost for a four-week schedule of 25 GRPs per week on the ABC Entertainment Network?
2. Based on adult CPRP figures, what is the cost for a four-week schedule of a total of 200 GRPs split evenly between NBC TalkNet and the CBS Network?
3. For an allocation of $250,000 split evenly between Mutual and CBS, how many total adult GRPs could be purchased (use CPRP to calculate)? How many thirty-second participations could be purchased under the same conditions (use thirty-second ROS costs)?
4. For an allocation of $300,000, how many weekly adult GRPs could be purchased on a four-week schedule if ABC's Contemporary Network were used (use CPRP to calculate)?

Exercise 17

Reference

Spot Market Radio Cost Estimator (Source 20)

Application

This source estimates the cost per rating point (CPRP) for groups of markets. Market costs shown are for ten markets in each group for the top fifty markets (five groups of ten markets). Markets have been listed in order by population. Cost shown is for one rating point for all ten markets in each group.

Situation

A planner is checking the cost of running radio spot schedules in major markets on behalf of a national temporary employment supplier of clerical help.

1. What is the CPRP for adult women in the top thirty markets?
2. What is the CPRP for adult women in the top fifty markets?
3. If the *one month* schedule called for 50 GRPs per week (adult women), what would the total cost be for the top twenty markets?
4. For an allocation of $740,000 and a goal of 50-adult-women-GRPs per market per week, how many weeks could you schedule for the top thirty markets?

Exercise 18

Reference

Daily Newspaper Cost/Coverage Estimator (Source 21)

Application

This source covers open costs and coverage for ranking newspapers in the top twenty markets.

Situation

A planner is seeking open cost estimates for a proposed 1,000-SAU-column-inch campaign. The minimum is 1,000 column inches per market.

1. What would be the total cost combined for New York, Boston, and Philadelphia?
2. What would be the total cost combined for Detroit, St. Louis, and Houston?
3. Will an allocation of $750,000 purchase 1,000 inches in New York, Los Angeles, and Chicago? Show the total cost for these three markets.
4. Will an allocation of $270,000 purchase 1,000 inches in Denver, Atlanta, and St. Louis? Show the total cost for these three markets.

Exercise 19

Reference

Standard Rate and Data Service Newspaper Costs (Source 22)

Application

This is an authoritative source for current national account space rates for daily newspapers.

Situation

A newspaper planner is checking costs for a newspaper buy in Rochester, New York, for a Detroit auto account.

1. What is the open black-and-white column inch rate for a weekday morning schedule?
2. What is the open black-and-white column inch rate for a Sunday schedule?
3. Current plans suggest use of 2,000 inches within the contract year. What are the rates per inch for both the morning and the Sunday editions?
4. What is the *total cost* for 2,000 inches in morning editions? These are all black and white.
5. What is the total cost for fourteen full pages in Sunday editions? All units will be black and white with three colors.

Exercise 20

Reference

SRDS Magazine Costs (Source 23)

Application

The source is used to calculate projected costs for individual magazines.

Situation

A planner for a video equipment manufacturer is estimating alternative schedule costs for *Video Review.*

1. What is the total cost for eight (four-color) pages plus two (two-color) half-pages to schedule over ten issues?
2. What is the total cost for ten (four-color) pages in regular issues plus one (four-color) third cover? These pages are scheduled for eleven separate issues.
3. What is the total cost for thirteen pages (four-color) in regular issues?

Exercise 21

Reference

Thirty-Sheet Outdoor Cost Estimator (Source 25)

Application

This multiple market estimator gives planners a typical monthly cost for a standard level of outdoor coverage.

Situation

A plan for a major distiller involves outdoor rental costs for various combinations of markets and length of showing (number of months).

1. What is the total cost of a three-month schedule for Miami-Ft. Lauderdale, Houston, Dallas-Ft. Worth, and Denver?
2. What is the cost for a six-month schedule for New York, Los Angeles, and Chicago?
3. If the campaign must run three months, how many markets (beginning with New York) could be covered for an allocation of $4,200,000?
4. If the campaign must run six months, how many markets (beginning with New York) could be covered for an allocation of $3,600,000?

Exercise 22

Reference

Nielsen Television Index Brand Cumulative Audience Report (Source 27)

Application

This source is used to evaluate the reach, frequency, and frequency distribution of a specific series of network programs.

Situation

A network planner is evaluating a scatter schedule for a major insurance firm. The estimated (precampaign) performance was anticipated as follows: 80 percent household reach with an average frequency of 6.5 times in a four-week period.

1. Was the household ("HH") reach estimate satisfied? Show the figure.
2. Was the average frequency estimate satisfied? Show the figure.
3. What percentage of the brand's total reach was delivered by the prime evening portion of the schedule? Show the figures.
4. If the media plan's recommended frequency range (effective frequency) is between two and seven exposure opportunities in a four-week period, what is the effective reach for the brand?
5. What are the total GRPs for the brand? What percentage of the gross rating points are within the two and seven exposure range?

Exercise 23

Reference

Spot Market Television Reach Table (Source 28)

Application

This table gives planners a rough approximation of reach by daypart for widely dispersed schedules (by GRP).

Situation

A planner is comparing reach levels between dayparts for a plaque-reducing toothpaste. The audience is adults.

1. How many GRPs does it take in early evening to equal the 41 reach shown in prime evening?
2. How many fewer GRPs does it take in prime evening to expose 68 percent of adults than it does to achieve that reach in early evening?
3. If average frequency is found by dividing GRP by reach, what is the average frequency of a 59 reach in late evening?
4. What is the average frequency of an 81 reach in prime evening?

Exercise 24

Reference

Network Radio Reach and Frequency Table (Source 29)

Application

This source offers alternative combinations of networks and GRP levels to estimate reach and frequency for adults 25+ years of age.

Situation

A planner for a car manufacturer is considering some network radio options. Questions involve working from reach goals and working from dollar allocations.

1. Write down the reach and frequency ranges available for 20 GRPs per week for four consecutive weeks.
2. What are the ranges for 100 GRPs per week for four weeks using three networks?
3. What scheduling options would offer a 25 or higher reach? List GRPs needed for four weeks and the number of networks necessary.
4. What scheduling options would offer a 4.0 or better average frequency? List GRPs needed and the number of networks necessary.

Exercise 25

Reference

Spot Market Radio Reach Table (Source 30)

Application

This source estimates exposure of adult listeners to radio by daypart and GRP level. Reach estimates are provided for one- and four-week schedules.

Situation

A media planner is using table in two ways: (a) to find the GRPs needed for desired reach level, and (b) to find reach level from a desired GRP level.

1. The plan would call for 200 GRPs per week in drive time. What is the estimated one-week reach? If continued, what would the four-week reach be?
2. How many ROS GRPs are needed to achieve a one-week reach level of 50?
3. The plan would call for eight weeks of 50 GRPs per week in drive time. What would the four-week reach be? What would it be if the GRPs were in ROS?
4. How many total GRPs would it take to achieve a 60 reach in ROS on a one-week basis?

Exercise 26

Reference

Daily Newspaper Reach Table (Source 31)

Application

This source allows newspaper planners to estimate the percentage of different readers exposed to a multiple insertion schedule in a single newspaper.

Situation

Bay City has 220,000 ADI households and 506,000 ADI adults. The *Bay City Times* has an audited daily circulation of 121,000. The schedule calls for one fifty-inch insertion to be run every other week.

1. What is the household coverage of the *Times*?
2. How many insertions will run in an average month?
3. What is the adult reach of this schedule?

Exercise 27

Reference

SMRB Individual Magazine Reach and Frequency (Source 32)

Application

Some magazines accumulate *different* readers as more issues are used. This is likely a reflection of out-of-home reading and newsstand sales. Planners seeking to maximize reach will often try to learn which magazine offers the most reach potential. The reward is more insertions for the magazines that do best.

Situation

A magazine planner has decided to use both *Outdoor Life* (*OL*) and *Popular Mechanics* (*PM*). The decision of how much space each will receive is, in part, dependent upon reach.

1. Which magazine would have the highest unduplicated reader audience after six issues? Show the reader impressions.
2. What would the gross (duplicated) reader impressions be for *OL* and *PM* if each received six-issue insertion orders?
3. How many GRPs would be generated by *OL* for a six-insertion schedule?
4. Look at the average frequency for *PM* on four issues. How was that figure calculated? Show the set-up of the calculation.

Exercise 28

Reference

SMRB Average-Issue Pair Duplications (Source 33)

Application

For schedules using two publications per month this table estimates the reach and frequency. For schedules using more than two publications, this information is used to prepare combination estimates used in formula projections such as Hofmans (see pages 78–79).

Situation

Planner has scheduled *Woman's Day* (*WD*), *Working Woman* (*WW*), and *Working Mother* (*WM*) in the same month. In preparation of the Hofmans's projection for the combination certain data must be prepared.

1. What is the total gross reader impressions of the three magazines?
2. What are the pair gross reader impressions for all possible pairs of the three magazines?
3. What are the unduplicated reader impressions for each possible pair?
4. What are the duplicated reader impressions for each possible pair?

Exercise 29

Reference

Outdoor Reach and Frequency Table (Source 35)

Application

The table is used to estimate monthly exposure for key target demographic segments.

Situation

Planning for a major distiller includes estimating the reach and frequency alternatives against a key target segment, upper income adults.

1. What is the reach and frequency estimate for this target segment if a 50-GRP daily schedule is used?
2. What is the reach and frequency estimate for this target segment if a 100-GRP daily schedule is used?
3. By what percent does reach and frequency increase when the daily schedule is raised from 50 to 100? Note: Subtract the difference and divide by the lower number. Multiply the division answer by 100 to get the correct decimal placement.
4. Which dimension (reach or frequency) increases the most (as a percentage) when the daily schedule is raised from 50 to 100 daily GRPs? To calculate the percentage of increase follow instructions in Question 3. What explains this situation?

Dual-Source Exercises

■   ■

The following problems will demonstrate how two sources of information must be combined to find the solution to the problem. As you begin to see how multisource situations are managed, you will understand how planners use media research and other data resources in the development of strategic plans.

Dual-source exercises are intended for students that already have experience with each individual source. We do not recommend that combination exercises be attempted until you have been "checked out" on each single source.

Exercise 30

Estimating Spot Radio Reach from Budgeted Dollars

Sources 20 and 30

A plan calls for a spot radio campaign of one month's duration in each of the top twenty markets. The target audience is adult men. The allocation to cover this portion of the campaign is $1,160,000.

1. Using the assumptions that the weekly schedules in each market will be identical in GRPs used, and the daypart will be morning and afternoon drive time, calculate the affordable one-week and four-week reach and average frequency.

Exercise 31

Estimating Radio Reach from Network Proposals

Sources 19 and 29

A network buyer has a $300,000 allocation for a December schedule. Based on the listed ROS rates for ABC Contemporary Network and the CBS Network answer the following questions:

1. Which network would offer the highest reach and frequency? Show the figures for each network. Use closest reach level to affordable GRPs.
2. What is the reach and frequency if the budget were split between the two nets as follows: 30 percent ABC and 70 percent CBS?

Exercise 32

Calculating Combined Reach of a Three-Magazine Schedule

Sources 33 and 34

A media researcher is evaluating the adult reader reach of various three-magazine combinations. For this projection, he will combine these magazines: *Woman's Day*, *Working Woman,* and *Working Mother.* Prepare the Hofmans calculation and answer these questions:

1. What is the gross reader impressions of the three magazines together?
2. What is the net (unduplicated) adult impression of the three magazines in combination? Show all figures including the Hofmans table.

Exercise 33

Outdoor (Thirty-Sheet) Cost Estimation

Sources 25 and 35

Planners for a premium-line automobile manufacturer are considering a three-month fall campaign in some key "resort-weather" markets: Los Angeles, Dallas-Ft. Worth, and Miami-Ft. Lauderdale. The target audience is upper-income managers-professionals. Fifty daily GRPs are desired.

1. What are the estimated monthly reach, frequency, and GRPs for this target audience?
2. To assist with production orders for paper, how many boards would be involved (all markets combined)?
3. What is the combined cost (all markets) for the three months?
4. What is the per-market cost per rating point? Assume a thirty-day month.

Exercise 34

Estimating Spot Television Costs Based on Reach Goals

Sources 18 and 28

A television advertising plan for the Chicago market in October and November calls for late evening (late fringe) programming that will deliver a 50–55 percent reach of adults per month (four weeks).

1. What is the correct CPRP to be used in this estimation?
2. How many monthly GRPs are needed to fulfill the reach requirements?
3. What is the estimated cost of this plan?

Exercise 35

Weighted Audience Profiles for Publications

Sources 11 and 12

A manufacturer of a "revolutionary" sun/skin product is planning a special introductory campaign. The audience is adult men and women with women rated as twice as good in prospect value as men. The pricing of the product (high) has also prompted consideration of adults with a high-income profile.

Evaluation of publications will be based on the gender readership factors from SMRB. The income factor will be merged from the Mendelsohn service. The relative weights are as follows:
Male Readers = 20 percent (.20), Female Readers = 40 percent (.40), and Better Income Readers = 40 percent (.40).

Publications to be evaluated are: *Sports Illustrated, Time, TV Guide,* and *USA Today.*

1. Prepare a *composite* weighted audience for each publication. Note that "composite" means to sum the series of weighted audience elements to a single audience figure for each.

Exercise 36

Using Brand Sales to Determine Spot TV Allocations

Sources 1 and 18

The brand management of Kellogg's Raisin Bran cereal is interested in testing a new television promotion in some selected New York State markets. The medium is spot television. The markets are Albany-Schenectady-Troy (AST), Buffalo (B), and Syracuse (S).

The campaign is scheduled for the second quarter. Prime evening is the daypart. The allocation is $175,000. The allocation per market will be based upon each market's share of the total Raisin Bran sales in the three markets.

1. What is the "current twelve-weeks" combined dollar sales in the three markets for Raisin Bran? Note that sales = brand share × market category sales.
2. What is each market's share of the combined "current twelve-weeks" sales?
3. Based on each market's share of sales, what is the dollar allocation for each market?
4. What are the (second quarter prime) CPRPs for each market?
5. What are the affordable GRPs in prime time for each market (based on the dollar allocation for each)?

Exercise 37

Estimating Adult Reach for Planned Newspaper Schedules

Sources 15 and 31

A newspaper planner is working on schedule variations for the San Antonio, Texas, market. The newspaper involved is the Sunday edition of the *Express*. The schedule calls for four (4) consecutive weekly insertions.

1. What is the *Express*'s household coverage of the ADI?
2. How many adults are in the ADI?
3. Based on the reach table, how many adult reader impressions can we expect from a single insertion?
4. Based on the table, what is the anticipated reach of adults from the planned schedule?

A·P·P·E·N·D·I·X·E·S

• Appendix A Media Calculation Guide* •

Print Readers per Copy

Print readers per copy is the average number of different readers who will come into contact with an average issue of a newspaper or magazine. The figure indicates the relation between circulation and the size of the reading audience. It tells how heavily each copy of the publication is used.

   Needed:

   A. The average number of readers of a typical issue of the publication.
   B. The average paid circulation (number of copies).

Formula:

$$\text{Readers per copy (RPC)} = \frac{\text{Number of readers of an average issue}}{\text{Circulation of an average issue}}$$

   Steps to work the formula:

1. Find the average number of readers.
2. Divide by the average circulation.

   Example:

Magazine M has an average paid circulation of 1,250,000 copies, with an average readership of 3,380,000 readers per issue. How many readers per copy does this magazine have?

$$\frac{3,380,000}{1,250,000} = 2.7 \text{ readers per copy}$$

Cost per Thousand (CPM)

Cost per thousand represents the relationship between the size of a media vehicle's audience (measured as households, adults, teens, etc.) and its cost in time or space. It is used to compare the cost efficiency of one vehicle with another, for example, one magazine with another or one radio station with another. The purpose is to gain the largest audience at the lowest cost. The cost is calculated *per thousand* to provide workable dollars-and-cents figures that are easier to compare.

   Needed:

   A. Gross impressions, that is, the number of households or persons exposed to a vehicle. (If the figures are given in GRPs, convert to numerical values by multiplying GRPs times the population base.)
   B. The cost of a single unit of advertising space or time. (Production costs are not normally included.)

*These formulas provide approaches to calculating some of the basic media statistics used in advertising.

Formula:

$$\text{Cost per thousand} = \frac{\text{Cost of media vehicle unit}}{\text{Gross audience impressions}} \times 1{,}000$$

Steps to work the formula:

1. Determine the number of gross impressions, households, or persons.
2. Divide the media unit cost by the number of gross impressions. This will give the cost per impression.
3. Multiply by 1,000 to convert to cost-per-thousand impressions.

Example:

A thirty-second commercial on station WSSS costs $850. The Anytown rating figures for WSSS indicate 58,000 adult women viewing at that time. What is the cost per thousand adult females?

$$\frac{\$850}{58{,}000} \times 1{,}000 = \$14.65 \text{ CPM}$$

An advertiser would pay $14.65 for each 1,000 female viewers on WSSS. This figure is commonly compared with the CPM at another station to determine which one is more economical.

Broadcast Rating

A broadcast rating is the percentage of a market's population (measured as households, adults, men, women, etc.) tuned in to a specific program, station, or network at a given time. The figure is given in percent.

Needed:

A. Number of people tuned to program.
B. Total size of the audience group.

Formula:

$$\text{Rating} = \frac{\text{Audience tuned to program}}{\text{Total audience population}} \times 100$$

Steps to work the formula:

1. From research sources, find the number of estimated viewers or listeners in the audience.
2. Divide the audience figure by the total possible television set ownership population of that audience.
3. Multiply by 100 to convert to percent.

Example:

Anytown has 625,000 persons in its broadcast area. An audience survey reports that a certain program has an audience of 110,000. What is the rating for the program?

$$\frac{110{,}000}{625{,}000} \times 100 = 17.6\% \text{ rating}$$

Broadcast Share of Audience

Broadcast share of audience is the percentage of all viewers or listeners who are tuned to a particular program, station, or network at a given time. The figure is calculated in percent.

Share of audience measures the audience size as a portion of those who are in the audience of *all* stations or programs at that time, whereas the rating is a measure of that audience as a portion of all who *could be* in the audience including those who are not viewing or listening at that particular time.

Needed:

A. The number of receiving sets, households, or persons tuned to a particular program.

B. The total number of sets, households, or persons tuned in to *all* stations at the time.

Formula:

$$\text{Share of audience} = \frac{\text{Program audience size}}{\text{Total audience at the time}} \times 100$$

Steps to work the formula:

1. From a research source, determine the estimated number of viewers or listeners for the program, station, or network in question.
2. From a research source, determine the total estimated number of viewers or listeners that are the combined audiences from all programs on at that time.
3. Divide the program audience by the total audience.
4. Multiply by 100 to convert to percent.

Example:

The Anytown radio audience figures look like this at noon Monday.

Station	Number of Listeners
A	1,200
B	1,500
C	1,400
	4,100

What is the share of audience for Station B?

$$\frac{1,500}{4,100} \times 100 = 36.6\% \text{ share}$$

Radio Cumulative Rating (Cume)

The radio cumulative rating is the percentage of different persons or households hearing a certain daypart segment during the week. It indicates the potential size of a station's audience during a week's time. It is also used to measure the total reach (unduplicated listenership). *Cume* is a slang broadcast advertising term for "cumulative audience."

Note that this is a measure of potential only, dependent on continuity in the advertising. To expose all of the audience in the cumulative rating, an advertiser would need to schedule a commercial announcement during every quarter-hour of the time period for the entire week.

Needed:

A. The total number of different listeners hearing a daypart segment on a Monday-through-Friday or a Monday-through-Sunday basis.

B. The total number of possible listeners in the station's broadcast survey area.

Formula:

$$\text{Cumulative rating} = \frac{\text{Unduplicated listenership by daypart}}{\text{Total population of listener area}} \times 100$$

Steps to work the formula:

1. From a rating report, determine the daypart cumulative audience size.
2. Divide the audience figure by the total population of the particular audience segment.
3. Multiply by 100 to convert to percent.

Example:

Station WZYX in Anytown has a cumulative audience of 6,400 unduplicated adult listeners tuning in at least once between Monday and Sunday at 6:00 A.M.–10:00 A.M. If there are 33,000 adults in the Anytown survey area, what is the station's cumulative rating for that time period?

$$\frac{6,400}{33,000} \times 100 = 19.4\% \text{ cume}$$

Gross Rating Points (GRPs)

A gross rating point is a way to express the accumulated audience impressions developed by using a series of advertisements. A typical example might include the combined audiences from a series of magazine insertions, a package of television announcements, and an outdoor posting schedule.

GRPs are basically the sum of the ratings; that is, add the ratings for a certain time period (usually given as the average GRPs per week measured during a 4-week period) to arrive at gross rating points. The figure is valuable because it combines indications of reach and frequency in a single calculation. GRP totals have been adapted in media planning as quick measures of advertising impact.

Needed:

A. Audience value of each vehicle, expressed as a percentage (that is, percent reach). All figures must be of the same category; you cannot mix households with adults, or men with total audience, and so on.

B. The number of times that each vehicle is used within the specified time period (that is, frequency of advertising insertion).

Formula:

$$\text{Gross rating points} = \text{Audience value in percent} \times \text{Schedule frequency}$$

or

$$\text{GRP} = \text{Reach}\% \times \text{Frequency}$$

Steps to work the formula:

1. Find the rating values of each vehicle. (If the data are "raw" numbers, convert to percentages.)
2. Multiply the rating values from each vehicle by the number of times the vehicle appears in the advertising schedule.
3. Add the multiplied GRP for each vehicle to gain a sum total GRP figure for the period.

Example:
Radio

Daypart	Rating × Spots per week		GRP
M–F 4:00 P.M.–6:00 P.M.	2.2	10	22
Sat. 10:00 A.M.–3:00 P.M.	1.5	4	6

Total GRP/Week = 28

Magazine

Publication	Average Issue Adult Women Readers × No. of Insertions		GRP
D	15	6	90
E	19	4	76
F	24	12	288

Yearly GRP = 454

Unduplicated Reach

Unduplicated reach represents, through statistics, the probabilities of exposing a percentage of the households or persons by advertising in a certain media vehicle. Reach is calculated over a set time period, usually four weeks. The figure provides an estimate of how many different prospects might be exposed to an advertising schedule.

Needed:

A. From research sources, determine the estimated unduplicated audience figure.

B. Determine the base audience population. (Because reach is a percentage, the net audience must be compared to the highest possible population figure, which is the universe or base figure.)

Formulas:
Single Vehicle Reach

$$\text{Unduplicated reach} = \frac{\text{Unduplicated audience impressions}}{\text{Base population}}$$

Multiple Vehicle Reach
(This multiple vehicle calculation is a rough estimate because it uses a standard figure in calculating the overlap audiences of two or more vehicles. If the actual unduplicated figures are known, they should be used instead of this formula. Note that all reach figures are expressed in percent.)

[(Vehicle A Reach) + (Vehicle B Reach)] − [(Vehicle A Reach) × (Vehicle B Reach)] = Combined reach of Vehicles A and B

Example:
An advertiser is using three magazines in an advertising schedule. Magazine A has a reach of 21 percent of the target group. Magazine B has a target reach of 15 percent, and Magazine C reaches 11 percent. What is the combined audience of all three magazines?

(A) 0.21 + (B) 0.15 =   0.36
minus (A) 0.21 × (B) 0.15 =   − 0.03

Equals 0.33 (or, 33%)

Then, to combine the AB combination with C

$$
\begin{aligned}
(AB)\ 0.33 + (C)\ 0.11 &= \quad 0.44 \\
\text{minus } (AB)\ 0.33 \times (C)\ 0.11 &= \ \underline{-0.04}
\end{aligned}
$$

Equals 0.40 (or, 40%) combined reach

Average Frequency of Exposure

Average frequency of exposure provides the repetition of exposure to a vehicle or a schedule of several vehicles. It is the number of times that the average audience exposed will likely see or hear the vehicles within a specified time period, usually four weeks.

Frequency is necessary to assure that a satisfactory portion of the audience reached will have adequate repeat exposure to remember or to react to the advertising message.

Needed:

A. The gross impressions from using a vehicle. (The impressions can be in "raw" numbers or in GRPs.)

B. The net impressions of a vehicle or vehicles. This is the unduplicated audience during the identical time period. (Again, figures can be "raw" numbers or percentages.)

Single Vehicle Formula:

$$
\text{Average frequency} = \frac{\text{Gross impressions}}{\text{Net impressions}}
$$

or,

$$
\text{Average frequency} = \frac{\text{GRPs}}{\text{Reach}}
$$

Example:

A magazine has an average single-issue audience of 20 percent reach to the target group, but using four issues will reach 30 percent of the target group. If the advertiser uses four issues, what is the average frequency?

$$
\text{GRP} = 20 \times 4 = \frac{80}{30} = 2.7 \text{ average frequency}
$$

Multiple Vehicles (for combined frequency) Formula:

$$
\frac{[(\text{Vehicle A Reach}) \times (\text{Vehicle A Frequency})] + [(\text{Vehicle B Reach}) \times (\text{Vehicle B Frequency})]}{\text{Unduplicated reach of A and B}}
$$

Example:

Using a certain advertiser's schedule, radio station WXXX will reach 15 percent of Anytown households with a 6.5 frequency. If station WYYY is added, with a 20 percent reach and a 7.0 average frequency, what will be the combined frequency?

$$
\frac{(15 \times 6.5) + (20 \times 7.0)}{32^*} = \frac{97.5 + 140}{32} = \frac{237.5}{32} = 7.4 \text{ combined average frequency}
$$

*The combined reach of 20 percent and 15 percent is 32 percent, using our unduplicated reach formula:

$$
[(0.20) + (0.15)] - [(0.20) \times (0.15)] = [0.35] - [0.03] = 0.32
$$

Arbitron Ratings Company
1350 Avenue of the Americas
New York, New York 10019

Birch Radio
44 Sylvan Avenue
Englewood Cliffs, New Jersey 07632

Broadcast Advertisers Reports, Inc.
142 West 57th Street
New York, New York 10019

Editor & Publisher Company
11 West 19th Street
New York, New York 10011

Institute of Outdoor Advertising
342 Madison Avenue
New York, New York 10173

Interactive Market Systems
360 North Michigan Avenue
Chicago, Illinois 60601

Leading National Advertisers, Inc.
136 Madison Avenue
New York, New York 10016

Mediamark Research, Inc.
341 Madison Avenue
New York, New York 10017

Media Records, Inc.
370 Seventh Avenue
New York, New York 10001

Mendelsohn Media Research
352 Park Avenue South
New York, New York 10010

Nielsen Media Research
Nielsen Plaza
Northbrook, Illinois 60062

PRIZM
260 Madison Avenue
New York, New York 10016

Sales and Marketing Management
633 Third Avenue
New York, New York 10017

SAMI/Burke Marketing Services, Inc.
800 Broadway
Cincinnati, Ohio 45202

Scarborough Research Corporation
44 Sylvan Avenue
Englewood Cliffs, New Jersey 07632

Simmons Market Research Bureau
219 East 42nd Street
New York, New York 10017

Standard Rate and Data Service, Inc.
3004 Glenview Road
Wilmette, Illinois 60091

Telmar Communications Corporation
90 Park Avenue
New York, New York 10016

Glossary of Advertising Media Terms

Accumulative audience. *See* Cumulative audience.

Across the board. A program that is broadcast at the same time period every day (*see* Strip).

Adjacency. A program or a commercial announcement that is adjacent to another either preceding or following, on the same station.

Affiliate. A broadcast station that grants a network an option of specific times for broadcasting network programming in return for compensation.

Agate line. Newspaper advertising space one column wide by one-fourteenth of an inch deep; often referred to simply as "line"; somewhat obsolete because most newspapers now use "column inch" measurements of advertising space, especially for national advertising.

Agency commission. Usually 15 percent, allowed to advertising agencies by media on the agencies' purchase of media space or time.

Agency of record. Advertising agency that coordinates an advertiser's promotion of several products handled by more than a single agency (*see* Blanket contract).

Agency recognition. Acknowledgment by media owners that certain advertising agencies are good credit risks and/or fulfill certain requirements, thus qualifying for a commission.

Air check. Recording a broadcast to serve as an archival or file copy.

Allotment. The number and type of outdoor posters in a showing (*see* Showing).

Alternate sponsorship. Two advertisers who sponsor a single program—one advertiser sponsors one week and the other sponsors the alternate week (*see* Crossplugs).

Announcement. An advertising message that is broadcast between programs (*see* Station break, Participation, Billboard), or an advertisement within a syndicated program or feature film; any broadcast commercial regardless of time length, within or between programs, that presents an advertiser's message or a public service message.

American Research Bureau (ARB). One of several national firms engaged in radio and television research; the founder of Arbitron ratings.

Annual rebate. *See* Rebate.

Area of Dominant Influence (ADI). Arbitron measurement area that comprises those counties in which stations of a single originating market account for a greater share of the viewing households than those from any other market; similar to Nielsen's Designated Market Area.

Audience. Persons who receive an advertisement; individuals who read a newspaper or magazine, listen to a radio broadcast, view a television broadcast, and so on.

Audience accumulation. The total number of different persons or households exposed to a single media vehicle over a period of time (*see* Cumulative audience).

Audience composition. Audience analysis expressed in demographic terms or other characteristics.

Audience duplication. Those persons or households who see an advertisement more than once in a single media vehicle or in a combination of vehicles.

Audience flow. The movement of a broadcast audience's attention from one station to another when the program changes, measured against the audience that stays tuned to the same station or network to view the new program (*see* Holdover audience).

Audience profile. The minute-by-minute viewing pattern for a program; a description of the characteristics of the people who are exposed to a medium or vehicle (*see* Profile).

Audience turnover. That part of a broadcast audience that changes over time (*see* Audience flow).

Audimeter. A. C. Nielsen Company's automatic device attached to radio or television receiving sets that records usage and station information (*see* People meter).

Availability. A broadcast time period that is open for reservation by an advertiser in response to an advertiser's or agency's initial inquiry (slang "avail").

Average audience. The number of broadcast homes that are tuned in for an average minute of a broadcast.

Average exposure. The average (mean) number of times that each audience member has been exposed to an advertisement.

Average net paid circulation. Average (mean) number of copies that a publication distributes per issue.

Back to back. Two broadcast programs or commercials in succession.

Basic rate. *See* Open rate.

Barter. An advertising medium that sells time or space in return for merchandise or other nonmonetary returns; also a television programming offer in which a station is offered a syndicated program in exchange for commercial positions within the program.

Billboard. An outdoor poster; cast and production information that follows a broadcast program; a six-second radio commercial; a short commercial announcement, usually eight or ten seconds in length, announcing the name of the sponsor, at the start and close of a program.

Billing. The value of advertising that is handled by an advertising agency on behalf of its clients (often called "billings"); the process of issuing invoices for media space and time that have been purchased.

Blanket contract. A special rate or discount that is granted by an advertising medium to an advertiser who promotes several products or services through more than one agency.

Bleed. Printing to the edge of the page, with no margin or border.

Block. Consecutive broadcast time periods.

Booking. Scheduling a broadcast program or commercial.

Brand Development Index (BDI). A comparative measure of a brand's sales in one market, compared with other markets, used to decide the relative sales value of one market versus another (*see* Category Development Index).

Break. Time available for purchase between two broadcast programs or between segments of a single program.

Broadcast Advertisers Report (BAR). A commercial broadcast monitoring service that is available on a network and market-by-market basis.

Bulk discount. A discount offered by media for quantity buys (*see* Quantity discount).

Bulk rate. *See* Bulk discount.

Business card. A small print advertisement, announcing a business, that does not change over time (*see* Rate holder).

Business paper. A publication that is intended for business or professional interests.

Buy. The process of negotiating, ordering, and confirming the selection of a media vehicle and unit; as a noun, the advertising that is purchased from a vehicle.

Buyer. *See* Media buyer *and* Media planner.

Buying service. A company primarily engaged in the purchase of media for advertising purposes; it supplants part of the advertising media function; also called "media buying specialist" or "time/space buying specialist/service."

Buy sheet. The form used by a media buyer to keep track of the data on a media selection "buy."

Call letters. The letters that identify a station; for example, WBZ-TV.

Campaign. A specific coordinated advertising effort on behalf of a particular product or service that extends for a specified period of time.

Car card. Transit advertisement in or on a bus, subway, or commuter train car.

Card rate. The cost of time or space on a rate card.

Carryover effect. The residual level of awareness or recall after a flight or campaign period, used to plan the timing of schedules.

Cash discount. A discount, usually 2 percent, by media to advertisers who pay promptly.

Category Development Index (CDI). A comparative market-by-market measure of a market's total sales of all brands of a single product category, used to evaluate the sales potential of a market for a product category or a brand (*see* Brand Development Index).

CC. The conclusion of a broadcast; for example, this program runs 11:30 P.M.—CC.

Center spread. An advertisement appearing on two facing pages printed on a single sheet in the center of a publication (*see* Double truck).

Chain. A broadcast network; also, a newspaper or magazine group of single ownership or control.

Chain break (CB). The time during which a network allows a station to identify itself; usually a twenty-second spot (slang "twenty"); now often a thirty-second spot plus a ten-second spot, with twenty seconds remaining for identification.

Checking. The process of confirming whether an advertisement actually appeared.

Checking copy. A copy of a publication that is supplied by the medium to show that an advertisement appeared as specified.

Circulation. In print, the number of copies distributed; in broadcast, the number of households within a signal area that have receiving sets; in outdoor, the number of people who have a reasonable opportunity to see a billboard.

City zone. A central city and the contiguous areas that cannot be distinguished from it.

City zone circulation. The number of newspapers that are distributed within a city, rather than in outlying areas.

Classified advertising. Advertising that is set in small type and arranged according to categories or interests.

Classified display advertising. Classified advertising of a larger size than most other classified advertising, possibly with headlines, illustrations, and so on; classified advertising with some of the characteristics of display advertising (*see* Display advertising).

Class magazines. Special-interest magazines with desirable upscale audiences.

Clearance. Coverage of national television households by the number of stations (or markets) accepting a network program for airing; also, gaining available time on stations to carry a program or commercial.

Clear time. The process of reserving time or time periods with a station or network; checking on available advertising time.

Clipping bureau. An organization that aids in checking print advertising by clipping the advertisements from print media.

Closing date. The final deadline set by print media for advertising material to appear in a certain issue; in broadcast, the term "closing hour" may be used.

Closure. A sale resulting from following up on an inquiry from direct mail advertising.

Column inch. Publication space that is one column wide by one inch high, used as a measure of advertising space.

Combination rate. A special discounted advertising rate for buying space in two or more publications owned by the same interests.

Commercial impressions. The total audience, including duplication, for all commercial announcements in an advertiser's schedule (*see* Gross impressions).

Confirmation. A broadcast media statement that a specific time is still open for purchase by an advertiser who is preparing a broadcast advertising schedule.

Consumer profile. A demographic description of the people or households that are prospects for a product or service (*see* Target group).

Contiguity rate. A reduced broadcast advertising rate for sponsoring two or more programs in succession; for example, an advertiser participating in two programs running from 7:00 P.M.–7:30 P.M. and then 7:30 P.M.–8:00 P.M. may qualify for a contiguity rate.

Controlled circulation. Circulation that is limited to persons who qualify to receive a publication; often distributed free to qualified persons.

Cooperative advertising. Retail advertising that is paid partly or fully by a manufacturer; two or more manufacturers cooperating in a single advertisement (slang "co-op").

Cooperative announcement. Commercial time in network programs that is made available to stations for sale to local or national advertisers.

Cooperative program. A network broadcast that is also sold on a local basis and sponsored by both national and local advertisers; for example, "The Tonight Show" (*see* Network cooperative program).

Corporate discounting. Incentives offered to advertisers with numerous brands of products; all of the corporation's advertising schedules are combined for a larger discount level.

Cost per rating point (CPR). The figure indicates the dollar cost of advertising exposure to one percentage point of the target group, audience, or population (*see* Rating point).

Cost per thousand (CPM). A dollar comparison that shows the relative cost of various media or vehicles; the figure indicates the dollar cost of advertising exposure to a thousand households or individuals.

Cost per thousand per commercial minute (CPM/PCM). The cost per thousand of a minute of broadcast advertising time.

Coverage. The number or percentage of individuals or households that are exposed to a medium or to an advertising campaign.

Cover position. An advertisement on the cover of a publication, often at a premium cost; first cover = outside front cover; second cover = inside front cover; third cover = inside back cover; fourth cover = outside back cover.

Cowcatcher. A brief commercial announcement at the beginning of a broadcast program.

Crossplugs. In alternating sponsorships, permitting each advertiser to insert one announcement into the program during the weeks when the other advertiser is the sponsor, maintaining weekly exposure for both (*see* Alternate sponsorship).

Cumulative audience. Cumulative broadcast rating; the net unduplicated audience of a station or network during two or more time periods; also used to describe how many different households or people are reached by an advertising schedule (also called "accumulative audience," "net audience," and "unduplicated audience"); technically, a cumulative audience is those persons who were exposed to any insertion of an advertisement in multiple editions of a single vehicle, whereas an unduplicated audience is those persons who were exposed to any insertion of an advertisement in a combination of vehicles or media, counting each person only once (slang "cume").

Cumulative reach. The number of different households that are exposed to a medium or campaign during a specific time.

Cut-in. The insertion of a local commercial announcement into a network or recorded program.

Dayparts. Specific segments of the broadcast day; for example, daytime, early fringe, prime time, late fringe, late night.

Deadline. The final date for accepting advertising material to meet a publication or broadcast schedule (*see* Closing date).

Dealer imprint. Inserting a local dealer's identification into nationally prepared advertising.

Dealer tie-in. A manufacturer's announcement that lists local dealers; not the same as "co-op."

Delayed broadcast (DB). A local station broadcasting a network program at a time other than its regularly scheduled network time.

Delivery. The ability to reach or communicate with a certain audience or number of people by using a particular advertising schedule; the physical delivery of a publication.

Demographic characteristics. The population characteristics of a group or audience.

Designated Market Area (DMA). A term used by the A. C. Nielsen Company; an area based on those counties in which stations of the originating market account for a greater share of the viewing households than those from any other area (*see* ADI); for example, Lake County, Illinois, belongs to the Chicago DMA because a majority of household viewing in Lake County is or can be ascribed to Chicago stations rather than to stations from Milwaukee or any other market.

Digest unit. *See* Junior unit.

Direct advertising. Advertising that is under complete control of the advertiser, rather than through some established medium; for example, direct mail or free sampling.

Direct mail advertising. Advertising sent by mail; also used to describe advertising in other media that solicits orders directly through the mail.

Direct marketing. Sales made directly to the customer, rather than through intermediaries or intervening channels; includes direct mail, direct advertising, telemarketing, and so forth.

Directory advertising. Advertising that appears in a buying guide or directory; advertisements in a store directory; for example, Yellow Pages advertising.

Display advertising. Print advertising that is intended to attract attention and communicate easily through the use of space, illustrations, layout, headline, and so on, as opposed to classified advertising.

Display classified advertising. *See* Classified display advertising.

Double spotting. *See* Piggyback.

Double spread. *See* Two-page spread.

Double truck. Slang term for a print advertisement that uses two full pages side-by-side, but not necessarily the two center pages; usually for a magazine advertisement (*see* Center spread *and* Two-page spread).

Drive time. Radio broadcast time during morning and evening commuter rush hours.

Earned rate. The advertising rate that is actually paid by the advertiser after discounts and other calculations.

Effective frequency. Level or range of audience exposure that provides what an advertiser considers to be the minimal effective level, and no more than this optimal level or range; also called "effective reach."

Effective reach. *See* Effective frequency.

Facing. A billboard location with the panels facing the same direction and visible to the same lines of traffic.

Fixed rate. An advertising rate for advertising time that cannot be taken away or "preempted" by another advertiser; usually the highest advertising rate; commonly used in broadcast advertising.

Flat rate. A print advertising rate that is not subject to discount.

Flight (flight saturation). Concentrating advertising within a short time period; an advertising campaign that runs for a specified number of weeks, followed by a period of inactivity (*see* Hiatus), after which the campaign may resume with another flight.

Floating time. *See* Run of schedule.

Forced combination. A policy to require newspaper advertisers to buy advertising space in both morning and evening newspapers owned by the same interests within a market.

Forcing distribution. Using advertising to increase consumer demand, thereby inducing dealers to stock a product; seldom used now.

Fractional page. Print advertising space of less than a full page.

Fractional showing. An outdoor advertising showing of less than 25 (*see* Showing).

Free circulation. A publication sent without charge; often with controlled circulation.

Frequency. The number of times that an average audience member sees or hears an advertisement; the number of times that an individual or household is exposed to an advertisement or campaign (frequency of exposure); the number of times that an advertisement is run (frequency of insertion).

Frequency discount. A reduced advertising rate that is offered by media to advertisers who run a certain number of advertisements within a given time.

Fringe time. Broadcast time periods preceding or following prime time; television time between daytime and prime time is called "early fringe" and television time immediately following prime time is called "late fringe."

Full run. One transit advertising car card in every transit bus or car.

Full showing. The number of outdoor posters that are needed to reach all of the mobile population in a market at least once within a thirty-day period (*see* Gross rating points); also called a 100 showing (*see* Showing).

General magazine. A consumer magazine that is not aimed at a special interest audience.

Giveaway. A free offer; a broadcast program that offers free gifts as prizes.

Grid card. Spot broadcast advertising rates that are set in a matrix format to allow a station to set rates based on current audience ratings and advertiser buying demand; for example,

	60-sec.	*30/20-sec.*	*10-sec.*
A	$250	$175	$125
B	245	172	123
C	240	170	121
D	230	165	120

Gross audience. The total number of households or people who are "delivered" or reached by an advertising schedule, without regard to any possible duplication that may occur; also called "total audience."

Gross billing. The cost of advertising at the highest advertising rate; the total value of an advertising agency's space and time dealings (*see* Billing).

Gross impressions. The total number of persons or the total number of audience impressions delivered by an advertising schedule (*see* Gross audience).

Gross rate. The highest possible rate for advertising time or space.

Gross rating points (GRPs). The total number of broadcast rating points delivered by an advertiser's television schedule, usually in a 1-week period; an indicator of the combined audience percentage reach and exposure frequency achieved by an advertising schedule; in outdoor, a standard audience level upon which some markets' advertising rates are based.

Gutter. The inside page margins where a publication is bound.

Half run. Transit advertising car cards in half the buses or transit cars of a system.

Half showing. A 50 outdoor showing (*see* Showing).

Head of household. The person within a family or household who is responsible for the major purchase decisions; sometimes, a male head and female head of household are considered separately.

Hiatus. A period during a campaign when an advertiser's schedule is suspended for a time, after which it resumes.

Hitchhiker. A broadcast advertising announcement at the end of a program that promotes another product from the same advertiser.

Holdover audience. Those persons tuned to a program who stay tuned to that station or network for the following program.

Horizontal cume. The total number of different people who were tuned to a broadcast station or network at the same time on different days of the week.

Horizontal publication. A business or trade publication that is of interest at one level or to one job function in a variety of businesses or fields.

House agency. An advertising agency that is owned or controlled by an advertiser.

Households using radio (HUR). *See* Sets in use.

Households using television (HUT). *See* Sets in use.

House organ. A company's own publication.

Identification (ID). A spot television commercial eight to ten seconds in length, during a station break; the last two seconds of the visual time may be reserved for showing the station call letters ("station identification"); a ten-second broadcast commercial announcement, sometimes referred to as a "ten."

Impact. The degree to which an advertisement or campaign affects its audience; the amount of space (full-page, half-page, etc.) or of time (sixty-second, thirty-second, etc.) that is purchased, as opposed to reach and frequency measures; also, the use of color, large type, powerful messages, or other devices that may induce audience reaction (*see* Unit).

Independent station. A broadcast station that is not affiliated with a network.

Index. A numerical value that is assigned to quantitative data for ease of comparison.

Individual location. An outdoor location that has room only for one billboard.

Insert. An advertisement that is enclosed with bills or letters; a one-page or multi-page print advertisement that is distributed with the publication and may or may not be bound into it.

Insertion order. A statement from an advertising agency to a media vehicle that accompanies the advertisement copy and indicates specifications for the advertisement.

Integrated commercial. A broadcast advertising message that is delivered as part of the entertainment portion of a program.

Island position. A print advertisement that is surrounded by editorial material; a print advertisement that is not adjacent to any other advertising; a broadcast commercial that is scheduled away from any other commercial, with program content before and after; often at premium advertising rates.

Isolated 30. A thirty-second broadcast commercial that runs by itself and not in combination with any other announcement; usually found only on network television.

Junior unit. Permitting an advertiser to run a print advertisement prepared for a small page size in a publication with a larger page size, with editorial matter around it in the extra space; similarly, using a *Reader's Digest*-size advertising page in a larger magazine is usually called a "Digest unit."

Key. A code in an advertisement to facilitate tracing which advertisement produced an inquiry or order.

Ladies of the House (LOH). A term used by A. C. Nielsen Company in some of its reports, referring to female heads of households.

Life. The length of time during which an advertisement is used; the length of time during which an advertisement is judged still to be effective; the length of time that a publication is retained by its audience.

Life-style profiles. Classifying media audiences on the basis of career, recreation, and/or leisure patterns or motives.

Linage. In print, the number of agate lines to be used for an advertisement or for a series of advertisements, now made somewhat obsolete by the declining use of agate-line measurements (*see* Agate line).

Line rate. The print advertising rate that is established by the number of agate lines of space used; somewhat obsolete because of the declining use of agate-line space measurements.

List broker. An agent who prepares and rents the use of mailing lists.

Local rate. An advertising rate offered by media to local advertisers that is lower than the rate offered to national advertisers.

Log. A broadcast station's record of its programming.

M. 1,000.

Magazine concept. Buying a certain number of broadcast announcements from a station with a certain guaranteed audience level, without selecting the specific times or programs.

Mail-order advertising. Advertisements intended to induce direct ordering of merchandise through the mail; the advertisements themselves are not necessarily distributed through the mail and may appear in other advertising media.

Make-good. A repeat of an advertisement to compensate for an error, omission, or technical difficulty with the publication, broadcast, or transmission of the original.

Market. *See* Target market and Target group.

Market potential. The reasonable maximum market share or sales level that a product or service can be expected to achieve.

Market profile. A geographic description of the location of prospects for a product or service; sometimes used instead of "target profile"; *see* Target Market *and* Target profile.

Market share. A company's or brand's portion of the sales of a product or service category.

Mat service. A service to newspapers that supplies pictures and drawings for use in advertisements; entire prepared advertisements may be offered ("mat" is slang for "matrix").

Maximil rate. The cost of an agate line of advertising space at the highest milline rate; somewhat obsolete as the usage of agate lines has declined.

Media buyer. The person who is responsible for purchasing advertising space or time; often skilled in negotiation with the media.

Media planner. The person who is responsible for determining the proper use of advertising media to fulfill the marketing and promotional objectives for a specific product or advertiser.

Merchandising. The promotion of an advertiser's products, services, and the like to the sales force, wholesalers, and dealers; promotion other than advertising to consumers through the use of in-store displays, guarantees, services, point-of-purchase materials, and so forth; display and promotion of retail goods; display of a mass media advertisement close to the point of sale.

Message distribution. Measurement of media audience by the successive frequency of exposure; for example, saw once, saw twice, and so on.

Metropolitan area. A geographic area consisting of a central city of 50,000 population or more, plus the economically and socially integrated surrounding area, as established by the federal government; usually limited by county boundaries (slang "metro area").

Metro rating. The broadcast rating figure from within a metropolitan area.

Milline rate. A comparison of the advertising-line rates of newspapers with uneven circulations by calculating the line-rate-per-million circulation; determined by multiplying the line rate by 1,000,000 and dividing by the circulation; now somewhat obsolete because of the declining use of agate-line measurements and advertising-line rates.

Minimil rate. The cost of an agate line of advertising at the lowest possible milline rate; somewhat obsolete as the usage of agate lines has declined.

Mood programming. Maintaining a single approach or characteristic in broadcast programming.

Net. Money paid to a media vehicle by an advertising agency after deducting the agency's commission (also, slang for "network").

Net unduplicated audience. The number of different people who are reached by a single issue of two or more publications (*see* Cumulative audience).

Network. In broadcast, a grouping of stations; an organization that supplies programming to a group or chain of stations.

Network cooperative program. A network program with provisions for inserting local commercials (*see* Cooperative program).

Network option time. Broadcast time on a station for which the network has the option of selling advertising.

Newspaper syndicate. A firm that sells special material such as features, photographs, comic strips, and cartoons, for publication in newspapers.

Next to reading matter. A print advertising position adjacent to news or editorial material; may be at premium rates.

Nielsen. The A. C. Nielsen Company; a firm engaged in local and national television ratings and other marketing research.

Nielsen Station Index (NSI). A rating service for individual television stations.

Nielsen Television Index (NTI). A national television rating service, primarily for network programming.

No change in rate (NCR or NCIR). Used when some other format or specification change has occurred.

O & O station. A broadcast station that is "owned and operated" by a network.

One time only (OTO). A commercial announcement that runs only once.

One-time rate. *See* Open rate.

Open-end transcription. A transcribed broadcast with time for the insertion of local commercial announcements.

Open rate. The highest advertising rate before discount can be earned; also called "basic rate" and "one-time rate."

Overrun. Additional copies of an advertisement beyond the number actually ordered or needed; extra copies to replace damaged outdoor posters or transit car cards.

Package. A series of broadcast programs that an advertiser may sponsor.

Package plan discount. A spot television discount plan for buying a certain number of spots, usually within a one-week period.

Packager. An individual or company that produces packaged program series; also called "syndicator."

Paid circulation. The number of print copies that are purchased by audience members.

Panel. A single outdoor billboard.

Partial showing. An outdoor showing of less than 25.

Participation. A commercial announcement within a broadcast program, as compared with one scheduled between programs; also called "participating announcement."

Participation program. A broadcast program with each segment sponsored by a different advertiser.

Pass-along readers. Readers of a publication who acquire a copy other than by purchase or subscription (*see* Secondary audience).

Pay cable. Cable television programming for which the audience must pay or subscribe.

Penetration. The percentage of households that have a broadcast receiving set; a measure of the degree of advertising effectiveness; the percentage of households that have been exposed to an advertising campaign.

People meter. Slang for a broadcast ratings measurement device that records individual audience members who are present during a program.

Per issue rate. A special magazine advertising rate that is determined by the number of issues that are used during the contract period; similar to a frequency discount, except not based on the number of advertisements, but rather on the number of issues in which an advertising campaign appears.

Piggyback. Slang for two of a sponsor's commercial announcements that are presented back-to-back within a single commercial time segment; for example, two thirty-second commercials in a sixty-second time slot; also called "double spotting."

Pilot. A sample production of a proposed broadcast program series.

Plans board. An advertising agency committee that reviews campaign plans for clients.

Plug. A free mention of a product or service.

Point-of-purchase advertising (POP). Promotions in retail stores, usually displays.

Position. The location of an advertisement on a page; the time when a program or commercial announcement will run in a broadcast; special positions may cost premium prices.

Potential audience. The maximum possible audience.

Preemptible rate. An advertising rate that is subject to cancellation by another advertiser's paying a higher rate, usually in broadcast; the protection period varies by station, and ranges from no notice to two-weeks notice or more (*see* Fixed rate).

Preemption. Cancellation of a broadcast program for special material or news; the right of a station or network to cancel a regular program to run a special program; a commercial announcement that may be replaced if another advertiser pays a higher or "fixed" rate.

Premium. An item that is offered to help promote a product or service; a higher-cost advertising rate (*see* Premium price).

Premium price. A special advertising rate, usually higher, for special positions or other considerations.

Preprint. Advertising material that is printed in advance of the regular press run, perhaps on another printing press with greater capability for color, and so forth.

Primary audience. Individuals in the print media audience who purchase or subscribe to the publication (*see* Secondary audience).

Primary household. A household in which a publication has been subscribed to or purchased.

Primary listening area. The geographic area in which a broadcast transmission is static-free and easily received.

Primary readers. Those persons who purchase or subscribe to a publication; readers in primary households.

Prime time. The hours when viewing is at its peak on television; usually the evening hours.

Product allocation. The various products that are assigned to specific times or locations in an advertiser's schedule, when more than one brand is advertised; the amount of the advertising budget that is allocated to individual products.

Product protection. A time separation between the airing of broadcast commercial announcements for competitive goods or services.

Profile. A term used interchangeably with "audience composition" to describe the demographic characteristics of audiences.

Program compatibility. Broadcast programming or editorial content that is suitable for the product or service that is being promoted; suitability of the advertisement or campaign theme with program content.

Progressive proofs. A test press run of each color in the printing process.

Projected audience. The number of audience members calculated from a sample survey of audience size; the number of broadcast viewers, either in total or per receiving set, based on the sample for the rating percentages.

Publisher's statement. The certified circulation of a publication, attested by the publisher and subject to audit.

Pulp magazine. A publication, usually printed on low-quality paper, with sensational editorial material; for example, a mystery, detective, or "TV/movie" magazine.

Qualified circulation. The distribution of a publication that is restricted to individuals who meet certain requirements; for example, member physicians are qualified to receive the *Journal of the American Medical Association.*

Qualified reader. A person who can prove readership of a publication.

Quantity discount. A lower advertising rate for buying a certain amount of space or time.

Quarter-run. One-fourth of the car cards that are required for a full run in transit; a card in every fourth transit system vehicle.

Quintile. One-fifth of a group; usage in advertising often refers to audience members who have been divided into five equal groups (quintiles), ranging from the heaviest to the lightest media usage levels.

Rate. A charge for advertising media space or time.

Rate book. A printed book that is designed to provide advertising rates for several media vehicles; for example, Standard Rate and Data Service.

Rate card. A printed listing of advertising rates for a single media vehicle.

Rate differential. The difference between the local and the national advertising rates in a vehicle.

Rate guarantee. Media commitment that an advertising rate will not be increased during a certain calendar period.

Rate holder. A small print advertisement used by an advertiser to meet contract requirements for earning a discounted advertising rate.

Rate protection. The length of time that an advertiser is guaranteed a certain advertising rate without an increase.

Rating. The percentage of the potential broadcast audience that is tuned to a particular station, network, or program; the audience of a vehicle expressed as a percentage of the total population of an area.

Rating point. A rating of 1 percent; 1 percent of the potential audience; the sum of the ratings of multiple advertising insertions; for example, two advertisements with a rating of 10 percent each will total twenty rating points.

Reach. The total audience that a medium actually reaches; the size of the audience with which a vehicle communicates; the total number of people in an advertising media audience; the total percentage of the target group that is actually covered by an advertising campaign.

Reader interest. An expression of interest through inquiries, coupons, and so forth; the level of interest in various products.

Readership. The percent or number of persons who read a publication or advertisement.

Reading notice. A print advertisement that is intended to resemble editorial matter.

Rebate. A payment that is returned by the media vehicle to an advertiser who has overpaid, usually because of earning a lower rate than that originally contracted.

Reminder advertising. An advertisement, usually brief, that is intended to keep the name of a product or service before the public; often, a supplement to other advertising.

Rep. A media representative (slang for a national sales representative).

Replacement. A substitute for a broadcast commercial announcement that did not clear the original order, that is, that was not broadcast as specified on the advertiser's order.

Retail trading zone (RTZ). The geographic area in which most of a market's population makes the majority of their retail purchases.

Roadblock or roadblocking. Slang term for placing television announcements at the same time on two or more networks, or at the same time on several stations in a single market; used as a remedy to channel switching during a commercial break.

ROP color. Color printing that is done during the regular press run.

Run of paper (ROP). Advertising that is positioned anywhere in a publication, with no choice of a specific place for the advertisement to appear.

Run of schedule (ROS). Broadcast commercial announcements that can be scheduled at the station's discretion anytime; in some cases, the advertiser can specify or request certain time periods; for exmple, ROS 10:00 A.M.– 4:00 P.M. Monday–Friday.

Satellite station. A broadcast station in a fringe reception area, to boost the effective range of the main station's signal.

Saturation. An advertising media schedule of wide reach and high frequency, concentrated during a time period to achieve maximum coverage and impact (see Flight).

Scatter plan. Commercial announcements that are scheduled during a variety of times in broadcast media; usually, the advertiser is permitted to specify general time periods during which the commercials will be scheduled; also called "scatter package."

Schedule. A list of advertisements or media to be used in a campaign; a chart of the advertisements that have been planned.

Schedule and estimate. A data form submitted by an advertising agency to the advertiser prior to a firm media purchase; it contains price and audience goals and a proposed schedule.

Secondary audience. The members of a print media audience who do not subscribe to or purchase the publication (see Pass-along readers).

Secondary listening area. The outlying area in which broadcast transmissions are subject to fading or static; in television, the Grade 3 signal contour.

Self-liquidating point-of-purchase. Display for which the retailer pays part or all of the costs.

Self-liquidating premium. An item for which the cost is paid by the customer; the price that the consumer pays covers the manufacturing cost of the premium.

Self-mailer. A direct-mail item that is mailed without an envelope.

Sets in use. The percentage of households that have broadcast receiving sets that are operating at one time within a market area; because many households have more than one receiving set, "households using television" and "households using radio" are the current common terms.

Share of audience. The percentage of sets-in-use (and thus of HUT or of HUR) that are tuned to a particular station, network, or program (slang "share").

Share of voice (SOV). The proportion of advertising expenditures that are made for a brand versus competitive brands.

Shopping newspaper. A newspaper-like publication that is devoted mainly to advertising, often distributed free to shoppers or to households (slang "shopper").

Short rate. Money that is owed to a media vehicle by an advertiser to offset the rate differential between the earned rate and the lower contracted rate.

Showing. The number of outdoor posters that are necessary to reach a certain percentage of the mobile population in a market within a specified time; many outdoor markets are now purchased by gross rating points (see Full showing and Gross rating points).

Sixty. Slang for a one-minute broadcast commercial announcement.

Soap opera. Slang for a continuing broadcast dramatic serial, usually a daytime program.

Space buyer. The person who is responsible for purchasing advertising in newspapers, magazines, and business publications, and sometimes outdoor and transit (see Media buyer).

Space position value. A measure of the effectiveness of an outdoor poster location.

Spectacular. A large outdoor lighted sign.

Split run. Testing two or more print advertisements by running each only to a portion of the audience, usually in a single issue.

Sponsor. An advertiser who buys the exclusive right to the time available for commercial announcements in a given broadcast program or segment.

Spot. The purchase of broadcast slots by geographic or station reakdowns; the purchase of slots at certain times, usually during station breaks; the term "spot" can refer to the time used for the commercial announcement or it can refer to the announcement itself.

Standard Metropolitan Statistical Area (SMSA). *See* Metropolitan area.

Station break. The time between broadcast programs to permit station identification and spot announcements; slang for a twenty-second broadcast announcment.

Station clearance. *See* Clear Time.

Station identification. The announcement of station call letters, usually with broadcast frequency or channel, and station location.

Station option time. A broadcast time for which the station has the option of selling advertising.

Station posters. Advertisements consisting of posters in transit stations.

Strip programming. A broadcast program or commercial that is scheduled at the same time of day on successive days of the week, either Monday through Friday or Monday through Sunday (*see* Across the board).

Subject to non-renewal (SNR). Commercial time that is available for purchase if the current advertiser does not renew.

Sunday supplement. A newspaper section in magazine format; also called "magazine supplement" or "magazine section" or simply "supplement."

Sustaining period. A period of time during an advertising campaign when advertisements are used to remind the audience of the product or service or of the campaign; often, a time of reduced advertising expenditures following the introductory flight.

Sweep. The period of the year when a ratings service measures the broadcast audience in the majority of the markets throughout the country; for example, surveys that are scheduled for November 2–24 would be referred to as the "November sweep."

Syndicated program. Broadcast program that is sold to individual stations, rather than appearing on a network.

Syndicator. Television program distributor who works with reruns or new programs on a market-to-market basis (*see* Packager).

Tabloid. A newspaper of the approximate size of a standard newspaper folded in half (slang "tab").

Tag. Dealer identification, usually added to the end of a broadcast commercial announcement to indicate where the product or service being advertised can be purchased in the local market.

Target group. Those persons to whom a campaign is directed; those individuals with similar characteristics who are prospects for a product or service; also called "consumer profile."

Target market. The geographic area or areas to which a campaign is directed; the areas where a product is being sold or introduced; also called "market profile."

Target profile. A demographic description of the target groups, often including the geographic target markets.

Tearsheet. A publication page with an advertiser's message, sent to the advertiser for approval or for checking.

Teaser. An advertisement that precedes the major portion of an advertising campaign, intended to build curiosity.

Telemarketing. Selling by use of telephones, either initiating the calls or receiving orders.

Ten. Slang for a ten-second broadcast commercial announcement.

Thirty. Slang for a thirty-second broadcast commercial announcement.

Throwaways. Free shopping newspapers.

Tie-in. *See* Cooperative advertising *and* Dealer tie-in.

Till forbidden (TF). A newspaper insertion order abbreviation; run the advertisement until told to stop.

Time buyer. The person who is responsible for purchasing advertising on radio and television (*see* Media buyer).

Time period rating (TPR). The rating for a particular broadcast time period, regardless of the program that was broadcast during that slot.

Time sheet. A form used by a time buyer to keep track of the data on a media buy; also called a "buy sheet"; the form used to keep track of how advertising agency personnel use their time, for application in billing purposes.

To be announced (TBA). Used as a notification in broadcast program schedules.

Total audience. The number of all the different homes or individuals who are tuned to a broadcast program for six minutes or longer.

Trade paper. A specialized publication for a specific profession, trade, or industry; another term for some business publications.

Traffic count. The number of persons who pass an outdoor panel location.

Trim size. The final magazine page size, after it is trimmed.

Turnover. The frequency with which the audience for a broadcast program changes over a period of time (*see* Audience turnover).

Twenty. Slang for a twenty-second broadcast commercial announcement; also called a "chain break" or "station break."

Two-page spread. A single print advertisement that crosses two facing pages; also called "double spread" or "double truck" (*see* Center spread *and* Double truck).

Unduplicated audience. The total number of different people who were exposed to an advertisement or campaign through multiple insertions in more than one media vehicle (*see* Cumulative audience).

Unit. Advertising unit; the form and context in which an advertisement appears in a media vehicle; for example, full-page, half-page vertical, center spread, black and white, back cover, two colors; thirty-second commercial, ten-second ID, and so on.

Upfront buying. Initial purchasing of network television advertising by firms wishing to have optimal selection of available programs; reserving advertising time on network television programs when the seasonal schedule is first announced; this tactic often requires longer schedules and higher prices.

Usage level. Classifying media audiences by the amount of the product or service they use.

Vehicle. An individual outlet of an advertising medium, such as a certain magazine or a specific broadcast station or program.

Vertical cume. The total number of different people who were tuned to successive broadcast programs.

Vertical publication. A business or trade publication that is of interest to all levels or job functions within a single business or profession.

Vertical saturation. Many broadcast commercial announcements scheduled throughout the course of a single day, generally designed to reach many different people, in an attempt to reach a high percentage of the broadcast audience.

Wait order. An instruction or request to delay publication of a print advertisement; also, but seldom, used in broadcast.

Waste circulation. The readers of a publication who are not prospects for the product or service being advertised; advertisement distribution in an area in which the product or service is not distributed.

Index